The

EVERYTHING®
Middle East Book

Dear Reader:

As you pick up this book and begin to read, know that you will encounter something other than a dispassionate treatise on the history of the Middle East. This part of the world has seeped into every corner of my being. As a result, you will find relevant information and genuine passion born out of a curious mind and a compassionate heart. Though most books approach the Middle East with a type of dry scholasticism (reminiscent of those monotone instructors we've all had), I have created a unique resource grounded in historical fact and illuminated by current realities.

With the keys I have provided, you will unlock more than simple head knowledge. Instead, you will open a new realm of practical understanding and educated conviction. Though some have written this area off as a hopeless quagmire of violence and hatred, your minds and hearts will be opened to the vitality of a troubled, yet beautiful land. It is my hope that every person reading this book will be given fresh eyes for the people of the Middle East. May this be the beginning of something new in your life as you seek truth and pursue peace.

Jacob M. Foline

The EVERYTHING® Series

Editorial

Publishing Director	Gary M. Krebs
Managing Editor	Kate McBride
Copy Chief	Laura MacLaughlin
Acquisitions Editor	Eric M. Hall
Development Editor	Karen Johnson Jacot
Production Editor	Jamie Wielgus
Technical Reviewer	Amanda Roraback
	Smokey Ardisson

Production

Production Director	Susan Beale
Production Manager	Michelle Roy Kelly
Series Designers	Daria Perreault
	Colleen Cunningham
Cover Design	Paul Beatrice
	Frank Rivera
Layout and Graphics	Colleen Cunningham
	Rachael Eiben
	Michelle Roy Kelly
	John Paulhus
	Daria Perreault
	Erin Ring
Series Cover Artist	Barry Littmann

Visit the entire Everything® Series at www.everything.com

THE
EVERYTHING®
MIDDLE EAST
BOOK

The nations, their histories,
and their conflicts

Jacob M. Fellure

Adams Media
Avon, Massachusetts

To my son Malachi, born September 11, 2001. May this book, just as your birth, be a message of hope in the midst of hate.

An Everything® Series Book.
Everything® and everything.com® are registered trademarks of F+W Publications, Inc.

Published by Adams Media, an F+W Publications Company
57 Littlefield Street, Avon, MA 02322 U.S.A.
www.adamsmedia.com

ISBN: 1-59337-053-9
Printed in the United States of America.

J I H G F E D C B A

Library of Congress Cataloging-in-Publication Data
Fellure, Jacob M.
The everything Middle East book / Jacob M. Fellure.
p.   cm.
(An everything series book)
ISBN 1-59337-053-9
1. Middle East. I. Title. II. Series: Everything series.
DS44.F45   2004
956–dc22   2004002186

This publication is designed to provide accurate and authoritative information with regard to the subject matter covered. It is sold with the understanding that the publisher is not engaged in rendering legal, accounting, or other professional advice. If legal advice or other expert assistance is required, the services of a competent professional person should be sought.

> —From a *Declaration of Principles* jointly adopted by a Committee of the American Bar Association and a Committee of Publishers and Associations

Many of the designations used by manufacturers and sellers to distinguish their products are claimed as trademarks. Where those designations appear in this book and Adams Media was aware of a trademark claim, the designations have been printed with initial capital letters.

This book is available at quantity discounts for bulk purchases.
For information, call 1-800-872-5627.

Contents

Top Ten Reasons You Need *The Everything*® *Middle East Book* / x

Introduction / xi

What Do You Mean by "Middle East"? / 1
Origin of the Term **2** • Orientalism Exposed **3** • Geographic Boundaries **6** • Ethnic and Linguistic Groups **8** • Common Religion **9** • Culture and History **9** • Social Identity **10** • Conservative and Liberal Definitions **11** • Boundaries for This Book **12**

The Cradle of Civilization / 13
Components of a Civilization **14** • The Sumerians **14** • The Egyptians **17** • The Phoenicians **20** • The Hittites **21** • The Babylonians **23** • The Hebrews **24**

Rise of the Empires / 27
Components of an Empire **28** • The Assyrians **28** • The Chaldeans, a.k.a. Neo-Babylonians **31** • The Medes **33** • The Persians **35** • The Greeks **37** • The Romans **39**

Ancient Judaism / 41
The Sons of Jacob and Their God **42** • From Slavery to Wandering **44** • Moses and the Levitical Law Code **47** • Conquest, Kingdom, and Captivity **49** • The Message of the Tanakh **51**

5   Early Christianity / 53

First-Century Judaism **54** • The Concept of Moshiach **56** • Yeshua and His Followers **57** • Execution and Persecution **59** • Growth from Jerusalem and Antioch **61** • The Letters **62** • The Church and Rome **64**

6   The Byzantine Empire / 67

Emperor Constantine's Conversion **68** • New Religious Freedom **69** • Holy Hermits **71** • Politics and Religion **72** • Looking Inside and Out **75** • Justinian's Creations and Conquests **77** • Division and Decline **79**

7   Early Islam / 81

Ancient Arabia **82** • The Seventh Century **84** • Muhammad and His Followers **86** • Growth from Medina **88** • Death, Division, and Domination **90** • The Qur'an and Hadith **93**

8   Islamic Empires and European Colonies / 97

Umayyads in Damascus **98** • Abbasids in Baghdad **101** • Umayyads in Spain **104** • Fractured Fraternities **105** • When Turks Attack **106** • Europe to the Rescue—Everyone Loses **108** • Expulsion of the Infidels **109**

9   A New Empire Is Born / 113

The Aftermath of Defeat **114** • Osman's Empire **116** • Constantinople and Cairo Fall **117** • Sultan Süleyman and Ottoman Expansion **121** • Turkic Rivalries **122** • Euro Power **124** • Division and Decay **125**

10   World War and Change / 127

Choosing Sides **128** • Lawrence or Arabia? **130** • Settling Dust and Changing Maps **132** • Winds of Nationalism **135** • Memories of Imperialism **138** • Birth of the Nations **139**

Modern Middle East Mosaic / 143

Urban and Eclectic **144** • Kurds **145** • Armenians **147** • Circassians **148** • Assyrians **149** • Copts **151** • Berbers **152** • Jews **153** • Islamic Offshoots—Reformers or Heretics? **154**

Israel/Palestine—All Eyes on Jerusalem / 159

Aryanism, Zionism, and Exodus **160** • Declaration of State and War **161** • The Fix of '56 **164** • Six Days in '67 **165** • War of Atonement **167** • Peace Camps and Refugee Camps **168** • Suicides, Strikes, and Settlements **172**

Egypt—Heart of the Arab World / 179

Remnants of Imperialism **180** • Nationalism and Revolution **182** • Nasser's Pan-Arabism **183** • Sadat's Peace **186** • Radicals Reborn **189** • President Mubarak—Stayin' Alive **190**

Saudi Arabia—Crossroads of Islam / 195

Hashemite Protectors and the House of Saùd **196** • What's a Wahhabi? **196** • God's Black Gold **200** • Bin Laden's Bucks **202** • All Roads Lead to Mecca **207** • Times, They Are a-Changin' **208**

Iraq—British Colony to Ba'thist Beginnings / 211

Ousting Ottomans and Housing Hashemites **212** • Independence with Strings **213** • Kingless Kingdom **215** • Instability and Revolutions **216** • Starting the Ba'th **217**

Iraq—The Rise and Fall of Saddam Hussein / 221

The Boy from Tikrit **222** • At War with Iran **224** • At War with the World **226** • Suppression, Sanctions, and Suffering **228** • Between Iraq and a Hard Place **231**

Iran—The Shi'ite State / 235
Dynasties and Divisions **236** • America and the Shah **239** • Seeds of Revolt **241** • Khomeini's Student Revolution **242** • Ayatollahs and Politics **244** • Winds of Change **248**

Turkey—Modern and Democratic / 251
Young Turk Takeover **252** • From the Ashes of Empire **254** • Atatürk's Radical Reforms **256** • Kemalist Clergy **259** • Internal Struggle—East or West? **262** • One Nation Looking Forward **265**

Tackling the Tough Issues / 269
Understanding Shame/Honor Societies **270** • Is Islam a Violent Religion? **273** • Islamic Revivalism and Militancy **276** • Between Frustration and Aggression **277** • Clashing Civilizations or Civilized Collaboration? **278**

Where's the Peace? / 281
Border Disputes **282** • Ethnic Divisions and Religious Differences **283** • Ideological Differences and Political Agendas **287** • Historical Memory **288** • Your Place in This World **289**

Appendix A • Timeline: Prehistory to the Present / **291**
Appendix B • Further Reading and Resources / **298**
Index / **301**

Acknowledgments

Thanks to: my wife, Elicia Fellure, for being so supportive of my work and understanding of my obsession with the Middle East; Dr. William Watson, for your scholarly insights on the early Christian and Islamic periods; Dr. Richard Cahill, for your valuable information on the Arab-Israeli conflict and your inspirational life; Samuel Allen, for sharing your keen knowledge of warfare and the ancient world; Jason Bolt, for your research and perspectives on the Republic of Turkey; Moxie Java, for providing me delectable Mint Mochas every morning and free Internet access throughout the day; Java Lounge, for your unique atmosphere, quiet cubbyholes, and tasty treats; and the countless shopkeepers, homemakers, shepherds, officials, scholars, professionals, and students in cities and villages throughout the Middle East, who have shown me undeserved hospitality and have opened my eyes to the rich beauty of their ancient lands.

Top Ten Reasons You Need
The Everything® Middle East Book

1. Process more of what you see and hear in the media.
2. Find important background information concerning the ongoing violence in Israel/Palestine, Iraq, and other nations.
3. Learn interesting facts about the ancient and modern Middle East.
4. Discover the strategic importance and cultural significance of this region.
5. Form a more accurate opinion of your nation's involvement in the Middle East.
6. Develop a clearer perspective of Judaism, Christianity, and Islam.
7. Better understand Middle Eastern coworkers, neighbors, students, etc.
8. Debunk stereotypes and misconceptions about the region and its people.
9. Discover the reasons many Muslim and non-Muslim nations are frustrated with the United States.
10. Discuss current events intelligently.

Introduction

▶ YOU MAY HAVE PICKED UP THIS BOOK to explore the turbulence of the Middle East or maybe to brush up on names and dates for an upcoming exam. Good, you have come to the right place! What you may not know is that you have also begun a journey of self-discovery. Whether or not you consider yourself "civilized," you are part of a civilization that has borrowed many of its systems and traditions from people who once lived in the Middle East.

From the birth of civilization in Sumer (modern Iraq), with the first organized religion, government, and written language, to the beginnings of monotheism, which conceived Judaism, Christianity, and Islam, most people will find some connection to the Middle East. For those who feel an ancient spiritual or physical connection to this region, it is often an uncomfortable reality. Even after recognizing the origins of your moral, civil, or religious perspectives, you many find it difficult to relate to the very peoples and cultures that birthed these norms.

In the twenty-first century, the Middle East may appear more a graveyard of cultures than a delivery room. Dominated by religious extremism, tyrannical regimes, poverty, and war, this seems hardly a place to call home. In the following pages, you will not only learn more about your ancient connections to this area, you will also find valuable information about the peoples, cultures, and politics of the modern Middle East.

Since September 11, 2001, the global media has been saturated with information about the Middle East and Islam. From sound bytes, talk shows, and all the experts, the average person has gotten more disjointed information than anyone could handle. Who can make sense of it all? You can!

The purpose of this book is to provide you with a foundation upon which all of this random information can be placed. This is not another piece of sensationalized frontline reporting. Rather, it is a useful tool that will bring context, balance, and perspective to the misunderstood Middle East.

Through brief histories, you will better understand the ancient and modern backgrounds of current peoples and conflicts. You will be challenged to step outside of yourself and away from extremes. Interesting facts and thought-provoking questions will offer you a fresh set of eyes to view the Middle East. This book will be your media survival guide as you grapple with the complexities of this diverse region.

So, put on your *kafeyah* (traditional headdress) and get on your camel, because you are invited to journey into the unknown realm of Moses and Ali Baba. In the end, you may be surprised to find yourself cruising through the land of pop stars Shakira and Tarkan in a brand-new Mercedes, watching MTV from a mobile satellite link. As they say in Egypt, *Ahlan wa-sahlan* (Welcome)! Ɛ

Chapter 1

What Do You Mean by "Middle East"?

The term "Middle East" may seem self-explanatory, but nothing could be further from the truth. The origins of this term and its contemporary boundaries are almost as misunderstood as the region itself. After reading this chapter, you will have developed an important understanding of the Middle East that will serve as a foundation for the rest of this book.

Origin of the Term

You have chosen to explore the region known as the Middle East. From the beginning, you must "Orient" yourself. Yes, you must literally find your bearings, but you must also look back to the roots of the Western world's understanding of the lands to the east, known as the Orient.

The Orient

As Westerners began to study the geography and history of the East, they borrowed the Latin term *oriens,* rising sun. They proceeded to divide the Orient into three areas:

- **Near East**—the eastern lands closest to the West, stretching from the eastern Mediterranean Sea to the Persian Gulf.
- **Far East**—the portion of the Orient farthest from Europe, found along the Pacific Ocean.
- **Middle East**—the region not exactly near or far, found between the Persian Gulf and Southeast Asia.

ALERT!

Don't be confused by the term "Near East." It is simply the more traditional name for the region we call the Middle East today.

In the early 1900s, American naval officer Alfred Thayer Mahan began using the term "Middle East." This new name for the old "Near East" stuck. By the beginning of World War II, the average Westerner knew the Middle East as the area bounded by the Black Sea (to the north), the Arabian Sea (to the south), the Indus River, in modern-day Pakistan (to the east), and the Mediterranean and Red Seas (to the west).

The Media East

Most people have a subconscious definition of the Middle East that has been formed by the media. From those brave journalists with their satellite phones, armchair America awaits live images and commentary from the front lines. Without ever really defining the term, news anchors and columnists often refer to the Middle East.

The problem is not with the quality or validity of the information given but with this lack of context. Unless the viewer happens to have a good understanding of Middle Eastern history and culture, the apparent chaos and volatility of the region is frustrating. The average person ends up thinking something like this: "Muslims are involved, and there is some type of unrest, so it must be happening in the Middle East."

Regardless of whether this is your perspective, the media has probably played a large role in shaping your understanding of the area. In fact, most Westerners have been influenced by something even more powerful than the media, known as Orientalism.

Orientalism Exposed

Have you ever wanted to experience just one of the 1,001 Arabian nights? Does the sensual lure of the harem make you dream of being a sultan? Do you want to know the secrets of the Ancient Arabic Order of the Nobles of the Mystic Shrine? Okay, how about settling for a drag off the fine Turkish tobaccos found in a Camel cigarette? The exotic images brought to mind by these questions are a result of what the renowned scholar Edward W. Said called "Orientalism."

In 1978, Professor Said, a Palestinian-American born in Jerusalem, published a book called *Orientalism,* in which he questioned the validity and motivation behind many Western perceptions of the Middle East. Whether through Mark Twain's caricatured Middle Eastern travelogue or the imagined Orient of recent popular culture, Westerners have been exposed to a voluptuous and mysterious Middle East that, for the most part, does not exist.

Ali Baba and the Reality Thieves

The *1,001 Arabian Nights* is a legitimate piece of Middle Eastern literature. Originally called *alf layla wa layla* (one thousand nights and a night), these stories were recited orally by professional storytellers and also written down in Arabic. Thanks to England's Captain Sir Richard Francis Burton, these stories were translated into English and brought to the West. However, instead of being recognized as stories or clever parables, they quickly gained notoriety as the histories of a distant and mysterious land. As a result, to this day, many people think of the region in terms of flying carpets, genies in lamps, bloodthirsty Sultans, and seductive belly dancers.

FACT

According to the 2002 *World Factbook,* published by the U.S. Central Intelligence Agency (✍ *www.cia.gov*), over half of the world's 6.3 billion inhabitants are Christian, Muslim, or Jewish. That means more than 3 billion people find their spiritual heritage in the Middle East.

The Hair-Raising Harem

The harem was a real part of Middle Eastern culture. From the Arabic *haram* (meaning forbidden or sacred), the harem was an area designated "for women only." It was a sanctuary for all the women of the house in the event that men from outside the family were to visit.

The harems of royalty were unique in that they contained both wives and concubines. The women were guarded by eunuchs who, by nature of their physiognomy, were unable to disrupt the sanctity of the harem. Although the sultan could have sexual relations with any of his wives or concubines, it was forbidden for him to engage more than one woman at a time. In addition, many of his marriages were the result of political alliances rather than passionate relationships.

It is unfortunate how the concept of the harem (certainly foreign to the Western mind) was distorted and mythologized. The idea of the harem as a sexual playground of naked concubines is really a product of the early twentieth-century American imagination. Western painters, filmmakers, and playwrights used the myth of the harem as cover to explore their own sexual fantasies, bringing their viewers to a new level of misconception.

The Shriner's Circus

If you want to know the secrets of the Shriners, you will have to do more than wear the fez and drive mini-motorcycles in parades. In fact, you will have to go through a series of rituals that are said to have come directly from Ali, son-in-law and nephew of the prophet Mohammad. You will learn common Arabic phrases like the greeting *as-salaam aleikum* (peace be upon you), use the Islamic calendar, and attend meetings in "mosques" named after Middle Eastern cities. You will be given Lawrence-of-Arabia–style clothing and will even talk about making a pilgrimage similar to the Islamic hajj to Mecca, Saudi Arabia. With all of this "Middle Eastern" flair, the Shriner initiate could easily think he had converted to Islam. In fact, he has merely taken part in a fabricated fantasy.

The Shriners were founded in the late 1800s when two American men, drunk with Orientalist folklore, decided to create their own fraternal order. They were not alone in their fascination with the exotic—by 1922, over 500,000 Americans were members of the Ancient Order of the Nobles of the Mystic Shrine, better known as the Shriners.

The ancient nation of Egypt is still a vibrant cultural and intellectual center, with masterful art, music, dance, and literature. Naguib Mahfouz, one of Egypt's greatest writers, has received international acclaim for his many novels and screenplays, including *The Cairo Trilogy* and *Children of the Alley*. In 1988, at the age of seventy-seven, Mahfouz was awarded the Nobel Prize in Literature.

Mythology and Marketing

As for that Turkish Camel cigarette, again an Orientalist haze has clouded reality. In the late nineteenth century, rolled cigarettes were viewed as an Oriental luxury, available only to the wealthy. When U.S. technology was developed for the mass production of rolled cigarettes, marketing campaigns targeted this popular perception. With names like Fatima Turkish Blend, Mecca Brand, Mogul Egyptian, or Omar Turkish cigarettes, tobacco companies suggested that the smoker had the pleasures of the sultan at his or her fingertips. No doubt, colorful images of mysterious veiled women and powerful turban-clad Sultans added to the cigarette mystique, but it is also true that the roots of Orientalism were already in place.

As you can see, the media and popular culture together have created a certain perception of the Middle East. While this perception may contain seeds of truth, it is definitely not totally accurate. In the following pages, you will find the facts you need to develop an educated understanding of the diverse regions we lump together under one name.

Geographic Boundaries

One obvious way you can define the region's location is by finding its geographic heart. Experts and news junkies alike agree: The Middle East lies somewhere on the eastern shores of the Mediterranean. As you will quickly discover, the boundaries beyond this central point are harder to determine.

Political Boundaries

Will you draw the northern border of the Middle East in southeastern Europe, at the border between Turkey and Bulgaria, or should it stop short of Turkey at the Syrian border? And the eastern perimeter, should it extend through Central Asia all the way to the Pakistan/India border, or go only as far as Iraq? Should the southern line be drawn to include the African nations of Sudan and Somalia, or should it stop at Jordan and Saudi Arabia? Finally, should the western boundaries stop at the edge of the Asian continent, on the Israeli/Egyptian border, or do they stretch across North Africa to the Atlantic shores of Mauritania and Morocco? These are tough questions. To answer them, we start by looking at the landscape.

FACT

"Sahara" is an Arabic word meaning "desert." Early Arab merchants traveling across this massive hot spot called it like they saw it—the desert.

Certain realities on the ground provide obvious boundaries for the region. For instance, the Black Sea, Caucasus Mountains, and Caspian Sea combine to form a point where the area naturally breaks from the West to become the East. Similarly, the Mediterranean Sea is a significant border in any definition of the Middle East. The Sahara is another important, natural dividing line between the Arabized lands of North Africa and the more indigenously African regions to the south. Finally, the Indus River winds its way through modern Pakistan as a definitive boundary. Historically, this river was the easternmost edge of the early Islamic empires. The Indus remains an important line of cultural and ethnic division, separating the more Persianized Pushtun and Baluchi peoples from the more stereotypically "Indian" Punjabi and Sindhi groups.

Isn't It All Desert?

Although most people think "desert" when they think Middle East, the region's geography and climate is as diverse as that of the United States. Much of the Arabian Peninsula is made up of hot sandy desert lands, but even Arabia cannot be characterized as uniform. Along its western borders, mountains as high as 12,000 feet tower above the temperate Red Sea coast, while in the southeastern nation of Oman, mountains of similar stature line the entrance to the Persian Gulf's crystal blue waters.

ALERT!

At this point, you may find your gut instinct telling you where to draw these boundaries. On the other hand, you may be thinking the Middle East is as difficult to define as the parameters of infinity. Hang in there; with a few more pieces of the puzzle, you will begin to see the full picture!

Massive evergreens pepper the snow-covered slopes of Lebanon's ski resorts, while sunbathers enjoy its sandy beaches. The lush forests of Turkey's Black Sea coast give way to mountain peaks higher than any Rocky Mountain high, while its Mediterranean resorts rival the famed Greek Isles. The Fertile Crescent is a well-watered region that stretches all the way from Israel's coastal plain, through northern Syria, and down the banks of Iraq's Tigris and Euphrates Rivers. These lands are rich with plant life, waterfalls, and wildlife. Along with the marshy banks of the Nile River in Egypt, the Fertile Crescent has been the breadbasket of the Middle East for nearly 10,000 years. With so much diversity in landscape and climate, it is a wonder that anyone would say, "Isn't it all desert?"

Ethnic and Linguistic Groups

Ethnicities and languages also help to define the region. You can easily tell if one person is from an Arabic background and another is Swedish. Even if both are speaking English, things like skin tone, hair color, and facial structure indicate that each is from a different region. Similarly, it doesn't take a linguist to hear the difference between languages like Russian and Swahili. Ethnic and linguistic similarities and differences help to determine whether someone is European or Southeast Asian. Despite the many ethnic and linguistic differences within Europe, some groups share certain connections that make them all European. As you begin to explore the Middle East, you will find three major groups:

- **Arabs**—Numbering somewhere around 300 million, they are in the majority in the area from Syria (north) to Yemen (south) and Oman (east) to Morocco (west).
- **Turks**—Also known as Turkic peoples, this group numbers over 100 million. They are in the majority in the area from Turkey and Azerbaijan to the former Soviet republics of Central Asia.
- **Persians**—Over 30 million Farsi-speaking people are in the majority in the area from Iran to parts of Afghanistan and Pakistan.

FACT

The phrases *Ash-sharq al-awsat* (Arabic), *Ortadoğu* (Turkish), and *khAvareh MeeyAneh* (Farsi) all translate as "Middle East."

Many use the term "Arab world" interchangeably with "Middle East," but the region cannot be so easily defined. A portion of the Middle East can be called the Arab world, but with significant Turkish and Persian populations in predominantly Arabic lands and vice versa, in the end the lines cannot be so neatly drawn according to ethnic and linguistic groups. In addition, minority groups like the Kurds, Jews, Armenians, Circassians, and Berbers complicate the issue even further.

However, boundaries must be drawn at some point, even if they are not perfect. Should the Middle East include Pakistan, even though most of its inhabitants are neither of Arabic, Turkish, or Persian background? If not, should the Kurdish regions of northern Iraq, eastern Turkey, and western Iran be excluded from the Middle East? To answer these questions, let's examine the religious aspects of these lands.

Common Religion

Religious allegiance can be a powerful adhesive or a dangerous explosive. From the beginning of recorded history, the Middle East has seen its share of both.

Today, Islam is the predominant religion from North Africa to Southeast Asia. This region is known as the Muslim world. We've already discussed the overlap between the Arab world and Middle East; the Muslim world is yet another overlay in this complex part of the globe.

The Arab and Muslim worlds are distinct from one another and from the Middle East. Although all three are related, each is a separate entity. Nevertheless, the common beliefs and practices of Muslims in this region do help differentiate it from neighboring areas, where Islam is not the popular religion.

More than 90 percent of the Middle East's people are Muslims. However, not all Arabs are Muslims, not all Middle Easterners are Arabs, not every Muslim is an Arab, and not every Middle Easterner is a Muslim.

Islam is often the common denominator for the region's diverse tribal, ethnic, and linguistic groups. As you will discover in Chapters 7 and 8, Islam is more than a religion. It is a complete system that determines a culture's law, economics, military strategy, politics, and even personal hygiene. Given this information, you can see why Islam is such an important factor. Still, it is not the only issue defining the Middle East.

Culture and History

The Middle East can be defined in a cultural sense as an area of the world where Islamic traditions are the norm. Even though close to 50 million Middle Eastern people are not Muslims (roughly 10 percent), Islam has influenced the cultural norms and history of the region. Not only that, but Arabian culture is a great influence on the nearly 40 percent of Middle Easterners who do not consider themselves Arabs. Arabic phrases like *as-salaam aleikum,* literally meaning "peace be upon you," are spoken by non-Arab Muslims across the globe. Pre-Islamic traditions, mannerisms, rituals, and clothing styles, originating from Arabia, have been influential across Africa and Asia. Even the Arabic alphabet has been adopted by non-Arab cultures, such as the Turkic and Farsi speaking peoples of Central Asia.

From the world's first civilization in southern Mesopotamia (now modern Iraq), to the Ottoman Empire's 500-year reign over the Middle East, the peoples of this land have a shared history. The many differences between them have caused conflict among the diverse peoples of this region. Nevertheless, they share a deep sense of heritage and connection to the land that is hard for Westerners to comprehend. Five thousand years of conflicts and alliances have forged a people with a common memory of the past that is affecting their future.

An unmistakable pride permeates the peoples of the Middle East, as they are well aware of their ancient roots and not-so-distant greatness. Because of these common memories, many people find themselves shamed and frustrated by the region's current state of affairs. In an attempt to regain lost honor, many refer to the years of British and French colonialism as the cause of their present impotency. In addition, many look to the United States and its current influence and see the footprints of yet another exploitive empire.

Social Identity

The last piece to this puzzle is a conglomerate of all the previous pieces. Social identity is difficult to define, yet at the same time it is one of the most recognizable aspects of the Middle East. Considering geographic location, ethno-linguistic background, religious affiliation, cultural norms, and regional history, is there a common identity? Despite obvious difference, is there one factor or combination of factors that connects diverse groups? Islam could be said to be this cultural glue, but many non-Muslims consider themselves Middle Eastern. The Arabic language could arguably be the common thread, but what about all of the groups who don't speak Arabic? You must consider all of the factors to effectively define the Middle East.

Conservative and Liberal Definitions

After exploring these issues and many more, experts have defined the Middle East in several ways. By looking at the most limited definition on one hand and the most generous on the other, you will see the wide spectrum of ideas related to this question.

Finding the middle of the Middle East—along the eastern shores of the Mediterranean Sea—is a point that most people can agree on. This central location is in fact the most conservative definition. Based largely on geographic location, at the expense of other important factors, this definition includes only the countries of Syria, Lebanon, Israel, Palestine, and Jordan.

What about the birthplace of Islam, Saudi Arabia? How about Turkey, the center of regional power from the fifteenth to the twentieth century? What about Iraq, home to the imperial Islamic city of Baghdad? Among other places, what about Egypt, the largest Arab country on the planet? This definition is much too limited.

At the other extreme, the most liberal definition uses Islam as the common bond and appears to be almost the same as the Muslim world, minus India and Southeast Asia. This perspective would add to the conservative definition the North African countries of Mauritania, Western Sahara, Morocco, Algeria, Tunisia, Libya, Egypt, Sudan, Eritrea, Djibouti, and Somalia; the island nation of Cyprus; the West Asian countries of Turkey, Armenia, Azerbaijan, Iran, Iraq, Kuwait, Saudi Arabia, Bahrain, Qatar, United Arab Emirates, Oman, and Yemen; the Central Asia "stans," which include Kazakhstan, Turkmenistan, Uzbekistan, Kyrgyzstan, Tajikistan, Afghanistan, and Pakistan.

The problem with these parameters is that they might as well include parts of sub-Saharan Africa, Western China and Russia, India, and Bangladesh, as Muslims are the predominant inhabitants of these regions as well. For that matter, they should also extend their borders into the Balkans to include the largely Muslim areas in this part of the world. Again, defining the Middle East is a somewhat nebulous task, but Islam cannot be the lone factor.

FACT

When "stan" or "istan" appears at the end of a country's name, it means "the land of" whatever group is named. For example, Afghanistan means "the land of the Afghans."

Boundaries for This Book

Now that you have been thoroughly exposed to the issues surrounding the question, "What do you mean by 'Middle East'?" it is time for a definition. For the purposes of this book, the Middle East will be defined along the lines of the most liberal view. It will include all of North Africa (that is, above the Sahara), West Asia (minus Cyprus), and the Central Asian countries of Afghanistan and Pakistan. This will by no means silence the ongoing academic debate, nor should it be a rigid definition to die by. Instead, like life in the Middle East, this definition should be fluid and adaptable. Most likely you are a Westerner. As a result, you have in mind a tidy Western definition of the Middle East. But remember, you are exploring a region that often operates under the attitude of I.B.M.—not the technology giant, but an acronym for these Arabic phrases:

- *Inshaa Allah*—Literally translated as "God willing," but meant more like "hopefully."
- *Bukra*—Literally meaning "tomorrow," as in "We'll get to it later."
- *Ma leysh*—Don't worry about it!

Remember, the Middle East can be as hazy as its legendary sandstorms. Now that you are aware of the ways you have been influenced by the media and your culture, you can begin to expand your knowledge of a land that is both rich in history and relevant to the future. Ⓔ

Chapter 2

The Cradle of Civilization

The modern Middle East cannot be separated from its ancient foundations. By examining its rich historical soil, you will uncover the roots of the region's many contemporary issues. Starting from the dawn of civilization, along the Tigris, Euphrates, and Nile Rivers, you will discover the origins of such things as centralized government, organized religion, and written language. You are also likely to find a part of your own history.

Components of a Civilization

Imagine you have been stranded for years on a remote island. You rig together a small boat and set out for home. What would be your first word upon seeing the mainland? Civilization! That's right. No matter how much they may enjoy periods of solitude, at some level, most people desire the comforts and security of the civilized world.

What then is civilization? The encyclopedia calls it "an advanced state of cultural and material development . . . marked by political and social complexity and progress in the arts and sciences." For some people this clinical definition may hit home, but most people need something a little less academic. So, as you explore humanity's first civilizations, look for these simple components:

- Well-planned cities
- Large, centralized government
- Written language
- Organized religion
- Development of new technologies and skills
- Established trade networks
- Social class structures
- Appreciation of art and entertainment
- Professional military forces

The Sumerians

In Mesopotamia (now Iraq), more than 5,000 years before Abraham was born, the Ubaidian settlers arrived. Little is known of these ancient peoples, but most experts believe they came from the mountainous regions of contemporary eastern Turkey and northern Iran. By the fifth millennium B.C., they had developed small farming communities in the large fertile plain of the Euphrates and Tigris River valley. The rivers' constant supply of water ensured that their livestock and crops flourished. As word spread of the region's bountiful lands, people from surrounding areas came to share in the wealth. Before long, small Ubaidian farming communities grew into large multiethnic cities made up of people from around the Middle East.

FACT

"Mesopotamia" is a Greek word meaning "between the rivers." It refers to the lands that lie between the Euphrates and Tigris Rivers (in modern Iraq).

After centuries of intermarriage, the native tongue of an immigrant group known as the Sumerians emerged as the common regional language. Soon, this prosperous part of Mesopotamia was called Sumer, after the Sumerian newcomers. By 3500 B.C., the Sumerian civilization was in place, with the world's first large, well-planned cities, massive ziggurats (stepped pyramid-temples), and complex water-diversion and irrigation systems.

The city of Kish was the center of political power for the surrounding cities, with its well-organized government and impressive public works. From this metropolis, a priest-king ruled the region with power and authority given by the gods. Nearly all of Sumer's citizens were polytheistic, meaning they believed in many gods. As prudent bureaucrats, government-installed priests welcomed the various gods of the diverse peoples, admitting them into a structured national religion.

Gods and Stars

Sumerians satisfied their fascination with the skies by using tall ziggurat towers as both observatories and temples. Elements of astronomy and astrology guided worshippers to view the heavenly lights as signs from the gods. After years of intense study, priests developed maps of the skies that included many of the constellations (and that today's stargazers still use). Those priests were some of the first astronomers, with such an advanced knowledge of the stars that they could even predict lunar and solar eclipses.

Priests told complex stories explaining the powers of the gods and the ways they needed to be appeased. Animal sacrifices were the primary source of tribute, but gifts of fruits, vegetables, gold, and other valuables were also made. In addition, priests recited stories of the gods battling in the heavens and creating the universe. Other popular Sumerian epics remembered the details of past wars and the characteristics of heroic leaders.

One of the tales best known today is the *Epic of Gilgamesh*. Its theme—a man escaping a great flood in a boat full of animals—may sound familiar from a more recent source, the Old Testament. The *Epic of Gilgamesh* was recounted verbally until about 2500 B.C., when the Sumerians wrote it down. Today, the only remaining texts come from Assyrian scribes who copied this famous Mesopotamian tale onto clay tablets around 700 B.C.

Amazing Inventors

The Sumerians' inventiveness led them to many firsts. Sumerians invented the wheel around 3500 B.C. By the year 3200 B.C., they had created the world's first written language. This new script consisted of lines and triangular shapes organized into small crude pictures. These symbols were made by pressing the tip of a hard reed into a soft clay tablet, resulting in wedge shapes. When archeologists discovered this ancient style of writing, they called it "cuneiform," from the Latin word meaning "wedge."

FACT

Many ancient peoples borrowed the Sumerian cuneiform script to represent their native languages. In the Middle East today, many non-Arabic speakers use Arabic script. Similarly, Americans use Latin script even though they speak English.

Sumer was also the birthplace of the school. Although its primary function was to teach new scribes the art of reading and writing cuneiform, schools also taught some arithmetic. Students who showed exceptional promise and motivation could also take classes in religion, literature, and science in order to gain the more privileged social positions, such as priest or government official.

The Sumerians also conceived of such common ideas as the sixty-minute hour, the 360 degrees of a circle, wheeled vehicles, and the first synthetic material, known as faience. This manmade substance was meant to replicate the rare blue-colored gemstone, lapis lazuli. By mixing glass and copper ore under extreme heat, Sumerians were able to produce a blue-colored substance resembling the coveted precious stone.

Now it is time to journey south and west, to the banks of the Nile River. Here we will witness the birth of another civilization, one that today boasts the world's largest ancient monuments and the most well-preserved artifacts.

The Egyptians

No one knows exactly when the waters of the Nile River were first employed to support farming, but by the year 3500 B.C., the Egyptian civilization was already well established. The country was divided into northern and southern kingdoms. The northern area, defined by its low-lying marshlands, was known as Lower Egypt. The southern portion started above the marshlands, about 100 miles from the Mediterranean coast, and rose in elevation to the Nile's first waterfall (or cataract). Because of its higher elevation, this region was known as Upper Egypt.

E ALERT!

The Nile River flows south to north, from the Ethiopian Highlands to the Mediterranean Sea. This means that southern Egypt is higher in elevation than northern Egypt. Northern Egypt appears to be "upper" Egypt on a map, but it is really "lower" Egypt, because of its lower elevation.

In about 3100 B.C., a man known today as King Menes joined these two regions together and set up his capital city, Memphis. This united kingdom grew to become a world power that remained at the forefront of science and technology for thousands of years.

The Information Superhighway

The Egyptians used mathematics, physics, and astronomy to construct massive pyramids. Although the Great Pyramids of Giza have flat sides that form perfect triangles, the early Egyptian pyramids were almost identical to the terraced ziggurat pyramids of Sumer. This leads many to believe that the Egyptians borrowed more ancient Sumerian technology.

Not only is there an apparent technological connection between these two ancient cultures, but there is also reason to believe that there was a free exchange of astronomical and religious learning. The ancient Egyptians shared the Sumerians' fascination with the stars. In fact, the Egyptians had detailed maps of the stars that included many of the constellations identified first by Mesopotamian stargazers. From methods of water diversion and irrigation to production of the synthetic material faience, numerous parallels suggest a flow of information from the Euphrates and Tigris civilization to the peoples of the Nile Valley.

Egyptians were by no means just copycats. In fact, they were quite the opposite; they took Sumerian technology to another level with bigger and better creations. They also developed their own inventions and unique cultural and religious constructs.

Genius on the Nile

Egyptians used the Nile for irrigation, but it was also their maritime highway. Simple boats, fashioned from bundles of reeds, enabled citizens to travel the length of the kingdom comfortably and quickly. Eventually, large galley ships were built that allowed goods and people to the Nile and also to the unknown expanses of the Mediterranean Sea.

FACT

How about a beer? Germans weren't the first beer lovers. Artwork from both Mesopotamia and Egypt show the production and consumption of beer and wine as early as 2500 B.C.

A system of simple pictures, known today as hieroglyphics, was used by the people of the Nile to record everything from business transactions to military victories. Egyptians also developed a symbol for the number ten. This may not seem like a great achievement, but the new mark let them record 100 items with only ten symbols instead of 100 straight lines. Around 2800 B.C., Egyptians started making sheets from papyrus plants, the ancient precursor to paper. Papyrus quickly became the writing material of choice, as it was lighter than stone or clay tablets and could be rolled into a portable scroll. In fact, papyrus was adopted by many ancient peoples and was used by the Romans until about A.D. 300.

Paintings and carvings were often used to show the gods interacting with the pharaoh, reinforcing the common belief that the ruler was in fact a god-man. With the aid of the sun god, Re, the pharaoh would govern the land and ensure favor from the gods. Egyptians had a strong view of the afterlife, in which they believed their earthly bodies and possessions would be carried on into eternity. As a result, priests invented the first methods of embalming, known as mummification. To this day, modern morticians are unable to replicate the exact methods of preservation that have kept the bodies of pharaohs and farmers intact for thousands of years.

FACT

Did you know that Jacob, father of the twelve tribes of Israel, was mummified in Egypt? According to Genesis 50:1–3, "Joseph directed the physicians in his service to embalm his father Jacob. So the physicians embalmed him, taking a full forty days, for that was the time required for embalming. And the Egyptians mourned for him seventy days."

Ancient Egypt remains one of the most studied civilizations of all time, yet at the same time it is one of the most mysterious. From sci-fi movies to adventure thrillers, this land has provided the Western imagination with endless fuel for dreaming. Despite all of the fiction, one thing is certain: The modern inhabitants of Egypt are proud of their heritage. Even the largely Muslim city of Cairo acknowledges its polytheistic heritage, as statues of ancient gods and pharaonic trinkets are displayed in roundabouts and sold in bazaars. Whether or not today's Egyptian Arabs are direct descendants of the pharaohs, monuments of former greatness stand beside modern high-rises, blurring the millennia into one civilization—Egypt.

The Phoenicians

Around 2500 B.C., a Canaanite group, known today as the Phoenicians, established small settlements along the northeastern Mediterranean coast, in the area currently known as Lebanon. While the settlers borrowed many aspects of Sumerian culture, they enjoyed relative independence from the Mesopotamian and Egyptian power centers.

Many Phoenicians were craftsmen and farmers, yet the region's real strength was found in its relationship with the seas. From the coastal cities of Tyre, Sidon, and Byblos, the biggest and best ships of the time were built. Utilizing their own superior shipbuilding technology, Phoenician inventors used sails to propel their ships, rather than the bulky oars and rowing crews used by other seafarers.

As masters of the Mediterranean, Phoenicians were successful traders and explorers. They entered the Atlantic Ocean to trade with Britain and traveled south through the Red Sea to the tip of Africa. With their unique glassware and purple dye, Phoenicians traveled to distant lands and returned with loads of exotic merchandise. In addition to trading their goods with distant peoples, they were also responsible for spreading Middle Eastern civilization to those they met. The wealth and reputation of the Phoenician cities grew as they dominated the marine trade routes and established distant colonies, like the North African city of Carthage (in modern-day Tunisia) and Tarshish in southern Spain.

The Phoenicians developed the first phonetically based alphabet, which was the inspiration for the Latin script we use today. This form of writing was designed to simplify written language by using a single character to represent each sound.

The need to record information from large business transactions while traveling the seas pushed Phoenicians to abandon the complicated Sumerian cuneiform system and develop their own set of characters. The resulting system included twenty-two simple symbols to represent specific spoken sounds, rather than the complicated shapes and pictures used by other ancient peoples. This was the world's first alphabet, from which Hebrew, Arabic, Greek, and Latin alphabets would find their inspiration.

Although these wealthy traders dominated the seas, they were not as fortunate on land. For nearly half a century, ancient Phoenicia was occupied by foreign powers. Eventually, the weakening of these powers, combined with the maritime strength of the Phoenicians, brought Phoenician independence. A few hundred years later, they were again subjugated and enveloped into the bloodlines of Greek, Roman, and Arab conquerors. Today Phoenician pride is kept alive in Lebanon, as some citizens choose to identify with the fame of their ancient predecessors.

The Hittites

About 1,000 years after Menes united Upper and Lower Egypt, light-skinned Indo-Europeans known as Hittites conquered much of Asia Minor (modern-day Turkey). The Hittites proceeded to subdue the indigenous peoples, imposing their language, culture, and laws. This was the first civilization in Asia Minor; in addition, it was the first civilization comprised of peoples from the ethnic stock that would later populate Europe. Before long, Hittite aggressiveness led to clashes with Mesopotamian and Egyptian armies.

The Hittites were fierce and inventive warriors. In fact, they were the first to extract iron from ore. From this new metal, they made weapons that were much stronger than the bronze and copper ones used by everyone else. Their warrior ingenuity also produced some of the world's lightest and fastest chariots. Iron weaponry and high-tech chariots were a huge advantage on the battlefield, but over time knowledge of iron-working spread to Mesopotamia, Egypt, and beyond.

Not Just Warriors

One of the Hittites' most distinctive attributes was their strong emphasis on justice. Their extensive law codes were not unique, but the way the Hittites implemented them was unheard of elsewhere. Most ancient communities punished lawbreakers with violent retribution. The Hittites, however, approached criminals with a desire to restore both the victim and the criminal. They did this by forcing the criminal either to return the stolen property, plus an additional fee, or, if nothing could be returned, to pay a sufficient amount, as determined by a judge.

Having studied the ancient inhabitants of places known today as Iraq, Egypt, Lebanon, and Turkey, now consider the modern citizens of these countries. They see this ancient history as their heritage. They view these technological and scientific contributions as their own, and they cherish the power and majesty that once rested in their homelands as memories of the past and hope for the future.

Hittite Culture

As was the case with most ancient peoples, the Hittites believed there were many gods controlling peoples' emotions, the weather, fertility, war, and so on. The Hittite pantheon was made up of over a thousand gods, acquired from their Indo-European homeland, as well as Mesopotamia, Egypt, and other regions. Again, as in Sumer and Egypt, the Hittite king controlled religious and political life. Among the masses, the belief was that the king's interaction with the gods assured the health, wealth, and protection of their people. Storytelling and written literature were also important parts of Hittite culture. Scribes recorded historical and religious texts from the spoken Hittite language, using Sumerian cuneiform characters.

Cuneiform and gods weren't the only things the Hittites borrowed from other civilizations—everything from art and architecture to the use of the wheel came from other peoples. Although they introduced the world to iron, this warring people borrowed much more than they invented. Ultimately, the Hittites met the fate of their violent focus, as another invading European group, known only as "the Sea Peoples," destroyed their civilization in 1200 B.C.

The Babylonians

About the same time the Hittites were conquering Anatolia (modern-day Turkey), a tribe of Canaanites known as the Amorites moved into the central Mesopotamian region of Babylonia. They made the city of Babylon their base (near modern-day Baghdad), from which they conquered the armies of Mesopotamia. The Amorites quickly adopted the rich culture of the Sumerian civilization, which then came to be known as Babylonian civilization.

From the Sumerian story of the world's creation to their wedge-shaped cuneiform characters, Amorite scribes borrowed the history and culture of Sumer and made it their own. At the hands of the mighty warrior king Hammurabi, the new Babylonian kingdom spread its influence across the Fertile Crescent, from what is now the Persian Gulf all the way to the northeastern shores of the Mediterranean. Hammurabi was not only a skilled fighter, he was a great legislator as well. His detailed law code is the most comprehensive of any ancient civilization and is the inspiration of the popular saying, "An eye for an eye and a tooth for a tooth."

FACT

"If a surgeon has removed with the bronze lancet a cataract from a nobleman, and has cured his eye, he shall take ten shekels of silver. If it be a commoner, he shall take five shekels of silver." This edict, given by the Babylonian king Hammurabi in the 1700s B.C., is a snapshot of Babylon's detailed regulatory system, as well as its scientific, social, and economic situation.

From the birth of Babylon in 2000 B.C. to its destruction in 1530 B.C., the Babylonians carried the wonders of Sumerian civilization to new heights. Massive bridges, temples, and palaces remain to this day as testimonies of Babylon's greatness. As you will discover in Chapter 3, Babylon's power was not finished. After nearly a thousand years of dormancy, in 605 B.C. it was revived as the militant Chaldean or Neo-Babylonian Empire.

From Saddam Hussein's delusions of a revived Babylonian Empire to the impact of biblical Abraham (who was originally from the Babylonian city of Ur), this civilization has not been forgotten. In fact, thanks to the detailed writings of Abraham's descendants, a vivid picture of the entire region is available to the modern world.

The Hebrews

The Hebrew civilization doesn't start with a huge ethnic group or a mighty conquest, but with a single man and his family. Genesis 11:31 reads: "Terah took his son Abram (Abraham), his grandson Lot son of Haran, and his daughter-in-law Sarai, the wife of his son Abram, and together they set out from Ur of the Chaldeans to go to Canaan. But when they came to Haran, they settled there." From Abraham and his descendants the Hebrew civilization begins.

The biblical record explains that Abraham and his family were born and raised in "Ur of the Chaldeans." Most scholars believe this took place in about 1800 B.C., which would mean that the family lived in Ur when it was the most powerful city in Mesopotamia. The exact reason they departed from the comforts of city life is not known, but some have suggested that they may have been trying to escape the strains of Ur's swelling urban population.

Promises and Land

The text of Genesis goes on to say that Abraham and his family lived in Haran until after his father Terah's death. While in the city of Haran (today found in south central Turkey), Abraham heard the voice of his singular deity declaring, "Leave your country, your people, and your father's household, and go to the land I will show you." With these words in mind, Abraham traveled south, with most of his extended family, to the region of Canaan (modern Palestine/Israel), where he again heard a voice telling him, "To your offspring I will give this land."

Because of a famine in Canaan, Abraham and his relatives wandered into Egypt, where they were called Hebrews, from the Egyptian word meaning "wanderer." After living in Egypt for a short time, Abraham returned to Canaan, where he had many children, most notably Ishmael and Isaac. Both of these sons produced children, including Jacob and Esau from Isaac. Jacob proceeded to have twelve sons of his own, and these men would become the leaders of the twelve Hebrew tribes.

In the Middle East today, two groups see themselves as descendants of Abraham. Jews claim to be from the line of Isaac, and Arabs from the seed of Ishmael (*Isma`il* in Arabic).

Wanderers with Holy Words

To escape another famine, Jacob and his family wandered back into Egypt, just as Abraham had done. The biblical text goes on to say that they were very successful in Egypt, but that as a group, the Hebrews were eventually were forced into slavery. During 400 years of forced labor, the Egyptians continued to refer to the wanderers as Hebrews, but the descendants of Jacob (Israel) knew themselves as Israelites.

Upon their release from Egypt, there were likely over a million Israelites under the leadership of Moses. For close to forty years this wandering mass looked for Canaan; meanwhile, Moses recorded the five books known collectively as the Torah. This massive literary work was at the center of Hebrew civilization and remains to this day the culture's most significant achievement.

Kingdom of Conflict

After conquering the land of Canaan, in the middle of the thirteenth century B.C., the Israelites divided the land into Israelite tribal regions. Originally set up as a theocracy administered by priests, this was followed by a long period in which wise judges ruled the people. Around 1000 B.C., a traditional monarchy was set up. At this time a king ruled the nation but, as the kingdom was still religiously based, priests retained great power.

The best-known kings, David and his son Solomon, expanded Hebrew territory to run from the Euphrates River in the north to the Red Sea in the south. Solomon developed the capital, Jerusalem, into a magnificent city that included an opulent palace and a large temple dedicated to the one deity. Inside the holy city of Jerusalem, Solomon's Temple was the focal point of Hebrew consciousness, as it was the house of the only all-powerful God.

After Solomon's death in 930 B.C., the kingdom split, with Israel in the north and Judah in the south. Within 200 years, Israel was conquered and Judah remained the only Hebrew kingdom. Within another 150 years, Judah was also conquered. The term "Jew" was derived from "Judah," to refer to all surviving Hebrew people.

Less than 900 years after conquering Canaan, the Hebrews found themselves wandering once again, this time in Mesopotamia. It would be another half a century before they would return to Canaan, only for the region to be occupied thereafter by a succession of foreign empires. In A.D. 70, the Hebrews were forced once again to wander the earth in what is called the Diaspora, meaning "the spreading out."

You can see just how much the Middle East has given to humanity. As the descendants of the pharaohs, who built the pyramids, and of the Sumerians, who invented written language, it's easy to understand the pride of modern Middle Easterners. From the first city to the first wheel, you can see just how much the world has been influenced by the Middle East. So why is it that most people today don't also follow the polytheistic example of these civilizations? The answer to this question is found, as usual, in the Middle East. Ⓔ

Chapter 3

Rise of the Empires

Historical empires fought to take over large pieces of the planet. The Middle East has been ruled by indigenous empires from the inside out and by distant foreign regimes from the outside in. Nevertheless, the Middle East has been shaped by centuries of dictators, rebel revolts, and empires striking back.

Components of an Empire

Imperialism is arguably as old as civilization itself. The earliest organized governments sought to exert their power and authority over neighboring peoples and nations, causing some historians to define them as empires. For the purposes of this book, empires will be defined as strong, centrally organized entities that not only control close neighbors, but also expand their territories by subduing and integrating distant peoples into their domains. As you seek to understand the Middle East's turbulent history, look for these components in an empire:

- One all-powerful leader
- Sophisticated military forces
- Ever-expanding borders
- Organization of extensive territories
- Efforts to integrate diverse peoples
- Cultural, religious, and ideological control
- A massive capital city
- Attitude of global superiority

The Assyrians

Just over 5,000 years ago, the region of Assur (now northern Iraq) was under the influence of the great Sumerian civilization. The inhabitants of Assur, Assurians (Assyrians), borrowed nearly every aspect of Sumerian culture, including religion, law, and the cuneiform script. Within 1,000 years, the Amorites conquered Sumer, taking control of central and southern Mesopotamia from their capital city—Babylon. At about the same time, the Assyrians expanded their territory from northern Mesopotamia by colonizing parts of central Anatolia (Turkey).

By the 1800s B.C., Assyria's king, Shamshi-Adad, expanded his domains to cover a massive area from the southern Zagros Mountains (today, southwestern Iran) to the Mediterranean Sea. The king then divided his domain into provinces, appointed regents over these areas, connected the districts with a royal mail service, and regularly counted the people of his far-flung empire.

Because of these large-scale organizational efforts, Shamshi-Adad's kingdom is considered by many to be the world's first empire. Regardless of whether this was the first empire, it didn't last long. After only half a century, the Babylonian king Hammurabi conquered Assyria, putting an end to the kingdom. This began one of the Middle East's most violent and chaotic periods.

For nearly 300 years the region was ravaged, as various migrant invaders—Assyrians, Babylonians, Hittites, and Egyptians—took turns fighting one another. Although several of the invading peoples settled in the region and established kingdoms, instability and conflict characterized this bloody period. As a result of this long tumultuous time, the Assyrians were formed into a battle-hardened warrior nation. Eventually, they used their tenacity to revive the Assyrian Empire of old. This time, however, it would be a military state, known throughout the Middle East for its ferocious armies.

Revival

At some point around 1200 B.C., Assyria acquired the skill of iron-working, probably from a Hittite fleeing his conquered kingdom. Combined with other new technologies, this skill allowed Assyria to reassert itself as a regional power. By continually raiding neighboring territories, the Assyrians gained significant plunder and tribute. Because little was done to organize or annex conquered areas, Assyria expanded slowly for nearly 400 years. Then, in 745 B.C., a new king—King Tiglath-Pileser III—ascended to the throne with a view toward global domination.

The new Assyrian leader methodically planned his invasions and intentionally relocated conquered peoples from their homelands to other parts of the empire. One famous example of this policy was the conquest of the northern Hebrew kingdom of Israel, in which the Assyrians deported the Israelites to various locations in the empire. As a result, those tribes were lost to history, never to be heard from again.

By the late 700s B.C., the Assyrian king Sargon II had stretched the empire to cover the area from the Taurus Mountains (Turkey) in the west, to the Persian Gulf in the east. When Sargon's son, Sennacherib, came to power, he moved the imperial capital to Nineveh (modern-day Mosul, Iraq), home of the famous goddess Ishtar. In his new capital, the king enforced Assyrian rule, crushing even the smallest rebellions with swift brutality.

From Nineveh, Sennacherib's son, Ashurbanipal, continued in the ruthless Assyrian military tradition by conquering Memphis, Egypt's capital, and Susa, capital of the Elamite kingdom (modern-day southwestern Iran). Ashurbanipal not only continued to expand and organize Assyria's massive empire, he also sought to preserve Mesopotamian history, culture, and learning by collecting a huge library in Nineveh.

In 722 B.C., Assyrian armies (under the leadership of King Sargon II) conquered the northern Hebrew kingdom of Israel and deported its entire population, but they stopped short of taking the southern Hebrew kingdom of Judah. To this day, the fate of the Lost Tribes of Israel is a mystery, and the descendents of Judah, or "Jews," remain as the only recognizable Hebrews.

Changing of the Guard

The Assyrian Empire was in full swing, with territories including most of Egypt, the entire eastern Mediterranean coast, central Anatolia, Mesopotamia, and western Aryana (Iran). By all appearances it was the world's most powerful government, and there was no reason to think things would change. But after the death of Ashurbanipal, everything fell apart. It's unclear exactly what caused this rapid deterioration, but within twenty years of the king's passing, the Persians, Chaldeans, and Medes had conquered Nineveh and ended the 1,000-year reign of the Assyrians.

Although the Assyrian Empire vanished from the world stage, the people of Assyria remained in their northern Mesopotamian homeland. Under Median, Persian, Greek, and Roman rule, they preserved their ancient heritage. Eventually, Christianity became a unifying force that distinguished the Assyrians from other groups. To this day, the Assyrian Christians (known as the Nestorians) of Iraq, Iran, Turkey, and Syria differentiate themselves from neighboring Arabic, Kurdish, and Turkic peoples.

FACT

In 650 B.C., the Assyrian king, Ashurbanipal, built one of the ancient world's largest libraries. In 1929, archeologists uncovered this collection, finding over 20,000 cuneiform tablets with information about Middle Eastern history, literature, magic, chemistry, astronomy, and botany.

The Chaldeans, a.k.a. Neo-Babylonians

With the fall of the Assyrian war machine, the Chaldeans became the powerhouse of Mesopotamia. By 605 B.C., King Nebuchadnezzar II had declared Babylon (near modern-day Baghdad, Iraq) as the capital of his new or "neo" Babylonian Empire. After conquests in Syria, Phoenicia (modern-day Lebanon), and Egypt, Nebuchadnezzar moved into Judah, the only remaining Hebrew kingdom. By 586 B.C. he had captured its capital city, Jerusalem, and relocated Judah's inhabitants to Babylon. Using the wealth and manpower he had acquired through conquest, Nebuchadnezzar built Babylon into the largest, most impressive city of his time.

Babylon the Great

Spreading out over 2,500 acres, this magnificent city-state boasted more than 1 million citizens. The entire city was built with bricks ornamented with colorful tile pictures. Protected by 100-foot walls, the city was divided by the winding Euphrates River. The city's magnificent processional avenues were so awe-inspiring that many argued they should be named a wonder of the ancient world. Ornately crafted entrances, such as the famous Ishtar Gate, welcomed visitors and citizens to the majesty of Babylon. From extravagant palaces to soldiers' golden helmets, the wealth of Babylon was the envy of the world.

As the envy of the world, Babylon was also its target. In response, Nebuchadnezzar secured the borders of his empire with large walls and towers. For instance, at Babylonia's northeastern edge, the Medes were growing in strength. Nebuchadnezzar ordered a large wall to be built, and to this day, the ruins of the Median Wall can be seen in northern Iraq.

FACT

If you put all of Babylon's bricks end to end, they would encircle the planet fifteen times at its widest point.

In addition to building numerous palaces and defenses, Nebuchadnezzar also fashioned a massive ziggurat tower covered with trees, plants, and flowers. Many believe this towering desert oasis (commonly known as the "Hanging Gardens of Babylon") was built to comfort his wife, who was homesick for the mountainous landscape of her homeland in Media (present-day northwest Iran). Regardless of their purpose, these gardens, rising to heights of 300 feet, were unlike anything the ancients had ever seen. The technology used to transport water from the Euphrates River to high terrace gardens was a wonder in itself, but it was the Hanging Gardens of Babylon that were chosen as one of the Seven Wonders of the Ancient World.

The Chaldeans not only revived the ancient city of Babylon, they also continued the Mesopotamian traditions of astronomy, astrology, and mapmaking. Using clay tablets, Chaldean priest-astrologers mapped the world and the universe, placing Babylon at the center of the cosmos. A clear attitude of global superiority permeated the city and was under-scored by Nebuchadnezzar's declaration that Babylon was "the belly button of the world." Contrary to Chaldean propaganda, Babylon was not the center of the universe, but thanks to Babylonian scribes, some of the Middle East's most ancient literary and historical works were preserved.

Babylon Has Fallen

Despite the neo-Babylonian Empire's opulence and pride, its power was short-lived. After less than 100 years, the Persians took Babylon, bringing an abrupt end to the Chaldean Dynasty. As with the Assyrians, the people of Babylonia remained in Mesopotamia, though even as subjects of foreign kings, the Chaldeans retained their identity for hundreds of years. As early as the first century, they rejected their traditional polytheism and adopted Christianity. Today, Iraqi Catholics distinguish themselves from other Iraqi Arabs and Kurds by calling themselves Chaldeans.

FACT

During the Chaldean regime, Aramaic became the common language of the Middle East. As a result, Jesus Christ spoke a dialect of Aramaic nearly 600 years later. Today, Aramaic (also known as Syriac) remains the liturgical language of many Middle Eastern Christians.

The Medes

By helping to destroy the Assyrian Empire, the Medes found themselves on top in their corner of the world. At about the same time that the Chaldeans were setting up an empire from Babylonia, the Medes began to develop their regime from the heights of the Zagros Mountains (present-day western Iran).

The Medes used their newfound freedom to conquer parts of Anatolia (Turkey), Urartu (Armenia), Assyria, and Aryana (Iran). Soon other Aryan tribes, such as the Persians and Parthians, submitted to Median power. With an empire stretching from present-day Afghanistan to Turkey, the Medes controlled more territory than the former Assyrian Empire. Not only that, but they ruled over more land than their rivals, the Chaldeans.

ALERT!

Don't be confused by the term "Aryan"! In the twentieth century, Adolph Hitler idealized an ancient race of blond-haired, blue-eyed Europeans known as the "Aryans"—this was pure myth! In reality, Aryan tribes, such as the Persians, Medes, and Parthians, lived in the Middle East and were anything but European.

The Medes were relatively limited in their cultural and political development. As a result, they borrowed many things from the Assyrians and Urartians (Armenians). Median religion, however, was somewhat unique. The priestly tribe, known as the Magi, developed a complex tradition of stories to explain the natural world. What set the Magi's religion apart from other polytheistic groups was its dualism between good and evil gods. This worldview eventually influenced the prophet Zarathustra (also known as Zoroaster) who rejected the Magi's pantheon for a singular deity—Ahura Mazda.

Borders Without Orders

From luxurious palaces to well-engineered fortifications, the Median capital was impressive in appearance, but the empire as a whole lacked the organization and oversight of previous world powers. As a result, the Persian tribe was able to grow in strength. In, 550 B.C., they conquered the Median capital, claiming the empire for themselves.

After ruling only sixty years, the Medes lost their vast empire and became subjects of the Persians. But even as the Medes lost political control, Median religion continued to reign supreme long after the Persian takeover. The Magi remained the priestly tribe of the Persians until the emperor Darius rejected traditional beliefs for the teachings of Zoroaster.

FACT

After five centuries of the Persian Magi and their polytheism, the prophet Zoroaster claimed to be in contact with the one and only deity Ahura Mazda, meaning "Wise Master." He called his listeners to reject the many gods of the old Magi religion that he said was inspired by Angra Mainyu, translated as "Lie Demon." Although Zoroastrianism became the official religion of more than 1 million Middle Easterners, today there are only about 140,000 followers worldwide.

It is unclear exactly what happened to the Medes after the Persian takeover. Maybe they joined forces with their Persian cousins and helped to establish the world's most powerful empire. It's possible that they intermarried with Persians and ceased to exist as a distinct Median nation. Or perhaps they remained separate from the Persians and continued living in the mountaintops of their homeland. The world may never know exactly what happened to the Medes, but one thing is certain: Their conquests prepared the way for the Persians, who shaped the Middle East and nearly conquered the known world.

The Persians

As you read earlier, the Persians were an Aryan tribe that submitted to the power of their cousins the Medes. However, they eventually organized a revolt and overtook the Median Empire. With the Median territories under his belt, Cyrus, of the prominent Achaemenian family, built a Persian empire. In 539 B.C., he conquered Babylon, adding all of the Chaldean territories to his growing empire. Cyrus' grandson, Darius, took the Achaemenian Dynasty to another level by conquering lands as far east as the Indus River, in present-day Pakistan, and as far west as the Danube River, the border of modern-day Romania. With an empire stretching from Eastern Europe to India, Darius was responsible for more people and land than anyone up to his time.

Empire Management

Unlike his Median predecessors, Darius devised an ingenious organizational system to bridge the wide expanses of his empire. First, the Persian leader divided the empire into twenty regions, each governed by a leader known as the satrap. To ensure that none of his satraps were thinking of starting their own kingdom, Darius developed a secret service to inspect and investigate the various regions. Darius also undertook the daunting task of connecting the provinces with a system of roads. In addition, a royal mail service was established, allowing citizens and officials to communicate across the empire.

Another aspect of Persian management focused on setting standards. The popular Aramaic tongue was named the official language and, instead of cumbersome cuneiform characters, the Phoenician alphabet became the official Persian script. The Achaemenians also minted the first imperial currency and developed a standard system of weights and measures.

A universal law code brought uniform justice across the empire, and the Emperor Darius' conversion to Zoroastrianism established an official Persian religion.

This was the best-managed empire the world had ever seen.

Compassionate Imperialism

Known as the *shah an-shah* (king of kings), the Persian ruler made his position clear, but, compared to previous world empires, the Achaemenians had relative respect for the rights of their conquered peoples. In fact, when Cyrus conquered Babylon, he released the Jews and allowed them to return to Judah, where they remained under Persian rule with a certain amount of freedom.

ESSENTIAL

In 490 B.C., the Greeks miraculously repelled a massive Persian attack on the city of Marathon. With news of victory, their fastest runner set out to inform Athens, 26.2 miles to the south. Upon reaching Athens, the runner exclaimed *"Nike!"* meaning victory, before dropping dead of exhaustion.

The Persians continued to rule the Middle East with their compassionate brand of imperialism until a revolt erupted among their Greek subjects in Ionia (present-day western Turkey). Darius sent his armies to quiet the unrest, but the Athenians of neighboring Greece sent reinforcements as well, creating the first Greco-Persian war. The Persians came out on top in Ionia, but a clash of civilizations had begun.

The next half-century saw repeated conflicts in which the Persians burned Athens and the Greeks defeated Persian forces in both Greece and Asia Minor. Military defeats, infighting, revolts, and independent-minded satraps led to a serious weakening of the Persian Empire. Under the leadership of Alexander II (known as Alexander the Great), Greek forces pushed the Achaemenians out of Anatolia (modern-day Turkey) and proceeded to take the eastern Mediterranean coast, Egypt, and Mesopotamia. In 331 B.C., Persia itself came under Alexander's rule.

For another 1,000 years, as Greeks and Romans built their empires, Western forces reigned in the Middle East.

The Greeks

Greek civilization stretches back nearly 4,000 years, when a people known as the Hellenes began to develop a Mediterranean civilization that would become the backbone of Western civilization. In this book, however, the focus is mainly on their exploits in the Middle East.

In 334 B.C., twenty-year-old Alexander II of Macedonia led the world's first crusade of Western imperialism. From southeastern Europe, Alexander and his soldiers traveled thousands of miles, conquering the entire Persian Empire and part of India. From North Africa to Central Asia, Alexander and his men established colonial cities that eventually became centers of Greek culture. To this day, Middle Eastern cities such as Alexandria, Egypt, and al-Iskandariyah, Iraq, remain as monuments to this twenty-something world leader.

The Greco-Persian Wars were one of the most pivotal points in world history. Thanks to Alexander the Great's victories over the Persian Empire, Western civilization was shaped by Greek thinkers, such as Plato and Aristotle, instead of the shah or his Zoroastrian priests.

Even though Alexander was a Western conqueror, he saw himself as the successor to the Persian throne. He was responsible for opening the door for Greek culture to enter the Middle East, but he also brought the Middle East to the Greeks. In fact, Alexander and 10,000 of his men married Persian wives. Not only that, he adopted Persian dress and customs and was planning to make Babylon the capital of his empire. What was originally a clash of civilizations appeared to be changing into a marriage of civilizations. Who knows what would have happened if Alexander had carried out his plans. Instead, soon after returning to Babylon from his conquests, he died suddenly of a strange illness.

With Alexander's unexpected demise, it was unclear who would run the empire. As a result, it splintered into at least nine different kingdoms, some ruled by local leaders and others by Macedonian generals. By 300 B.C., four of Alexander's generals had regained control of Alexander's domains. Seleucus reigned over most of the former Persian territories; Ptolemy retained Egypt, the eastern Mediterranean coast, and part of central Anatolia; Lysimachus gained western Anatolia and Thrace (modern-day Bulgaria); and Cassander ruled over Macedonia and Greece. Not exactly a unified empire, nevertheless, it allowed for the influence of Greek culture on the Middle East.

East Meets West

Soon, Greeks flocked to Alexander's colonial cities, bringing their architecture, athletics, philosophies, political systems, and language. Like teenagers obsessed with MTV, Easterners looked to the Greeks for their social and cultural cues. From Egypt to Persia and beyond, a new Hellenistic culture emerged, as non-Greeks imitated Greeks. Eventually, Greek became the common language of the entire Middle East, and Greeks or Hellenized Easterners held all positions of power. Although some resisted Hellenization, the tides had changed, and Greek culture was firmly in place.

You may think Athens was the capital of the Hellenistic world, but in reality Alexandria, Egypt, was the center of Greek influence. Entering the city from any direction, ancients were awed by the brilliance of the Pharos, the gigantic lighthouse counted among the Seven Wonders of the Ancient World. From exotic markets to its distinctly Greek layout and architecture, Alexandria was the intellectual and cultural hub of the known world.

Egypt was aglow with enlightenment as philosophers and thinkers displayed more than 3,000 years of learning in museums, zoos, and the ancient world's largest library. With a multiethnic population of more than 1 million, Alexandria stood as a cosmopolitan beacon of human progress and ingenuity. Among Alexandrian's many astronomers, biologists, physicians, and mathematicians, Euclid's teachings remain as the foundation for modern geometry. From the romantic exploits of Cleopatra and Mark Antony to adventurous tourists in search of the Great Pyramid, Egypt was an exotic land of mysteries—just as it is today.

FACT

Persians and Hebrews were not the only ancient peoples to adopt Phoenician script; Greeks also borrowed this convenient form of writing, which was later passed on to us via the Romans. Just look at the word *alphabet*, which comes from the Greek letters *alpha* and *beta* but is also related to the Hebrew letters *aleph* and *bet* and the Arabic letters *alif* and *baa.*

Hellenism not only spread to the east, it also made its way into Western Europe. Specifically in the city of Rome, Greek ideas affected government, law, politics, and religion. Eventually, this Hellenized city-state expanded its control from the Italian peninsula to Spain, North Africa, Greece, and Asia Minor. By 133 B.C., even Alexandria aligned itself with the Romans, resulting in a new Western empire.

The Romans

As with the Greeks, the Roman story is one that starts well before the Roman Empire. From as early as 800 B.C., a people known as the Latins lived on the Italian peninsula. Around 250 B.C., they began more than a century of conflict with the North African powerhouse of Carthage.

Originally established by Phoenician traders, the city of Carthage (in modern-day Tunisia) grew to control most of North Africa, Spain, and the western Mediterranean islands. As Rome expanded its territory into the Mediterranean, the two powers collided, spawning a long conflict known as the Punic Wars.

In 218 B.C., after nearly fifty years of hostilities, a Carthaginian commander named Hannibal led an army of 40,000 men (and a large herd of elephants) from Spain across the Alps to destroy Rome once and for all. It was Hannibal's lifelong ambition to see a silence of the Romans, but instead it turned out to be a slaughter of his lambs (or to be more accurate, his elephants). In the end, Rome not only protected itself, it captured Carthage and added its territories to their emerging empire.

With most of the Mediterranean under its power, Rome proceeded to occupy the rest of the Middle East (minus Iran and Arabia). While Greek language and culture permeated the region long after Alexander's death, the strength of his empire was lost until the Roman conquests. Under the Pax Romana, or "Roman Peace," a Western empire once again controlled the east, but this time Latin was the imperial language and Roman order was preserved at all costs. Despite many changes, Rome continued to rule the Middle East in various forms until the seventh century A.D.

In the next three chapters, you will discover that the Roman Empire was transformed not by military might but by social forces in the Middle East. From the development of Judaism's monotheistic nation, to the religious groups it spawned, the following chapter lays a crucial foundation upon which your entire understanding of the modern Middle East will rest. Ⓔ

Chapter 4

Ancient Judaism

Out of the foggy details of ancient monotheism mentioned in Genesis chapters 1 through 11, the Hebrew Scriptures unveil a clear plan for a monotheistic nation, fathered by Abraham, Isaac, and Jacob. This chapter takes you through the birth of this nation and its resulting religious traditions. From the twelve sons of Jacob, to the Hebrew kingdoms they established, you will find a people whose faith and folly have shaped the religious fabric of the Middle East and much of the world.

The Sons of Jacob and Their God

According to the Book of Genesis, the promises God gave Abraham were passed through Isaac to Jacob (also known by the name Israel) and his twelve sons. In Genesis 35:23–26, these sons are listed as Reuben, Simeon, Levi, Judah, Issachar, Zebulun, Joseph, Benjamin, Dan, Naphtali, Gad, and Asher. Chances are you only recognize a few of these names, but in fact each of these men fathered a Hebrew tribe, which together came to be known as the Twelve Tribes of Israel.

The Favorite Son

The Book of Genesis explains that while living as nomads in Canaan (present-day Israel/Palestine), the sons of Abraham, Isaac, and Jacob lived quiet lives herding their livestock. The text explains that Jacob favored his son Joseph over the others, creating a serious sibling rivalry. Because of their jealousy, the brothers agreed to sell Joseph to a caravan of Ishmaelite merchants. The traders took him to Egypt, where he was sold to a high-ranking Egyptian official. After years of slavery and imprisonment, the text says that Joseph became the pharaoh's right-hand man.

ALERT!

Joseph was more than a shepherd! As the pharaoh's assistant, Joseph would have spoken Egyptian, become comfortable with the culture, and studied the ancient secrets of the pharaohs. Not only that, but the Book of Genesis records that Joseph was mummified and placed in a sarcophagus in typical Pharaonic style.

Eventually, because of a famine in Canaan, Jacob sent his sons to Egypt in search of food. To their horrific surprise, the brothers found Joseph in charge of the food distribution. Instead of killing them for their past treachery, Joseph made peace with his brothers and requested that his father Jacob come to Egypt. After receiving the invitation, Jacob, his sons, and all of their families left Canaan for Egypt. On the way, Jacob is said to have made a sacrifice to God, which was followed by a vision where he was told, "Go down to Egypt, for I [God] will make you into a great nation there."

Upon arriving in Egypt, Jacob and a few of his sons met the pharaoh and were given land in the district of Rameses. Just as the Egyptians had called Abraham a "Hebrew" (wanderer), Jacob and his offspring were given this title as they wandered into North Africa.

Israel's Faith

The Hebrew Bible gives detailed accounts of Jacob's life and interaction with his God. As a strict monotheist, he is said to have called upon everyone in his family to get rid of their foreign gods and idols. He built multiple altars for animal sacrifices, including the pillar at the city he named Bethel (meaning "house of God"), and received divine visions, including that of the famous stairway to heaven (known as Jacob's Ladder). Jacob even wrestled with God, giving him the name Israel (meaning "struggles with God").

Prophecies

From his deathbed, Jacob gathered his sons to pass the torch of the monotheistic nation. Jacob started by adopting Joseph's sons Ephraim and Manasseh, making them equal heirs. By doing this, Joseph's inheritance was doubled, as he moved from being the head of one tribe to the father of two tribal leaders. Jacob went on to tell each of his sons what role they and their descendants would play in the coming nation. In his prophetic statements, Jacob made ominous predictions for some of his heirs, while others were named as future leaders.

Jacob's most notable prophecy likened Judah to a lion and he said, "The scepter will not depart from Judah, nor the ruler's staff . . . until he comes to whom it belongs and the obedience of the nations is his." Eventually, Judah's sons did become the dominant Hebrew tribe and, to this day, the Jews are named after the tribe of Judah. In addition, the latter part of Jacob's statement established the concept of a powerful world leader, known as the "Lion of the Tribe of Judah," who would come to rescue the Israelites from oppression.

From Slavery to Wandering

The Book of Exodus begins by explaining that the Hebrews were extremely successful in Egypt, growing to such large numbers that the Egyptians saw them as a threat to national security. With the passing of Joseph and all of his brothers, a new pharaoh rose to rule the country. This king is said to have devised several plans to ensure the protection of his domains. First, he placed slave masters over the entire Israelite community, hoping to suppress any possibility of revolt. But the Hebrew population continued to multiply, causing the pharaoh to order the murder of all newborn Hebrew males.

If you've seen the animated film *The Prince of Egypt,* you know the rest of the story—around 1500 B.C., a baby boy was born to the tribe of Levi. The newborn's mother saved him from the pharaoh's edict by sending him down the Nile in a papyrus basket. The pharaoh's daughter found the child, adopted him, and named him Moses.

QUESTION?

How smart was Moses?
Growing up in the royal family, Moses was one of the most educated people of his time. As an heir to the throne, he would have received the most advanced training in everything from warfare to the sciences. With access to nearly 2,000 years of ancient writings, Moses was able to read Egyptian hieroglyphics, Phoenician script, and possibly even Mesopotamian cuneiform. It is clear that Moses spoke Egyptian and Hebrew, but it is also likely that he understood Aramaic and other regional languages.

Moses was raised as the adopted son of the king. Because of his privileged position, Moses was more than likely trained in Egyptian combat, sciences, literature, and more. Because of his upbringing, it is also likely that he felt he was above the law. In a fit of rage, Moses killed an Egyptian soldier and was forced to flee to the area of Midian (present-day northwestern Saudi Arabia). As a shepherd in Midian, Moses was watching his flocks when suddenly he encountered a voice speaking to him from a burning bush. Identifying itself as the God of Abraham, Isaac, and Jacob, the voice ordered Moses to go back to Egypt, liberate his Hebrew brothers and sisters, and take them to the promised land of Canaan.

Man on a Mission

After receiving a special staff from God, Moses left Midian and met up with his brother Aaron in Egypt. Together they are said to have approached the Egyptian king with the message, "The God of Israel says: 'Let my people go, so they may worship me.'" Because the Pharaoh refused to let them go, ten plagues are recorded to have been visited upon the Egyptians. The last of these included special instructions in which each Hebrew family was to make bread without yeast, and kill a lamb and place its blood on the doorframe of their house. This blood would be a sign for God's final judgment to pass over them.

When the prescribed day came, the Israelites followed instructions, and God passed over their sons. Meanwhile, the Egyptians found all of their firstborn sons and animals dead. This was the last straw, and the Pharaoh told Moses and Aaron to leave his kingdom immediately. Suddenly, Moses was leading over 1 million people out of Egypt to the land of Canaan. After 430 years, the exodus had begun!

FACT

Every year, modern Jews remember their liberation from Egypt by celebrating Passover (*Pesach* in Hebrew). In commemoration of the original Passover, a *seder* meal (meaning "ordered") is served, in which specific elements are meant to symbolize captivity in Egypt, the exodus, and promises yet to come.

Soon after leaving the Pharaoh's clutches, the Israelites realized the Egyptian army was coming after them. According to the Biblical record, the Hebrews were pinned in by Egypt's most advanced chariots and skilled horsemen on one side and a sea on the other. The terrified Israelites prepared for death as Moses raised his staff, summoning the power of his God to divide the waters. With walls of water on either side, the Israelites passed through the sea bottom to safety, but their pursuers were crushed as the sea collapsed on them.

The Mountain of God

Moving toward Canaan, the Israelites continued to experience supernatural wonders in the desert, as stagnant water was made drinkable, mysterious food called *manna* (meaning "What is it?") formed on the ground, and streams of water appeared from a rock. Three months into their journey, Moses had led the Israelites back to the region of Midian, to the Horeb Mountains where God had spoken to him from the burning bush. Here on a mountain called Sinai, Moses again experienced a raging fire from which the voice of God declared these, the Ten Commandments:

1. You shall have no other gods before me.
2. You shall not make for yourselves idols.
3. You shall not misuse the name of God.
4. Remember the Sabbath (*Shabbat* in Hebrew) by keeping it holy.
5. Honor your father and mother.
6. You shall not murder.
7. You shall not commit adultery.
8. You shall not steal.
9. You shall not give false testimony.
10. You shall not covet.

With the Ten Commandments as their new constitution, the Israelites remained in the vicinity of Midian (northwestern Saudi Arabia) for another year, as God continued to inspire Moses with laws for the community and festivals of remembrance to order each year. Moses recorded all of this in a document known as "The Book of the Covenant" (found today in Exodus 20:22–23:33). Eventually, Moses was again called to the mountaintop, where he is said to have received God's laws on stone tablets, as well as specific instructions for the building of a tent for worship and its furnishings, including a sacrificial altar, seven-branched lamp stands (known as *menorahs*), and the famed Ark of the Covenant.

Considered by many to be the very throne of God, the Ark of the Covenant was the most prized possession of the Israelite community. Measuring just under four feet in length and a little over two feet in width and height, this wooden chest, covered in pure gold, housed the stone tablets sent down from God. Although Indiana Jones may have discovered this holy relic in *Raiders of the Lost Ark,* outside of Hollywood productions, its location remains a debated mystery.

Movin' On

Even though the Israelites were monotheists, living in Egypt for more than 400 years had shaped their culture and beliefs, causing them to dabble in polytheism. Because Moses spent six weeks on Mount Sinai, the Hebrews thought he wasn't coming back. So they made a golden calf, put on their Egyptian jewelry, and threw a party. The cow was likely meant to be the Egyptian fertility god Apis, as the scriptures say the Hebrews "ate, drank, and indulged in revelry" in front of the cow.

As a result of this little lovefest, the sons of Levi were chosen (via Aaron) as the priestly tribe, and the Hebrews were ordered by God to leave Sinai. This began a forty-year period of desert wandering, in which the Torah was drafted and the nation of Israel was prepared to enter the promised land of Canaan.

Moses and the Levitical Law Code

With anywhere from 1 to 3 million people and their livestock, it was necessary for the Hebrews to live in tents as they moved between pasturelands and oases. In fact, the Book of Numbers (33:16–49) records that the Hebrews moved more than thirty times from Sinai until their arrival at the border of Canaan. As they wandered, Moses began to record a history of ancient monotheism, the Hebrew people, and the laws he was receiving from his God.

First, in about 1445 B.C., Moses is believed to have been inspired to write the Book of Genesis (*Bereishith* in Hebrew), followed by the Book of Exodus (*Shemoth*), and, about five years later, the Book of Leviticus (*Vayiqra*). Named after the Levite priests who were to enforce its laws, the Book of Leviticus influenced Judaism more than any of the Mosaic writings. As a monotheistic community, God's laws were indisputable and the priests were his administrators.

The first seven chapters of Leviticus established the role of animal sacrifice in ancient Judaism. Unlike previous references to sacrifice, the text goes into great detail, prescribing specific animals and procedures for certain sins and situations. The Book of Leviticus also established the Day of Atonement (*Yom Kippur* in Hebrew), as a day in which nearly everyone and everything in the community was cleansed with blood. According to the Hebrew law code, blood was necessary to cleanse the worshiper of his or her disobedience.

FACT

The Feast of Tabernacles (*Sukkot* in Hebrew) commemorates the forty years of wandering that occurred between the receiving of the Ten Commandments and the conquest of Canaan. From mega-cities to jungle villages, many Jews remember their forefathers' wilderness time by living for one week in an outdoor structure, known as a sukkot.

While explaining God's requirements for spiritual cleansing, the Book of Leviticus also clarified God's position on day-to-day actions and attitudes. For example, Abraham was said to have given 10 percent of his wealth to God, but the tithe (meaning "10 percent") was not established until the Book of Leviticus commanded it. As the Israelite's primary law code, it formed the community's judicial system and holy days, but the code also set standards for personal morality, hygiene, sexuality, diet, and so on. The Book of Leviticus endorsed capital punishment, but the overriding purpose of its laws was to limit retaliation by establishing a punishment equal to the crime. Line after line, the text explicitly guided the new nation with divine prohibitions, commands, and promises, bringing order to the lives of more than 1 million Hebrew people.

Moses and the Hebrew nation lived as desert nomads for another thirty years before they saw the Promised Land. Looking down on the city of Jericho, Moses completed a forty-year history of the wilderness wanderings by recording the number of men from each of the twelve tribes. Today, this ancient chronicle is known as the Book of Numbers (*Bamidar* in Hebrew). Finally, with the Israelites poised to enter Canaan, Moses was inspired to draft a second edition of the divine law code. Known as the Book of Deuteronomy (*Devarim*), this scripture restated and clarified God's promises and laws, ordered the nation to take Canaan by force, and established a man named Joshua as Moses' successor. With the death of Moses, Joshua assumed power and prepared to conquer Canaan.

"Remember the Sabbath by keeping it holy." Today, the Jewish holy day begins at sundown on Friday and continues until sunset on Saturday. For most Christians, Sunday is set aside to remember the day of Jesus Christ's resurrection, and Muslims devote Friday to special prayer services and religious activities.

Conquest, Kingdom, and Captivity

By 1400 B.C., the Torah of Moses was complete, and the Hebrews believed its message was clear. Abraham, Isaac, and Jacob had worshiped one God, who promised them a great nation that would bless the planet from a specific land, the region of Canaan. After more than 400 years of slavery and migration, the promised monotheistic nation wanted the land they had been promised.

As the Book of Joshua (*Yehoshua* in Hebrew) recounts, the city of Jericho was the first to be conquered. From there, the massive Hebrew armies overwhelmed the surrounding cities, including Hebron, Bethel, and Jerusalem. Eventually, the surrounding northern and southern regions fell, putting the Israelites in control of Canaan. Joshua is then said to have divided the land into tribal regions according to each tribe's population.

Kingdom Come

After Joshua's death, the Hebrew tribes declared the kingdom of Israel a theocracy, with their God as king; the Ark of the Covenant as his throne; the Torah of Moses as his royal law code; and judges, priests, and prophets as his officials. This style of government continued for nearly 300 years, until Saul was named king in 1050 B.C. Forty years later, David (from the tribe of Judah) was called to rule the kingdom. During his reign, Hebrew tribal divisions were mended, Israel's capital was moved to Jerusalem (along with the Ark of the Covenant), and the kingdom's territories were expanded.

QUESTION?

What is the official Jewish symbol?
Although the star of David (also called the shield of David) is recognized by many to be the symbol of Judaism, the menorah, a seven-branched lamp stand, is the most ancient symbol of the Jewish faith.

David's son, Solomon, continued his father's expansions by stretching Israel's domains to run from the Euphrates River in the north to the Red Sea in the south. In addition, he transformed Jerusalem into a beautiful city, building the famous Temple of Solomon as a home for God and his throne, the Ark of the Covenant. The blood of animals and the prayers of the faithful flowed from Jerusalem's magnificent temple, as it became the center of monotheistic worship for the next 1,000 years.

Solomon moved the Hebrew nation to a new level of success, but tribal alliances were starting to crack. Solomon's death in 930 B.C. split the Hebrews into two kingdoms, Judah in the south and Israel in the north. By 722 B.C., the northern kingdom of Israel was overrun by the Assyrian Empire. Meanwhile, the southern kingdom of Judah remained strong, until Chaldean armies captured Jerusalem and destroyed Solomon's Temple in

586 B.C. The Judeans were taken to Babylon, where they remained in captivity until the Persians conquered Babylon.

Jerusalem

Under Persian rule, the Jews were allowed to go back to Jerusalem, where they rebuilt their city, their temple, and their lives. Under successive Persian, Greek, and Roman occupations, the descendants of Judah continued to worship their God in Jerusalem, until Roman forces destroyed the temple and expelled them from the region. This great Diaspora, or scattering, forever changed the Jewish people and their religion, as once again they found themselves wandering.

The Message of the Tanakh

From Mount Sinai's Ten Commandments to the 613 laws found in the Torah, the law of Moses provided moral and judicial foundations for the Hebrew people. After the time of Moses, monotheism continued to evolve as poets, kings, and prophets were inspired to write about the one God.

For nearly 1,000 years the warnings, promises, and predictions of Isaiah, Ezekiel, Jonah, Malachi, and others were gathered to form a division of scriptures called the *Nevi'im* (Prophets). From the praises of David's Book of Psalms to the wisdom found in Solomon's Book of Proverbs, the Hebrews embraced a body of scriptures known as the *Kethuvim* (Writings). Together, these scriptures form the Tanakh, which is an acrostic for Torah, Nevi'im, and Kethuvim. If you are not from a Jewish background, you've probably never heard of the Tanakh, although you may recognize its other name, the Old Testament.

ESSENTIAL

The Tanakh, or Old Testament, is the most recognized religious text in the world, as more than half of the world's population considers at least parts of it to be sacred writings, especially the Torah and the Psalms of David.

With more than twenty-five authors writing it over a 1,300-year period, the Tanakh stands as the monotheistic masterpiece. Its message sustained the Jewish people through repeated occupations and prepared the way for new monotheistic movements, such as Christianity and Islam. To this day, it continues to influence the lives of monotheists around the globe, as they look to its pages for pictures of the past, direction for the present, and hope for the future.

Although various interpretations of the Tanakh have fueled conflicts in the Middle East and beyond, the text itself offers unmistakable themes of monotheism, morality, justice, and mercy. With room for healthy debate, the Scriptures must not be a source for violent separatists but instead a conduit for divine connection. In the following chapter, you will uncover the roots of a religion that transformed the Middle East, the Roman Empire, and ultimately the world. E

Chapter 5
Early Christianity

Apart of Judaism is the belief that God would send a messenger, a messiah (*Moshiach* in Hebrew), to liberate the Jewish people. Around A.D. 30, an obscure group of Messianic Jews claimed the long-awaited messiah had come. Branded heretics by some and persecuted by others, this small sect continued to gather new followers. Within 300 years, this form of Judean Messianism, known today as Christianity, spread across ethnic and religious lines, transforming the Middle East and much of the world.

First-Century Judaism

In about 150 B.C., after more than 100 years of Greek occupation, a Jewish family known as the Hasmoneans (also called the Maccabeans) reclaimed Judea, Jerusalem, and the Jewish Temple. The Hasmoneans proceeded to place one of their own into the position of high priest, displacing the Zadokite family, which had controlled the priesthood since the time of David. Later, another Hasmonean declared himself "King of the Jews," even though he was not from the royal line of David. As a result, the Zadokites and those who followed them protested the Hasmonean dynasty and priesthood, forming a puritan sect known as the Essenes. Eventually, in 63 B.C., the Roman general Pompey the Great occupied Judea, turning the Hasmonean leadership into subservient puppets of the empire.

FACT

Today, the Jewish holiday of Hanukkah commemorates the Maccabean victory over the Greeks, the subsequent cleansing of the Temple of Solomon in Jerusalem, and reinstatement of the sacrificial system in 165 B.C.

The Separatists

In the first century A.D., the Essenes (writers of the famous Dead Sea Scrolls) were one of four Jewish sects, along with the Sadducees, Pharisees, and Zealots. The Essenes were a tightly knit community of ascetics who separated themselves from what they considered to be a corrupted Hebrew kingdom and religious system. In their minds, they were fulfilling the words of the prophet Isaiah when he said, "In the desert prepare the way for the Lord; make straight in the wilderness a highway for our God" (Isaiah 40:3). There were several brands of Essenic Judaism, yet all Essenes strictly adhered to the words of the Tanakh, practiced elaborate water purification rites, rejected the Hasmonean priesthood and its sacrificial services, and believed that a great war was coming. With the "Sons of Darkness and the Wicked Priest" on one side and the "Sons of Light and the Teacher of Righteousness" on the other, the Essenes were eagerly awaiting their warlord messiah.

The Privileged

The Sadducees were a group consisting of both Hasmonean priests and Hellenized aristocrats. Like the Essenes, the Sadducees recognized the Tanakh as God's only message, which translated into conservative religious views. Rejecting other Jewish sects, they denied mystical beliefs such as the resurrection of the body and the existence of spirits and angels. As overseers of the Temple, its treasury, and the sacrificial services, Sadducees held considerable influence in Judea. In addition, they controlled the Jewish religious courts, the office of high priest, and were in close contact with Roman officials. Overall, members of this sect owed their privileged positions to heredity, wealth, and/or political maneuvering.

The Scholars

The Pharisees, on the other hand, were generally self-made men who had risen to prominence through their knowledge of the Hebrew Scriptures. With a strong emphasis on individual education, the Pharisees created a power base by using their interpretations of the Tanakh and exclusive knowledge of other traditions found in what they called the "oral Torah." Unlike the Sadducees, the Pharisees believed this oral Torah had been given to Moses on Mount Sinai but was never written down; instead, sages transmitted these traditions verbally through the centuries.

The verbal traditions of the Pharisees, or oral Torah, were finally written down in the second century to form the Mishna. Over the next few hundred years, more commentaries, known as the Gemara, were written to further explain the traditions. In the fifth century A.D., these rabbinical writings were gathered together to form the Talmud.

The Pharisees were extremely critical of the Hellenized Sadducees, rejecting their political connections to the Roman occupiers. In addition, the Pharisees desired to see the complete implementation of Halakah

(Judaic law). Based on their biblical interpretations and the traditions of their rabbis (teachers), this brand of Judaism focused almost entirely on morality, spirituality, and—to some degree—mysticism.

The Freedom Fighters

The Zealot movement was born from the resentment and frustration caused by continued Roman occupation. With Rome exerting more control over the Jewish people, this nationalistic resistance group was formed. Resorting to terrorism, guerilla warfare, assassinations, and open revolt, this sect employed common religious ideals and terminology to recruit followers and incite rebellion.

Viewed as fanatics by some and freedom fighters by others, Zealots preferred death to Roman domination. The first-century Jewish historian Flavius Josephus provides evidence of this mindset, as he tells of a group of Zealots defending the mountain fortress of Masada in A.D. 73. Josephus records that after months of besiegement, the Roman Tenth Legion finally breached the walls of the fortress. Rather than submitting to their conquerors, the Zealot men, women, and children submitted to death, committing suicide as a group.

The Concept of Moshiach

Moshiach is a Hebrew word that is literally translated "anointed one." The term was inspired by ancient Middle Eastern coronation ceremonies, in which kings were anointed with olive oil as a sign of their authority. Known to English speakers as the messiah or the Christ, moshiach has come to be one of the most controversial and influential religious concepts of all time.

Although many scholars believe the messianic idea was introduced well after the time of Moses, Jewish and Christian traditions contend this has always been a central theme in monotheism. References to the "Lion of Judah" and the "End of Days" in the Torah, combined with the prophets' detailed descriptions of a spectacular world leader and his utopian age of justice, have produced this powerful concept. Believed to be a warrior king from the royal line of David and a high priest after the priesthood of Zadok, numerous scriptures have been interpreted to describe everything from the moshiach's place of birth to his characteristics and purposes.

Is there a difference among the terms Moshiach, Messiah, and Christ?
Around 200 B.C., Hellenized Jews translated the Tanakh from Hebrew into Greek. In this translation, the word *christos* ("anointed one" in Greek) was used for the Hebrew word *moshiach*, also meaning "anointed one." As a result, the English terms "messiah" and "Christ" were derived from these Hebrew and Greek words, and mean the same thing.

Yeshua and His Followers

As Roman occupation forces tightened their grip on Judea, zealotry and messianism were at frenzied levels. In the midst of these turbulent times, a Jewish man named Jesus son of Joseph son of David (*Yeshua ben Yosef ben David* in Hebrew) gathered large crowds who had heard of his wise teachings and ability to heal the sick, raise the dead, and exorcise demons.

Because of his understanding of the Tanakh, authoritative declarations, birth in Bethlehem, and supernatural abilities, many believed he was either the messiah or a great prophet preparing the way. According to his followers, people from all walks of life listened to Jesus' teachings and sought his miracles. Fishermen, craftsmen, tax collectors, Zealots, Sadducees, Pharisees, and even Roman officials were attracted to this mysterious rabbi from Nazareth.

The Chosen One

Out of the curious crowds, twelve men in particular believed Jesus was the chosen liberator and decided to drop everything and follow him. For three years, these men are said to have traveled with Jesus, teaching people to love God and others in the true spirit of the Torah. In addition, they warned their hearers to prepare for the Moshiach's Kingdom, spoken of in the Prophets and Writings. Eventually, four of Jesus' followers—Matthew, Mark, Luke, and John—are said to have recorded his life story in what are now called the Gospels.

The End of Days

Messianic fervor surrounded Jesus, as is evident in the story of his entry into Jerusalem, found in the Gospel of Matthew 21:1–16. In this account, Jesus rode into the city on a donkey as a great crowd chanted, "Praise to the Son of David!" He is then said to have gone directly to the temple, where he overturned the merchants' tables and chastised the priest in charge of the temple for allowing its precincts to be corrupted.

To the twenty-first-century Westerner, the first part of the story may conjure up quaint memories of children and palm branches at a Sunday morning church service, but the second half may seem out of character for Jesus. Wasn't he a passive teacher of love and peace? For the Jewish masses living in an age of messianic expectancy, however, everything made perfect sense; this was the beginning of God's cleansing and liberation—the messiah had come!

ESSENTIAL

Most first-century Jews believed the messiah would be a spectacular warrior and leader. His appearance would signal the "End of Days" and the establishment of a perfect age of justice and righteousness. With the moshiach leading his holy armies, the oppressive Romans would be judged, and perfect law would govern the world.

According to the prophet Zechariah (Zechariah 9:9), the King Moshiach would enter Jerusalem, "righteous and having salvation, gentle and riding on a donkey." But this was just the beginning. The prophecy continues in the next verse, "He will proclaim peace to the nations, His rule will extend from sea to sea . . . to the ends of the earth." The passage goes on to describe a great battle and the ultimate victory of God and his chosen ones. To the oppressed masses of Judea, Zechariah's prophecy was coming alive; Jesus' humble entry was the quiet before the storm. Starting with the house of God, and ending with the Romans, it was time for action!

Execution and Persecution

Three days after entering Jerusalem, Jesus and his twelve closest followers sat down to eat the Passover seder meal. While many of them believed this was their last meal before the great battle, Jesus is said to have revealed that it was in fact the last supper before his death. According to the Gospel of Matthew, he asked his followers to think of the Passover matzo bread (representing life), as his body, and the third cup of wine (representing redemption), as his blood.

Within twenty-four hours, Jesus was arrested, convicted, and executed, Roman-style, nailed to a cross. Viewed as the messiah by some, a blasphemer by others, and a troublemaker by still others, his crucifixion dealt a deathblow to his followers. How could the mighty Lion of Judah, the warrior king, be dead? The Romans were still occupying the land, corruption remained in the religious leadership, and the one they were counting on was dead.

Renewed Purpose

The Gospels record that after three days, Jesus miraculously came back to life and visited his followers over a period of forty days. The Gospel of Luke explains, "[Jesus] said to them, 'Everything must be fulfilled that is written about me in the Law of Moses (Torah), the Prophets (Navi'im) and the Psalms (Kethuvim) . . . the Messiah will suffer and rise from the dead on the third day, and repentance and forgiveness of sins will be preached in his name to all nations, beginning in Jerusalem.'" With this clarification, Jesus' disciples believed his crucifixion was the initial phase of the moshiach's great purpose. He had come first to deliver the world spiritually, as a type of sacrificial lamb, and he would return later to deliver the world physically, as the conquering warrior king.

Before ascending to heaven, Jesus is said to have left his followers with these instructions, "Go and make disciples of all nations, baptizing them in the name of the Father and of the Son and of the Holy Spirit, and teaching them to obey everything I have commanded you." With these instructions, Jesus' disciples proceeded to spread his message, first in Jerusalem and eventually around the world.

The Acts of the Apostles (written by Luke, the author of the Gospel of Luke) records that there were about 120 disciples just after Jesus' ascension. Known as "Followers of the Way" or "Nazarenes," Jesus' disciples remained in Jerusalem, worshipping at the temple as a small Jewish sect. From the descriptions found in the Book of Acts, the Nazarenes followed communal and hierarchical structures, similar to those of the Essenes. In accordance with Jesus' teachings, the Nazarenes welcomed all people, calling them to repent of their sins, accept God's forgiveness, be washed physically in water, and follow the message of the Tanakh.

Miracles and Multiplication

The movement reportedly gained about 3,000 new followers after a spectacular event in which the Holy Spirit of God reportedly entered each of them, causing them to speak in various Middle Eastern languages. Despite imprisonment and protest from religious leaders, the group continued to spread Jesus' message of repentance and forgiveness of sins, growing to around 5,000 people. According to Acts 5:42, "Day after day, in the temple courts and from house to house, they never stopped teaching and proclaiming the good news that Jesus is the Messiah."

ALERT!

Don't be confused by the term "martyr." Although the term is used loosely today to refer to everything from freedom fighters to missionaries killed in car accidents, the early Christian martyrs were nonviolent people brutally tortured and murdered for their religious convictions.

Considered heretics by some and troublemakers by others, Jesus' followers faced increased resistance from all sides. The Book of Acts records this pressure going well beyond verbal abuse as a man named Stephen was stoned to death, becoming the group's first martyr. This event is said to have sparked a widespread persecution in which many were imprisoned or killed, forcing most of the disciples to leave Jerusalem.

Growth from Jerusalem and Antioch

Taking their new faith with them, many Nazarenes fled to Jewish communities across the Middle East. Soon the Jerusalem sect gained followers in Ethiopia, Egypt, Cyprus, Antioch (Turkey), Damascus (Syria), Rome, and beyond. While traveling to Damascus to suppress this growing sect, a Pharisee named Saul (who came to be known as Paul) is said to have had a vision in which Jesus ordered him, in effect, to stop the witch-hunt. As a result, Paul devoted his life to spreading the very message he once tried to destroy. Disciples such as Peter (also called Simon), James the brother of Jesus (also called Jacob), John, and Philip recruited many new followers from various Jewish communities, but Paul took his message to a new group, the non-Jews (called "Greeks"). Named "apostles," from the Greek word meaning "a person sent forth," charismatic teachers like Paul traveled the known world spreading Jesus' teachings.

By about A.D. 40, the city of Antioch (also called Syrian Antioch) became a hub for this young Messianic movement. As a sort of Eastern capital for visiting Roman emperors, Antioch was the empire's third largest city, boasting a multiethnic population of more than 250,000. Within the city's Jewish population, many decided Jesus was the long-awaited messiah. Soon the city's gentile citizens recognized a difference between those Jews who called Jesus the moshiach and those who did not. To distinguish between the two, those Jews who followed Jesus as the Christ were labeled with the Greek word *Christian,* as the Book of Acts 11:26 states: "The disciples were called Christians first at Antioch." Though predominantly Jewish, the church in Antioch also included some gentiles.

This dynamic created some disputes regarding the role of Mosaic law and other cultural issues.

With strong ties to the Jerusalem church, and its leader the apostle James, the Christians of Antioch received regular visits from Judean leaders. The apostle Peter eventually made his home in Antioch and, from this city, the apostle Paul and his companions took Jesus' message into Asia Minor (Turkey), Greece, and beyond. Within twenty years, Paul's efforts brought thousands of Jews and gentiles from across the Roman Empire into the Messianic sect known today as Christianity.

ALERT!

The followers of Jesus did not see themselves pioneering a new religion, but rather as continuing and fulfilling a very old one. As disciples of the messiah, they believed they were observing the true spirit of Judaism established in the law, the Prophets, and the Writings.

The Letters

With Christian communities stretching from Rome to Mesopotamia, the apostles were responsible for the lives of thousands from various religious and ethnic backgrounds. Not only that, Christian communities found themselves dealing with very different issues based on their location, ethnic makeup, and so on. Some groups were unclear about issues of faith and practice, while others were discouraged by the difficult and often dangerous life of a Christian.

Because of the apostle Paul's efforts, many churches were started, but most were left with only small oral accounts of Jesus' life and ministry. Among those from Jewish backgrounds, there were many questions about the relationship between their faith in Jesus and their Judaic traditions. For those from polytheistic backgrounds, it was unclear exactly how they should live in this new faith. Between Jews and gentiles, there were disagreements about observance of certain customs, and even between Jews there were arguments about how gentiles should conduct themselves.

As a result, the first formal Christian document was drafted in about A.D. 50 at the Council of Jerusalem. In this letter, the Judaic leadership decided upon standards for gentile followers of Jesus, sending the manuscript to Antioch with Jerusalem's full authority.

From Paul

Soon after this, while in Antioch, the apostle Paul drafted a long letter to the churches in Galatia, a Roman province in central Asia Minor (Turkey). This letter, known today as the Book of Galatians, was circulated among the Christian communities that Paul and Barnabas had established just a few years earlier. In these writings, Paul was inspired to clarify the message of Jesus' life, denounce those who were introducing false teachings, and remind the churches of his love for them.

Over the next twenty years, Paul continued to travel throughout the Mediterranean, establishing new Christian communities and writing letters to those he had been with. In these letters (known as the Pauline epistles), Paul emphasized such themes as personal salvation through Jesus' atonement, the Jewish sacrificial system and priesthood, aspects of Christian living, and requirements for leadership in the community. As he and his audiences both faced persecution and death, his words were often meant to encourage faith and hope in the face of tremendous adversity. Despite some apparent cultural biases, Paul's message of social equity can be seen in his famous statement, "There is neither Jew nor Greek, slave nor free, male nor female, for all are one in Christ Jesus" (Galatians 3:28).

From Peter, James, John, and Judah

While Paul was writing his letters, the apostle Peter wrote several times to the churches in Asia Minor. Having been arrested and beaten for his faith, Peter wrote to people who were facing similar discrimination, hate crimes, imprisonment, and threats. His words encouraged Christians to stay strong in their devotion to God through tough spiritual times and physical suffering. In the end, Peter reminded the faithful to live holy lives, as the messiah would return to establish "a new heaven and a new earth."

Along with James, the brother of Jesus, John (author of the Gospel of John) and Jude, the brother of Jesus (also called Judah), also wrote letters to Christians scattered throughout the Roman world. Similar to Paul's and Peter's writings, these letters were meant to clarify the promises of God, the role of Jesus as the Anointed One, and to direct various Christian communities in issues concerning life and doctrine. In addition, these authors saw their share of danger, earning them the right to encourage Christians around the world to press on, overcoming evil with good and meeting persecution with prayer.

The Gospels, the various epistles, and the Book of Revelation form the Christian Scriptures, known as the New Testament. With twenty-seven books, written by at least eight authors over a period of about seventy years, many Christians believe these writings to be a divinely inspired addition to the Hebrew Scriptures. While considerable debate exists regarding the exact nature of these texts, most experts agree early Christian leaders penned them in the first century.

The Church and Rome

Less than thirty years after the death of Jesus, the apostles Paul, Peter, and James, along with many other Christians, had been martyred for their beliefs. About the same time, Jerusalem erupted in a massive revolt against its Roman occupiers. In response, Roman forces overwhelmed the city, destroying the sacred Jewish temple in about A.D. 70. Hundreds of thousands of Jewish men, women, and children were killed, taken to Rome as slaves, or forced to flee Judea. The Jerusalem church met the same fate, as they were murdered, enslaved, and exiled alongside their Jewish brothers and sisters.

Displacement

After the destruction of the temple and the subsequent Diaspora, only the Pharisees survived to maintain traditional Judaism. Sadducee priests could no longer perform their temple duties, and the group's aristocrats lost their wealth and political clout in the war. The Zealots were exterminated in the streets of Jerusalem or committed suicide in sieges, as in the famous Masada story. Finally, the Essenes remain a mystery; some believe Roman forces killed them all, while others contend they joined with the Jerusalem church, following Jesus as the moshiach.

As part of the Diaspora, Christians from Judea found themselves under increasing pressure. Roman intolerance for Christianity forced them to meet in caves, catacombs, and secret places to avoid detection. Amid rumors of disloyalty to the empire and evil practices in their ceremonies, new believers from Antioch to Rome faced uncertain times. It was in this setting that the apostle John was exiled to the island of Patmos, off the west coast of Asia Minor.

From the solitude of this island, in about A.D. 95, John is said to have received a prophetic vision in which he was shown the "End of Days." Known as the Book of Revelation (*apocalypse,* in Greek), the prophecies found in its pages were meant to comfort the oppressed with the knowledge that good would ultimately triumph over evil. With vivid pictures of cataclysmic events, culminating around the return of Jesus and his messianic kingdom, this is the only prophetic book in the Christian Scriptures.

Martyrs

From Egypt to Mesopotamia, Christians faced brutal death sentences with surprising courage, bringing new converts with every drop of blood. In fact, the phrase, "The blood of the martyrs is the seed of the Church" was coined as a result of the growth experienced during intense Roman persecutions. The most famous of the early martyrs was Ignatius, leader of the Antioch church, who was fed to wild animals in about A.D. 100. Along with Ignatius, countless other known and unknown martyrs lost their lives while spreading Jesus' message of repentance, love, and forgiveness.

Through suppressing Jewish revolts and attempting to eliminate the instability brought by the Christian movement, Rome quickly attacked what it could not control. In A.D. 135, a messianic figure known as Simon bar

Kochba, led the remaining Jews of Judea in a violent revolt against the Roman Empire. After reclaiming Jerusalem and the Temple Mount, many believed he was the moshiach, but Roman forces crushed his rebellion, and all Jews were forbidden Jerusalem and Judea. While nationalistic Jewish revolts could be put down, Christianity's seemed only to grow during Roman persecutions.

FACT

Fish, anyone? During Christianity's early years, the sign of the fish is said to have become a secret symbol among the faithful. From the Greek phrase "*Iesous* (Jesus) *Christos* (Christ) *Theou* (God) *Yios* (Son) *Soter* (Savior)," the acronym *ichthys* (the Greek word meaning "fish") was developed, hence the "Christian fish."

By A.D. 284, the Emperor Diocletian found himself ruling a weakened empire crumbling from the inside out. In an effort to revive his ailing domains, he divided them into an eastern and western empire and ruled over both from his new eastern capital of Nicomedia (modern-day Izmit, Turkey) in Asia Minor. In his new city, Diocletian adopted Middle Eastern customs and ceremonies, instituted major economic reforms, and in A.D. 303 ordered an intensified persecution of all Christians.

From Jewish Messianism to the relentless travels of a Pharisee named Paul, the story of Jesus' life inspired a new era of monotheism. By the early fourth century A.D., Christianity was more than a sect. From North Africa to southern Europe, the Roman Empire was losing its power, not to a rival empire, but to a religious movement. In the following chapter you will see the winds of change in full force, as Christian communities move from persecution to power.

Chapter 6

The Byzantine Empire

After one of the most brutal periods of persecution, the Church suddenly found itself not only accepted, but also endorsed by the empire. The resulting "Christianized" Roman Empire, known as the Byzantine Empire, produced one of the most influential religious/political movements of all time. But, as with all world powers, this empire's days were numbered. Internal political/doctrinal divisions and ongoing conflicts with foreign powers weakened the empire, bringing it to its knees, and led to its eventual demise.

Emperor Constantine's Conversion

In A.D. 306, following the reign of the Emperor Diocletian, Flavius Valerius Constantinus (Constantine the Great) assumed the position of co-emperor, ruling the western half of the Roman domains. With the intense power struggles between Constantine and the eastern emperor, Lucinius, the empire found itself in rapid decline, battling internal and external attacks.

In one such internal conflict, Constantine was preparing to battle against a rival Italian leader when he is said to have had a supernatural encounter that changed his life. As a solar henotheist, Constantine believed he was in close contact with the Roman sun god, Sol, and is even said to have had a vision of this god. But this vision was different. On the eve of battle, Constantine was reportedly instructed by Jesus Christ to inscribe the first two letters of the Greek word *Christos*, X (chi) and ρ (rho), on the shields of his men, thus ensuring their victory. The following day, as he was going into battle, he believed he saw a cross over the sun with the message, "In this sign conquer." Constantine was victorious over his rival, and his victory inspired him to credit the sign of the cross and the monogram of Christ ($X\rho$) for his success.

FACT

The Greek monogram of Christ, X (Chi) overlaying ρ (Rho), is found across the Middle East and Europe in ancient and modern churches. From the Greek word *Christos*, the letters chi and rho are usually accompanied by the first and last letters of the Greek alphabet, alpha and omega. Altogether, this revered symbol signifies the belief that Jesus is both the messiah and the eternal God.

According to the fourth-century theologian and historian Eusebius, in A.D. 312 Constantine converted to Christianity, thus becoming the first Christian emperor. The following year the emperor issued the Edict of Milan, which called for an immediate end to all persecution of Christians throughout the empire. With the support of Constantine, the Church gained new legal rights and considerable financial support from the state. With the marriage of Church and state, each influenced the other, though Christian communities experienced the biggest changes, as their leadership was suddenly empowered and employed by the empire. In addition, many Roman citizens aligned themselves with Christianity, given the religion's imperial stamp of approval.

New Religious Freedom

Although doctrinal details and issues of church government had been debated for nearly 300 years, most disputes were resolved locally or were overshadowed by the constant threat of persecution. In the absence of oppression, and with the addition of political power, what were once minor disagreements became major divisions. On the teaching of subjects from the nature of Christ to questions of moral conduct and salvation, charismatic teachers gathered followers, spreading their ideas throughout the Middle East and Europe. Soon, large-scale controversies arose in which heated and often violent debates pitted Christian against Christian, with each accusing the other of heresy.

In A.D. 324, Constantine became the sole ruler of both the successful eastern and fledgling western portions of the empire. As the undisputed Roman ruler, Constantine proceeded to revive his lands with the unifying power of his new religion. By reorganizing his military forces, implementing governmental reforms, and minting new gold coins, Constantine prepared the way for his broad-based plans for Roman revival.

Council of Nicaea

With the purpose of establishing Christian unity, Constantine organized the Council of Nicaea (modern-day Iznik, Turkey) in A.D. 325. The major doctrinal controversy to be addressed was the question of Christ's nature. On one side was Arius of Antioch, who contended that Jesus was not of the same substance as God, and on the other was Athanasius of Alexandria, who argued that Jesus was of the same substance as God. After debating the issue, 318 bishops (church leaders) drafted the famous Nicene Creed, declaring Jesus as divine and of the same substance as the Father. Because Arius rejected the council's decision, he was banished to Illyria (present-day Albania) and his movement, called Arianism, was deemed heretical.

The council also determined such things as the official date for celebrating Christ's resurrection (the Sunday after the Jewish Passover) and the roles of certain church leaders. At the conclusion of these proceedings, Constantine and his mother, Helena (a recent convert to Christianity), traveled to Jerusalem and Bethlehem, ordering the construction of church buildings over the reported sites of Jesus' birth and crucifixion. According to some traditions, Helena was even said to have found parts of the original cross.

Today, Orthodox, Catholic, and Protestant churches continue to follow some form of Athanasius's view, believing that Jesus was of the same substance as the Father. Nevertheless, small groups, such as the Jehovah's Witnesses, hold to the Arian view that Jesus was created by the Father and was not divine.

The New City

The following year, Constantine planned the construction of a new capital over the small Greek city of Byzantium. After four years of massive building projects, the "new Rome" was finally complete. On May 11, A.D. 330, Constantinople (now Istanbul, Turkey) was consecrated in a sacred ceremony and established as the new capital of the Roman Empire.

Situated on a small peninsula, known as the Golden Horn, and surrounded by the crystal-blue waters of the Sea of Marmara and the Black Sea's Bosporus waterway, the city was both beautiful and well fortified. From its ornate palaces and mosaic courtyards to its terraced garden parks and magnificent Roman architecture, Constantinople is said to have dwarfed Rome in splendor. With typical Roman baths and communal public toilets, a hippodrome, theaters, a polo field, and gymnasiums, Roman heritage was alive and well in this eastern city. As a sign of the empire's distinctly Christian orientation, the Church of Hagia Eirene (meaning "Divine Peace") was built in the heart of the majestic city.

Imperial power had shifted to Byzantium (Constantinople), leaving the city of Rome to deteriorate with little in the way of influence or resources. After watching a Middle Eastern religion transform the Roman Empire, most Middle Easterners quickly adopted Christianity as well. Constantine had succeeded in reviving the empire, but now it would be protected by Christ, and its people would be called Christians.

FACT

Despite countless wars and the ongoing Israeli/Palestinian conflict, Constantine's Church of the Nativity remains standing in the West Bank city of Bethlehem, the oldest basilica in the world.

Holy Hermits

One response to the religious freedoms offered by the Byzantine Empire was the Christian monastic movement. For hundreds of years, many Christians had found spiritual strength through enduring persecution and poverty. Now, with a Christian emperor and the Edict of Milan protecting them, Christians were able to speak and move freely. For some, this "easy" life was unfulfilling and allowed for fleshly distractions. In an attempt to regain the spiritual focus of Christianity's unpopular days, some chose to seclude themselves from society, denying their bodies basic comforts.

This ascetic lifestyle was by no means unique to Christianity. Certain Hindus, Buddhists, Greek brotherhoods, and Jewish groups (such as the Essenes) separated themselves from the world, pursuing a monastic life. The Christian monastic movement originated in Egypt around A.D. 300, with a man named Anthony of Alexandria. As the first Christian monk, Anthony taught the earliest known rules for Christian monasticism, which were recorded by the famous bishop and theologian Athanasius.

Soon, Christians across the Middle East were choosing the monastic life instead of the world's vices and riches. For example, Basil the Great was a member of a wealthy family from central Asia Minor. After receiving a topnotch education in Athens and Constantinople, Basil visited several well-known monks in Egypt and Syria. The devotion of these hermits inspired Basil to reject the privileged life for a path of poverty, meditation, and learning. Around A.D. 360, Basil founded the Basilian monastic order, whose rules remain the model for nearly all of today's Middle Eastern monks.

Finally, a man named Simeon of Antioch took his spiritual quest to the extreme, living atop a sixty-foot pillar for more than thirty years. Known as Stylites (from the Greek word *stylos,* meaning pillar), Simeon and others like him gave up all physical pleasures, enduring cold nights, wet winters, and scorching heat atop their pillars. Viewed as a wise holy man, Simeon's eccentric ways attracted both Christians and polytheists from around the Middle East. Following Simeon's death in A.D. 459, many decided to follow his example, living atop pillars to escape the world's carnality. Eventually, an entire complex was built around his pillar, which became a destination for pilgrims traveling between Jerusalem and Constantinople.

Politics and Religion

In Constantinople, imperial power combined with the divine order, blurring political and religious lines. For the first time Christians were influencing the state from the inside, but at the same time, the state was able to control Christianity. Politics and religion were inseparable, as doctrinal issues became government concerns and church leaders suddenly had the ear of the emperor. Christians enjoyed individual religious liberty, but at the same time the Church became entangled in state affairs.

Following the death of Constantine, the Byzantine Empire continued to evolve as a Christian world power. Constantine had managed to unite the eastern and western Roman domains, but the longevity of this union was by no means guaranteed. With the knowledge that religion could be an adhesive or an explosive, doctrinal controversies were as much a part of the state's business as tax plans and battle strategies.

Council of Constantinople

Under the Emperor Theodosius I, religious and political conflicts threatened the union of the empire. As a result, the emperor made a concerted effort to unify his realm under the banner of Christianity. After stamping out the last bits of polytheism, Theodosius proceeded to call a church-wide council (similar to Constantine's Council of Nicaea) to solidify Christian orthodoxy.

The Council of Constantinople (held in contemporary Istanbul, Turkey) convened in A.D. 381, attended by 150 bishops, the emperor, and his bureaucrats. In the end the bishops upheld the decisions of the Council of Nicaea, condemned several movements as heretical, and affirmed the doctrine of the Trinity, establishing that the Holy Spirit was of the same substance as the Father and the Son. In addition, the council decided that the bishop of Constantinople was second in command to the bishop of Rome.

Although Constantinople's decisions did set standards for Christian orthodoxy, they did not end disagreements and power plays. In fact, the empire was soon divided again, with Valentinian III ruling the "Latin" West and Theodosius II overseeing the "Greek" East. With leaders dogmatically supporting various points of theology, religious issues were often manipulated according to political aspirations and alliances.

Today, many Orthodox churches recite their liturgies in Greek, while the tradition of most Catholic churches was Latin. The use of Greek or Latin stems all the way back to the political and cultural differences found between those aligned with Constantinople in the east and those aligned with Rome in the west.

Council of Ephesus

In this vein, Theodosius and Valentinian called yet another church-wide council. The Council of Ephesus (in present-day Selchuk, Turkey) was held in A.D. 431 to deal with the growing controversy of Nestorianism. This argument began when Nestorius, bishop of Constantinople, refused to use the title "mother of God" for Jesus' mother, Mary. Arguing that Jesus was actually a divine person *and* a mortal person, both acting with one purpose, Nestorius and his followers would only recognize Mary as the mother of the human Jesus.

With Cyril, the bishop of Alexandria, leading the movement against Nestorianism, the council decided that Nestorius' teachings were heresy. In their estimation, Jesus was divine; thus, Mary was the "mother of God." As a result, Nestorians were forced to leave the empire, fleeing to Mesopotamia, Persia, India, China, and Mongolia. In these lands, Nestorians found many converts, eventually establishing a strong Nestorian church movement.

FACT

The Nestorian Church (also known as the Assyrian Church) remains to this day, with about 200,000 members living in Iraq, Syria, and Iran. The Nestorian Church once boasted much larger numbers, but nearly a third of all Nestorians were killed during World War I. In addition, many Nestorians have either converted to Islam over the centuries or joined other Christian movements.

Council of Chalcedon

Within twenty years, the issue of Christ's nature had once again made its way to the political stage, as a Byzantine monk named Eutyches began teaching the doctrine of Monophysitism. Eutyches taught that Jesus was one divine being, with no human aspects. At the request of both Rome and Constantinople, a fourth church council was called in A.D. 451 to again establish an orthodox view of Christ's nature.

Held in what is now the Istanbul suburb of Kadikoy, Turkey, the Council of Chalcedon was attended by 600 bishops, who drafted the Chalcedonian Creed. In this document, church leaders came to a type of compromise between Nestorianism and Monophysitism, called Diophysitism. In this view, Jesus possessed two natures, divine and human, but these natures were unified in one person.

Rejected by most Middle Eastern churches (most notably the Egyptian, or "Coptic," and Syrian, or "Syriac," Churches), the Council of Chalcedon created great political and religious divisions that have continued into the twenty-first century. Although Church councils established orthodox dogma, they did not achieve the unity desired by most Byzantine emperors. Instead, the state's orthodoxy moved what likely would have been ecclesiastical debates to another level. As "heretics" were persecuted and exiled over issues of theology, many Byzantine subjects (especially

Egyptians and Syrians) became disenchanted with the leadership in Constantinople.

ALERT!

Don't be confused by all of these terms. **Nestorians** believe Jesus was two distinct individuals, one divine and one mortal, acting as one in purpose. **Eutychans** (also called **Monophysites**) believe Jesus was not human, but was one fully divine being. **Diophysites** believe Jesus had two natures (divine and human), which were unified in one person.

Looking Inside and Out

Political/religious conflicts weren't the only concern of the Byzantine emperor; foreign empires and invaders were a constant threat. By the early fifth century, a Turkish-speaking people known as the Huns had appeared from Central Asia to challenge Rome and the northern Byzantine territories. By A.D. 432, the Huns had gained so much power that Rome began to pay them not to attack Italy. About the same time, the Sassanian Empire of Iran began to challenge the eastern Byzantine borders, leading to nearly 200 years of conflict.

Turkic Trouble

With Constantinople and Rome operating independently, a young warrior named Attila united the Hunnish tribes and made his move on the Byzantines. By A.D. 447, this Turkic commander and his skilled cavalrymen had defeated Theodosius II, taking most of Asia Minor, minus the city of Constantinople. If not for a lack of siege technology, Attila would likely have taken the city as well, gaining the throne of Byzantium and changing the course of history. As it turned out, Constantinople survived but was forced to give the Huns part of the Balkans and a considerable payment of tribute.

From his new Balkan domains, Attila, known to Christians as "the scourge of God," moved toward Italy with his eyes fixed on Rome. Aided by his new Germanic subjects, the Ostrogoths (eastern Goths), Attila and the Huns went after the Romans, who were aided by another Germanic group, the Visigoths (western Goths). The Romans succeeded in defending themselves, but soon the Huns regrouped and took most of northern Italy. Because of Attila's sudden death, the city of Rome was spared, but the Western empire was all but dead. In A.D. 476, Roman power was finally destroyed. Germanic warriors overran the city, leaving Constantinople as the sole protector of Roman power and culture.

FACT

In the modern Republic of Turkey, schoolchildren begin their study of Turkish history with the famed Turkic leader Attila the Hun.

Sassy Sassanians

Viewing themselves as the revived Persian Empire, members of the Sassanian family moved in the spirit of Achaemenian conquerors such as Cyrus and Darius the Great. Stretching from Mesopotamia to northern India, their empire quickly grew in wealth and might. Largely because of its position along the central corridor of the famed Silk Road, Persia played a lucrative role in connecting the markets of the East and West. The Sassanians managed to resurrect the splendor of the Persian kings, but they lacked the massive territory of the Achaemenians. In a type of déjà vu reality, the Persian Sassanians would have to clash with the "Greek" Byzantines, if they were to revive Persia's former glory.

With an evolved form of Zoroastrianism as their state religion, Sassanians saw little distinction between "church" and state. Like the Byzantines, the new Persian Empire was interested in keeping order. As a result, other religions were tolerated, but at times their followers met severe persecution. Nestorian Christians were able to thrive within Sassanian domains, but this was largely because they had been excommunicated from the Byzantine Church, which ensured they would not align with the Western enemy.

For nearly 300 years, Syria and northern Mesopotamia became a proving ground for these two world powers. In their battle for supremacy the Sassanians and Byzantines traded blows, conquering and reconquering each other's lands. The region of Armenia, in eastern Anatolia (Turkey), also found itself between two giants. Although the kingdom of Armenia was not part of the Byzantine Empire, its common Christian faith made the Armenians natural allies. Nevertheless, the Sassanians also had considerable influence in Armenia, as their powerful military was a constant threat. Eventually, Armenian lands were partitioned between the Byzantines and Persians, then fully conquered by the Sassanians, and later given limited autonomy under Persian rule.

Formerly known as the kingdom of Urartu, the Armenian Kingdom was the first to accept Christianity as a nation in A.D. 301.

Justinian's Creations and Conquests

Out of the ashes of Attila's conquests in the West and draining wars with the Persians in the East, the Byzantine Emperor Justinian boldly moved to revive Roman glory. Starting in A.D. 527, Justinian's organizational efforts, massive building projects, and relentless military campaigns not only restored Roman glory, they began a new golden age of Byzantine greatness.

Divine Order

Declaring himself Christ's coruler on Earth, Justinian combined political and religious offices to solidify his complete authority. Although a large bureaucracy administered imperial affairs, the emperor had the final word in foreign and domestic policies. In addition, Justinian's wife, Theodora, held considerable influence as empress, involving herself in both politics and diplomacy.

As Christ's coruler, Justinian recognized his responsibility to maintain justice and order. To fulfill these duties he organized a new body of civil law based on ancient Roman laws, imperial decisions, and other legal texts. As Byzantium was now a Christian empire, Justinian revised or deleted many old laws according to biblical principles. The resulting law code remained the primary source for medieval Western lawmakers and has even influenced contemporary international law.

Divine Mortar

The new emperor also desired to elicit his subjects' respect by building awesome monuments, many of which pushed the technological limits of the time. Large basilicas and monuments were built across the empire, including the massive Church of St. John, built over what was believed to be the apostle John's grave. Although this church was destroyed in the fourteenth century, its ruins can still be seen in the Turkish city of Selchuk, near the ancient city of Ephesus.

QUESTION?

How is Christianity observed in the Middle East today?
Today there are about fourteen million Christians living in the Middle East. With large populations in Egypt, Iraq, Israel/Palestine, Lebanon, and Syria, various brands of Orthodox, Catholic, and Protestant Christianity are observed.

The most impressive of Justinian's creations was the Hagia Sophia (the church of divine wisdom), completed in A.D. 537. This feat of architectural genius amazed sixth-century observers as much as it does modern spectators. Its massive dome, combined with the sheer beauty of its ornate mosaics, silk curtains, and marble pillars (some of which were taken from the Ephesian Temple of Artemis), gave worshipers a taste of divine glory and Byzantine power.

Divine Borders

Justinian's judicial and aesthetic efforts aside, the emperor's highest ambition was to see the empire's borders expanded, especially in Europe. At the expense of his eastern borders and imperial treasury, Justinian waged a massive war from land and sea to reclaim the West. Eventually, his armies repossessed Italy and southern Spain from the Germanic invaders, as well as Sicily, most of North Africa, parts of Arabia, and the Black Sea coast. In addition, after more than 200 years of conflict, the mighty Persian Empire was forced to sign a peace treaty in recognition of Byzantine superiority.

Justinian had succeeded in creating a colossal world empire, complete with a comprehensive law code, monumental structures, and vast domains. Although this was the high point of Byzantine power, it was to be short lived. Financial stresses, combined with ecclesiastical, domestic, and foreign conflicts, created rapid decline that would eventually bring the empire to ruin.

Division and Decline

Within 100 years of Justinian's victorious conquests, the empire was in trouble. With imperial coffers depleted, taxes were raised, causing resentment throughout the provinces. In addition, the army and navy were exhausted from repeated foreign attacks and revived fighting with Persia. As a result, both Byzantine and Persian armies were weakened and demoralized.

About this time, Arab armies appeared from Byzantium's southeastern borders, taking the Byzantine province of Syria in about A.D. 630. Within a decade, the Sassanian Empire was defeated as the Arabs conquered Persia and then the wealthy Byzantine province of Egypt. By about A.D. 670, Arab cavalrymen had advanced through Anatolia to the gates of Constantinople, where they were eventually forced to retreat. The Arabs had dealt a major blow to the empire's territories, but the most devastating defeats would come from within.

The Big Split

For the first 300 years of Christian history, the fish and dove were symbols commonly used to represent Jesus Christ and the Holy Spirit. After the conversion of Constantine and the subsequent blending of Greco-Roman and Christian cultures, many pictures and symbols were used to depict Jesus, Mary, and other revered Christians, known as saints. Borrowed from pre-Christian depictions of gods and goddesses, these icons, or sacred images, were used by the Byzantines to convey biblical stories in a way that new converts and illiterate worshipers could understand.

The Byzantine Church continued to employ icons in their basilicas until the eighth century, when Emperor Leo III outlawed icons, deeming them idolatrous remnants of paganism. This ideology, known as iconoclasm, spread throughout the Eastern Church, but was quickly condemned by the western Bishop of Rome. This created a major division between the Western (Latin) and Eastern (Greek) churches that would never be fully repaired. By 1054, residue from the iconoclast debate, combined with heated disputes over Church leadership and authority, had led to a permanent separation of the Eastern (Greek) Orthodox and Western Roman (Latin) Catholic churches.

A State of Decline

This "Great Schism," as it came to be known, left the Byzantine Empire isolated and in a state of decline. As internal power struggles and the external military defeats chipped away at this former world power, Constantinople continued to rule smaller portions of its former territories. Foreign invaders, including the European Crusaders, pillaged Constantinople's legendary wealth, causing successive emperors to relinquish more and more territory, until only the walled city remained. After ruling the Mediterranean world for 700 years and trying to stay afloat for another 400, Byzantium was finally sunk. On May 29, 1453, Turkish forces captured the city, renaming it Istanbul (although it remained "Constantinople" in both formal and informal usage until its renaming at the fall of the Ottoman Empire in the 1920s), and making it the capital of their new Islamic empire.

ESSENTIAL

Contrary to popular belief, "Istanbul" does not mean "the city of Islam." After conquering Constantinople, the Turks used its common Greek name, *"Stan Poli,"* meaning "the city," which they pronounced "Istanbul."

From the seventh-century Arab invasions to four centuries of Turkish onslaughts, Constantinople had battled Muslim armies for nearly 800 years, but what was this new religious faith? Where did it come from, and what did its followers believe? In the next chapter, these questions and many others will be addressed as you discover the birth and spread of Islam. Ⓔ

Chapter 7

Early Islam

Viewed as a poet by some and a trouble-maker by still others, Muhammad ibn Àbdullah believed he was a messenger of God. In the tradition of Abraham, Moses, and Jesus, Muhammad was to be the champion of monotheism among his polytheistic tribesmen. After facing severe persecution, Muhammad's followers (known as Muslims) gained a political foothold in Arabia, allowing Islam's message to travel beyond the sands of Arabia. Muhammad united the country, and within 100 years of his death, an Islamic empire stretched across the continent.

Ancient Arabia

Although most information about pre-Islamic Arabia was written after the seventh century A.D., a hazy picture of ancient Arabia can be distilled from Sumerian, Assyrian, and other sources. Known in Islamic records as the *Jahiliyyah,* meaning the "Age of Ignorance," the pre-Islamic period has often been mistaken as a time of cultural and intellectual darkness. To the contrary, as far back as 3000 B.C., port cities lined the coast of the Persian Gulf. Teeming with international businessmen, colorful spice markets, and busy shipping centers, these unique Arabian towns were lively and diverse.

Saba'

Of all pre-Islamic Arabian civilizations, the southern kingdom of Saba', or Sheba, was the most impressive. Due to the biblical account of Solomon and the Queen of Sheba, many are aware of this kingdom's existence, but most are not familiar with its history or grandeur. Established sometime around 1000 B.C., in present-day Yemen, archeologists have uncovered the Sabaen culture's magnificent walled cities and fortresses, complete with temples, multilevel homes, dams, and irrigation systems.

FACT

The Sabaens worshipped many gods from their temples, including the sun goddess Shamsh and the star god Athar, but the most powerful deity was believed to be the god Mukah. Interestingly, these ancient Sabaen names have influenced modern Arabic words. For example, the Arabic *shams* means "sun," and *muqaddas* means "holy."

With their ability to irrigate large portions of land, most Sabaen families lived as farmers, but the kingdom's wealth and power was afforded by their control of the trade route between India and the Middle East. Indian spices, as well as gold, silver, and coveted Arabian incense flowed from Sabaen ports to desert caravans, making Saba' an important player in the economics of the ancient Mediterranean world.

Bedouin and Rock City

While stationary civilizations were found along the coastal regions, mobile nomadic tribes ruled most of Arabia's interior. Known as Bedouin (desert nomads), these tribes were involved in the transportation of goods from Saba' to the rest of the Middle East. With their livelihood connected to the trade routes, various Arab tribes organized, raided, and protected caravans. In addition, some tribes managed oasis settlements, such as Mecca and Yathrib (later called Medina), which were formed along the main north-south trade route, in the western Arabian Hijaz region.

About 500 B.C., Arab nomads calling themselves Nabataeans settled in what is now southern Jordan, at the north end of the trade route between Arabia and the Mediterranean. By 100 B.C., the Nabataeans had established an impressive capital city, known today as Petra, in an area that was both defensively and economically strategic. In this magnificent city, large tombs, homes, temples, and other structures were fashioned within the red stone cliffs of a rocky desert canyon.

From their rock-hewn capital, the Nabataeans established settlements throughout the region, eventually controlling a kingdom that stretched from the Red Sea to Damascus. The physical location of their kingdom put the Nabataeans in direct contact with the Mediterranean world and its technologies, as well as Phoenician script, which they adapted in their own style. Other Arab tribes eventually borrowed this Nabataean script, which became the basis for all forms of Arabic writing.

Although most Arabs claim to be descendants of Isma'il (Ishmael), it's not that simple. Isma'il's offspring are part of the crowd, but there are actually many non-Ishmaelite Semitic tribes that have produced nearly 300 million people from Africa to Asia who consider themselves Arab.

Although Petra flourished for several hundred years as a trading center, the Roman Empire's growth brought the Nabataean kingdom under foreign rule, eventually making it a part of the Roman province of Arabia in about A.D. 100. Over the next 500 years, other Arab tribes continued to establish small kingdoms and tribal confederacies, but none equaled the glory of the Sabeans or Nabataeans. By the late sixth century, Arabia found itself on the outskirts of the Byzantine and Sassanian empires. Arab tribes enjoyed independence, for the most part. They lacked unity and, for that matter, power, but within a short time they would find both.

The Seventh Century

Around A.D. 600, the city of Mecca, in modern-day Saudi Arabia, had blossomed into a prosperous oasis town. Benefiting from its position at the intersection of two major caravan routes and its status as a religious/cultural center, the city became very wealthy. As shrewd businessmen, Mecca's ruling tribe, the Quraish, used their resources to provide legendary hospitality to travelers and pilgrims alike.

The Culture of Mecca

As a religious center, Mecca was home to the famed Ka'ba, a cube-shaped building that housed 360 statues of Arabian gods. Each year, pilgrims from across Arabia traveled to Mecca, paying homage to the gods by offering animal sacrifices and making several laps around the Ka'ba. In addition, worshipers revered the Ka'ba's mysterious black stone (possibly a meteorite) by kissing it during their march around the sacred building. As the vast majority of Arabs were polytheistic, many rituals and beliefs reflected their desire to appease the gods and repel spirits known as jinn.

FACT

"I will grant you three wishes . . ." The popular Western image of the genie in the lamp was inspired by the ancient Arabian belief in beings known as jinn. These humanlike spirit beings were thought to wreak havoc on unprotected humans, even entering their bodies at times.

As a cultural center, Mecca was home to artisans, poets, and musicians who made their living from the city's reliable flow of traders and pilgrims. Of all the local artists, poets were the most respected. In fact, poetry was the most popular form of entertainment, making talented orators comparable to modern-day Hollywood stars. From romantic stories of brave warriors to the hilarious accounts of foolish men, spectators paid performers according to their skill. Verbal masters also received handsome sums for their freestyle flattery of wealthy individuals. With magical monologues and ingenious imagery, Meccan poets amazed the masses with rhythmic rhyming, arguably rivaling today's rappers and MCs.

Religious Soup

Although most Arabs in the early seventh century were polytheistic, several other traditions found their way into this region. Several shades of Christian thought (likely including some obscure groups deemed heretical by the Byzantine Church) had made their way into the Arabian Peninsula. Judaism was also a noticeable movement within Arabia. Not only had Jews gained prominence in the city of Yathrib along the Yemen-to-Syria trade route, but they also controlled the northern oasis town of Khayber. In addition, the former kingdom of Saba' (in present-day Yemen) saw many polytheists convert to Judaism, including the king.

With monotheists settling in oasis towns and moving across Arabia's trade routes, some Arabs began to question the existence of one all-powerful God. A mysterious group, known as the Hanifs, moved toward a more monotheistic view. Although the details are hazy surrounding their exact theology, it seems the Hanifs elevated one deity, known as "The God" (*Allah* in Arabic), to the highest position above lesser Arabian gods and goddesses. Although the Hanifs didn't gather many followers, times were changing, as new ideas simmered in the desert.

It was in this religious soup that Muhammad ibn Abdullah, a forty-year-old Meccan from the Quraish tribe's Hashemite clan, began to question his family's traditions. Were there many gods, one God in charge of lesser gods, or one singular deity? If only one God existed, who was following the right path, the Jews or the Christians? To find answers, Muhammad secluded himself in the mountains near Mecca, fasting and meditating for weeks on end. Then one day everything changed!

Muhammad and His Followers

According to Islamic sources, in A.D. 610, while meditating in a cave outside Mecca, Muhammad was gripped by a being (believed to be the angel Gabriel) that ordered him in Arabic, "*Iqra'*!" meaning "recite" or "read." Muhammad and the presence are then said to have gone back and forth several times, with Muhammad saying he could not read and the being declaring "Recite!" as it choked him. In great pain, Muhammad exclaimed, "What should I read?" The being is then said to have answered, "Recite! In the name of your Lord, who created man from a clot of blood. Recite! For your Lord is the most generous, He who has taught man by the pen things they know not" (Qur'an 96:1–5). Following this encounter, Muhammad returned to the city, confused and trembling with fear. Thinking he had gone insane or possibly been possessed by evil jinn, he consulted his wife Khadijah, who convinced him he was to be a prophet in the tradition of Abraham, Moses, and Jesus.

The Prophet

As Muhammad's first convert, Khadijah, a wealthy Meccan businesswoman, supported her husband both financially and emotionally in his new prophetic role. The next convert to Islam (which in Arabic means "submission [to the will of God]") was Muhammad's ten-year-old cousin Àli, followed by other friends and family, bringing the total number of followers, known as Muslims (in Arabic, "one who submits"), to about forty.

ALERT!

Don't be confused by the Arabic words Islam and Muslim. Islam (meaning "submission [to the will of God]") refers to a religious tradition, while Muslim (which translates to "one who submits") denotes a person who is following the religion of Islam.

In Arabia's great poetic tradition, Muhammad amazed crowds with his use of the Arabic language, yet the meaning of his messages often left his listeners puzzled. While Mecca's poets were frequently thought to receive their words from jinn, Muhammad believed the God of Abraham was inspiring his prose. In fact, as he called his listeners to monotheism and morality, he claimed to be repeating the very words of the God (*Allah* in Arabic). In response, some began to memorize his sermons, while others recorded them on animal skins and sheets of papyrus.

Quraish Quarrels

Soon, persecution from the polytheistic Meccans forced most of the Ummah (Muslim community) to flee to the Christian kingdom of Abyssinia, found in modern-day Ethiopia. With most of his followers safe in Abyssinia, Muhammad remained in Mecca, vehemently opposing idol worship at the Ka'ba. As more Arabs accepted his message, Muhammad instituted a bold break from Meccan tradition, calling all Muslims to pray in the direction of Jerusalem, the city of the only God.

In A.D. 620, Muhammad's wife, Khadijah, and uncle, Abu Talib, both died. Although he inherited his wife's fortune, the absence of his uncle's political influence removed his assurance of protection. In this tribal society, family connections and alliances guided all aspects of life, and with the passing of Khadijah and Abu Talib, Muhammad was no longer protected from those who saw him as a threat. As a result, powerful members of the ruling Quraish tribe began a plot to kill Muhammad and stop his message, which was threatening their business and traditions.

FACT

From ancient times the Arab peoples have followed a lunar calendar, which makes each year a little more than 354 days long. In addition to this moon-based system, the Islamic calendar starts in "the year of the Hijra" (*anno hegirae* in Latin, or A.H.), on July 16, 622, when Muhammad and his followers escaped from Mecca to Medina. Because of these two factors, the date June 22, 2003, on the Christian calendar is the equivalent on the Islamic calendar of Rabi` al-Thani 22, 1424 A.H.

After hearing of the Quraish leaders' plan, Muhammad decided to flee, accepting an earlier invitation to come to the city of Yathrib. Known as an honest man and wise leader, Muhammad was invited to mediate between tribal disputes, which were threatening the stability of the city. In A.D. 622, Muhammad and his followers escaped at night to Yathrib, which was later named Medina, or *Medinat an-Nabi* (meaning "city of the Prophet"). This secret night journey, known as the Hijra, was so significant to the survival of Islam that it marks the beginning of the Islamic calendar.

Growth from Medina

Muhammad was extremely successful in his new home, bringing peace to the city's warring tribes and attracting many followers. In Yathrib, Jews, Christians, and Muslims lived in peace under the wisdom of their new leader. By mending relationships between warring tribes, Muhammad created a loyal and unified city. Although Meccan armies continued to hunt Muhammad, their advances were always turned back.

Separating Sheep from Goats

After several years, Muhammad had gained many new converts in Yathrib and the surrounding areas, though the Jewish tribes never accepted him as a prophet of God. Eventually, Muhammad's teachings clearly separated Islam from the traditions of Judaism. One example of this shift was Muhammad's revelation stating that the direction of prayer should be changed. Originally, Muslims were instructed to pray toward Jerusalem, but now they were to face Mecca. In addition, Muslims were called to continue with the pre-Islamic tradition of annual pilgrimages to the Ka'ba, but as Muslims they would pray to the only deity, called *Allah* in Arabic.

Muhammad's teachings also addressed basic Christian theology. "They do blaspheme who say: God is one of three in a Trinity: For there is no god except one God"(Qur'an 5:76). There is also the passage, "That they said (in boast), 'We killed Christ Jesus the son of Mary, the Apostle of God'; but they killed him not, nor crucified him, but so it was made to appear to them . . . for of a surety they killed him not"(Qur'an 4:157). This declaration, in direct opposition to the foundational Christian belief of Jesus' sacrificial death, combined with other teachings, caused many Arab Christians to question the validity of Muhammad's prophetic claims.

Wearing Many Turbans

As a religious leader, Muhammad taught his followers to preach the message of Islam, but he also established laws and social norms for individuals and the community, known collectively today as *Sharià*. In addition, Muhammad trained his followers to fight for the will of God and the survival of Islam. Muhammad ordered his followers to raid caravans. Over time, the communities whose caravans had been raided banded together to stop Muslim banditry. Many battles ensued, but the Muslims were nearly always victorious, convincing many tribes to join Muhammad as the victorious Arab commander.

Even though Islam started in Arabia, and the first Muslims were Arabs, today Arabs make up less than 10 percent of the world's 1.3 billion Muslims.

Muhammad was a clever military leader, choosing his battles wisely. In A.D. 630, after winning many campaigns and repelling repeated Meccan attacks, 10,000 Muslim warriors moved on Mecca and took the city without a fight. The victorious Muslims proceeded to cleanse the Ka'ba of its idols.

With Yathrib (Medina) as Muhammad's political hub and Mecca as his religious center, many tribal leaders saw the tides changing, causing them to join the new Islamic movement. As clan solidarity and tribal honor were foundational aspects of Arab culture, thousands accepted Islam along with their leaders. Only two years after the taking of Mecca, nearly all of the Arabian Peninsula was united under the leadership of Muhammad, but this would all be threatened very soon.

Death, Division, and Domination

In A.D. 632, after returning to Medina from a pilgrimage to Mecca, Muhammad developed a sickness that eventually took his life. On his deathbed Muhammad is said to have challenged his followers to continue spreading Islam all the way to Constantinople. At the age of sixty-three, the founder of Islam passed on, marking the end of his revelations and the beginning of turmoil and division in the House of Islam (*Dar al-Islam* in Arabic).

Splinters and Successors

At Muhammad's sudden death, he had named no successor and had no biological son. This presented a huge problem for his followers, as no clear leader could be agreed upon. A major dispute arose regarding who should be the new leader, known as *Khalifah* (or caliph), Arabic for "successor." Two camps arose, one proclaiming Muhammad's son-in-law and cousin, Ali ibn Abi Talib, as the rightful successor, and the other insisting upon Muhammad's closest friend, Abu Bakr as-Sadiq. This division has continued through the centuries, with one group calling themselves *Shià* (from the Arabic phrase *Shiàt Àli,* meaning "partisans of Ali"), and the other calling themselves *Sunni* (from the Arabic root meaning "custom" or "practice").

FACT

Of the more than one billion Muslims living around the globe, Sunnis make up about 85 percent, while Shi'ites are about 15 percent.

In addition to the conflict regarding leadership, issues of tribal unity put the very future of Islam in question. As you read earlier, many clan leaders had followed Muhammad because of his military success and leadership capabilities. Now, with no clear leader, many tribes went their own way, refusing to pay the required *zakat* (religious tax) to Medina.

In one of Islam's most crucial moments, Abu Bakr saved the deteriorating confederacy by challenging tribal leaders to follow the living

God despite the death of Muhammad. As a result of his boldness, many tribes gained respect for Abu Bakr, resulting in his election as the fist successor to Muhammad. After being named caliph, Abu Bakr organized war parties to subdue those tribes that had abandoned their commitments to Islam. In what became known as the Wars of the Apostasy, Muslim forces succeeded in stamping out all rebel groups, making them sign peace treaties recognizing Islamic rule.

Conquests of the Caliphs

Through internal disagreements and bloody Arab-on-Arab wars, the Islamic armies moved forward in conquest into the Byzantine and Persian Empires. After leading the faithful for only two years, Abu Bakr died, but not before pointing to Ùmar ibn al Khattab as the next caliph. As Muhammad's second successor, Ùmar found himself responsible for defending and expanding the borders of the new Islamic empire.

The Arabic word "jihad" is possibly one of the most controversial words of the twenty-first century. On one hand, groups using the name jihad violently struggle against "infidels," fueling the belief that jihad means "holy war." On the other hand, hundreds of thousands of Muslims around the globe interpret jihad to be a nonviolent struggle against personal impurity. With various shades and interpretations of this word, it is literally translated as "a struggle," yet this particular struggle is an act of worship, with expected rewards.

On the western front, in Syria and Palestine, Muslim armies moved forward, defeating Byzantine forces left weakened by years of war with the Persians. With a similar situation in the east, depleted Persian forces lost battle after battle to Muslim war parties. By A.D. 640, Ùmar's men had subdued Persia, Egypt, and most of the eastern Mediterranean, including the ancient cities of Damascus and Jerusalem.

Dealing with Diversity

The Muslim world had become more than an Arab confederation, as Ùmar's domains included non-Arab Egyptians, Syrians, Mesopotamians, Persians, and others, as well as substantial Christian, Zoroastrian, and Jewish populations. In order to manage these diverse lands, the caliph divided his realm into provinces, appointed governors for these areas, and implemented new systems for taxation. This system included the *jizyah* tax levied on non-Muslim subjects, who were not allowed to serve in the Muslim army.

In some cases, Christians and Jews converted to Islam to avoid the non-Muslim taxes and the social stigma related to being a dhimmi, or "protected" non-Muslim. Many others converted to be on the winning side, or because of frustration with the Byzantine Church, while others truly believed Muhammad to be the final messenger of God. In the same way, many Zoroastrians wanted to avoid the challenges created by dhimmi status—as a result, most rejected the Sassanian state religion with the fall of the empire.

In A.D. 644, after ten years of managing the Ummah (Muslim community) and working to expand Muslim domains beyond Arabia, Caliph Ùmar was assassinated, making Ùthman ibn Àffan the third caliph. From the Umayyad clan, Ùthman was said to be a soft-spoken leader, lacking the persona of his predecessors. Nevertheless, Ùthman managed to develop the first Muslim navy and establish a standard version of Muhammad's revelations, known as the Qur'an.

The Qur'an, Islam's most sacred text, derives its name from the Arabic verb *qara'a* (meaning "to recite"), which is also the root of the command *iqra'*, meaning "Recite!"—believed to be God's first utterance to Muhammad.

Civil Blood Makes Civil Hands Unclean

Despite his mild manner, Ùthman's decisions created many enemies. In creating an official version of the Qur'an, he had also ordered the burning of all other collections, causing some to resent his actions and leadership style. Ùthman had also relieved several officials of their duties, which translated into additional resentment throughout the Muslim community. In this climate, a disgruntled group from the Egyptian garrison camp of al-Fustat (near modern-day Cairo) traveled to Medina and murdered Ùthman as he was praying.

With Ùthman's assassination, Àli ibn Abi Talib became the fourth caliph, but not without great consequence. In fact, several of Muhammad's close friends and one of his wives, À'isha, moved to the Mesopotamian city of Basra to establish an opposition movement. In what turned out to be the first Muslim civil war, Àli's forces crushed the rebellion in the conflict we know now as the Battle of the Camel.

Àli then moved the capital of the Muslim state from the Arabian city of Medina to Kufa, in modern-day Iraq. Soon another civil war began as a rebellious governor from Syria, from the prominent Umayyad family, moved against Àli's government. Although this rebellion was put down quickly, events were set in motion that would ultimately end Àli's life and begin a new Arab dynasty.

In A.D. 661, Àli was assassinated, ending a string of rulers known as the "rightly guided caliphs." For the next chapter in Islamic history, internal divisions, corruption, and family power plays would be signatures of the caliphate. With Àli's death, his son Hasan was named caliph, but only a year later Hasan submitted to the Umayyad family and their claim to the caliphate. With the Umayyads taking control, the capital was moved from Kufa to the ancient Syrian city of Damascus, were it would remain for nearly 100 years.

The Qur'an and Hadith

According to Islamic beliefs, Muhammad's first angelic experience was only the beginning. From this visitation in A.D. 610 until his death in 632, a series of revelations was given to Muhammad in the cities of Mecca and Medina. These encounters came to him in various forms but were said to be none other than the exact words of God, as witnessed by their unparalleled poetic beauty and intricacy.

Collecting the Codex

Although Muhammad's teachings were memorized and written down by many of his followers, no official compilation of these teachings was formed until sometime between A.D. 644 and 656. Known as the Qur'an, these revelations are divided into 114 chapters (*surahs* in Arabic) and more than 6,000 verses, or *ayas*. The Qur'an's major themes include God's oneness, rules for moral living, the unquestionable authority of Muhammad, and the coming Judgment Day. Reading the Qur'an is considered a sacred event, in which the worshipper is believed to be enunciating the very words of God in the same rhythmic fashion as they were first revealed. As it is believed to contain the exact expressions of God, the true Qur'an can only exist in Arabic, and any translation is considered a mere shadow of the Qur'an.

Following Muhammad's Example

According to one Qur'anic injunction, "Your companion (Muhammad) is neither astray nor being misled, nor does he say (ought) of (his own) desire. It is no less than inspiration sent down to him . . ." (Qur'an 53:2–4). This was interpreted to mean that God inspired everything Muhammad did. For example, the way he ate, walked, talked, prayed, and so on was exactly the way God wanted all humans to operate. Every aspect of Muhammad's life was to be mimicked, no matter how small or seemingly insignificant.

In addition, another Qur'anic mandate declared, "He who obeys the Messenger (Muhammad), obeys God" (Qur'an 4:80).

With this understanding that Muhammad's opinions and actions were inspired, the emerging Muslim community recognized the importance of emulating and obeying Muhammad. As a result, they began to record the things he said and did apart from his Qur'anic revelations. The "practices" or "customs" of Muhammad (*Sunnah* in Arabic) were narrated from Muslim to Muslim, until the history was eventually codified into an enormous body of writings known as the Hadith. In these records, Muhammad's decisions, actions (both public and private), along with many other details of his life are listed for the Ummah to reference.

As Muslim mothers began to teach their children in the ways their mothers had taught them, the examples found in the Hadith came to indirectly influence the majority of day-to-day Muslim life—even more so than the Qur'an!

While the Qur'an is revered as Islam's most sacred book, the sayings and actions of Muhammad, found in the Hadith, guide the majority of an observant Muslim's daily life.

Basic Components

From the Qur'an and Hadith, Muslims have derived basic components to define their religion. The following are the common beliefs and practices, known as "Iman":

- One God (Allah)—All-powerful, all-knowing, merciful creator of all things
- Heaven and hell—The places to which every human will be resurrected, judged, and given eternal paradise or pain, according to their deeds
- Angels and jinn—Two distinct races of created beings, each of which can be good or evil. (*Shaitan,* or "Satan," is considered to be an evil jinn)
- The prophets—Holy men sent throughout history as messengers of God, including Adam, Noah, Moses, Jesus, Muhammad, and many others (Muhammad is considered the greatest and final prophet)
- The sacred Scriptures—Four divinely inspired books, including the Torah of Moses, Psalms of David, Gospels of Jesus, and Qur'an. (The Qur'an is believed to be the greatest book and the only unchanged scripture)

There are also "din," the religious practices and beliefs that define the Muslim religion:

- Profession of faith (*Shahada*)—Saying with intent, "There is no god, except God and Muhammad is the messenger of God"

- Daily prayers (*Salaah*)—Five prayers completed each day, at prescribed times, with set words, and predetermined movements, while facing Mecca
- Alms-giving (*Zakat*)—Offering at least 2½ percent of an individual's wealth to the poor
- Fasting (*Sawm*)—Abstaining from all pleasures (including food, drink, sex, smoking, and so on) during the daylight hours of the month of Ramadan
- Pilgrimage (*Hajj*)—Traveling to the city of Mecca, Saudi Arabia (at least once in one's lifetime) to perform various rites at the Ka'ba and other significant locations

From the deserts of Arabia, Islam emerged not only as a religion but an all-encompassing system. The words of the Qur'an and the examples in the Hadith produced an Islamic way to do just about everything. From the rules of war to proper hygiene, there were divine guidelines for all aspects of life. *Sharià* (sometimes translated "Islamic law") was to influence every part of the Muslim state and the people within its borders, both Muslim and dhimmi (non-Muslim).

By the end of the seventh century, Islam had gathered the momentum needed to conquer the entire Middle East, North Africa, parts of Europe, and Central Asia. In the centuries to come, tolerant (almost secular kingdoms) and rigid dictatorial regimes would emerge, with Muslim rulers as diverse as the peoples they led.

In the next chapter, you will experience the ebb and flow of nearly 700 years of Islamic civilization. From the Arab Umayyad Empire to later Turkic Sultanates, Muslims continued to evolve in their understanding of Islam and its practical application. While Europe was mired in the Dark Ages, the Middle East was actively pursuing knowledge, leading the way in areas of science, technology, philosophy, and the arts. Muslims had defined themselves as a civilization, ensuring that Islam would be a lasting force for ages to come. Ⓔ

Chapter 8

Islamic Empires and European Colonies

As Muslim empires rapidly expanded their territories, the Byzantine Empire continued to lose ground. Despite great divisions and continued civil wars, a series of Islamic regimes ruled the Middle East and parts of Europe with great success. From the advances of Islamic scholars, scientists, and architects to the bloody wars of occupation waged by European Crusaders, the Middle East was forever changed by an unparalleled period of conflict and transformation. This chapter offers background information you will need to understand the modern Middle East.

Umayyads in Damascus

As you read in the previous chapter, the Caliph Àli was assassinated, making his son Hasan leader of the faithful. Within a year, Hasan abdicated the caliphate to the Syrian governor, Muàwiyya, of the Umayyad family. This transition of power began a new age, in which the Muslim community would no longer be managed by pious elected leaders but by a series of predetermined wealthy kings.

For almost ninety years, the Umayyad dynasty guided the house of Islam from their opulent Syrian capital, Damascus. The Umayyads appointed Arab Muslim governors to oversee their territories, but many non-Arab or non-Muslim officials were allowed to continue leading their communities. Beyond that, educated Jews, Christians, and Zoroastrians were utilized to teach Muslims. In the great schools of Alexandria, Damascus, Antioch, and Edessa (modern-day Sanli Urfa, Turkey) Christian monks educated their Muslim conquerors in subjects such as history, philosophy, and the sciences. In addition, Byzantine and Sassanian government structures were often left in place, Greek and Persian languages were commonly used, and *masjids* (Muslim houses of worship) were built using Roman architectural styles.

FACT

How about a cup of joe? While the exact origins of the coffee bean are debated, most historians agree it was first brewed in Arabia around A.D. 675. If this is true, maybe it should be called a cup of "Yu," from the Arabic form of Joseph, *Yusuf*.

With the Muslim conquests of predominantly Christian lands, Islam and Christianity were coexisting like never before. When Muslim men married Christian women, their offspring were often Muslim in name, with the beliefs of their Christian mothers. According to one Muslim historian, important members of the Umayyad armies were "Arab like strangers . . . Muslims with the characteristics of Christians." As a result of these influences, a mystical undercurrent appeared within Islam by the mid-seventh century.

Blood of the Martyrs

After the death of Muàwiyya in A.D. 680, Umayyad rule was challenged as Àli's second son Husayn traveled to Mesopotamia, gathering supporters from those loyal to his father. Umayyad armies quickly engaged Husayn and his Shi'ite followers, killing them at a place called Karbala' (in present-day Iraq). Instead of ending the Shi'ite movement, the death of Husayn actually gave new life to the partisans of Àli. Also, many dissatisfied Muslims rallied behind the image of Husayn's martyrdom in their opposition to the Umayyads of Damascus.

To this day the city of Karbala', Iraq, remains one of the holiest cities in Islam, especially for Shi'ites. An annual pilgrimage to the city commemorates Husayn's martyrdom, with reenactments of his death and loud displays of mourning, including self-inflicted beatings. The death of Husayn plays such an important role in the Shi'ite movement that it is often compared to the crucifixion of Jesus in the Christian tradition.

A New Master

Of all the Umayyad caliphs, Àbd al-Malik left the greatest legacy. During his reign from A.D. 685 to 705, Àbd al-Malik used his power to do the following:

- Reorganize the imperial system of taxation.
- Make Arabic the official language (instead of Greek or Persian).
- Mint the first Islamic currency (replacing Byzantine and Sassanian coinage).
- Establish an imperial postal service.
- Re-edit the Qur'an (adding vowel signs).

Àbd al-Malik also placed new restrictions on non-Muslims and non-Arab Muslims, causing great resentment and sporadic revolts. In one such conflict, an uprising in the city of Mecca was suppressed by Umayyad troops and catapults, leaving the Ka'ba in ruins. While Àbd al-Malik instituted positive reforms, he ultimately desired complete control of his domains. Any threat of opposition, Arab, Muslim, or otherwise would be met with swift and severe punishment. Not even the holy city of Mecca and its sacred Ka'ba were safe from Àbd al-Malik.

While trying to maintain order on the home front, Àbd al-Malik expanded Islam's territories to include new far-flung lands. In North Africa, Umayyad armies conquered the indigenous Berber tribes, moving to the shores of the Atlantic Ocean. Later, an Umayyad military leader named Tariq crossed from North Africa to Spain through an area later known as Jabal Tariq. This Arabic name was then corrupted in European languages to become "Gibraltar" (as in the Rock of Gibraltar). Eventually, Muslim forces continued through the Iberian Peninsula into southern France, only to be turned back outside of Tours (about 100 miles outside of modern-day Paris).

In the east, Muslim forces proceeded through the mountains and high plateaus of Persia to Central Asia, where they encountered warriors from nomadic Turkic tribes. After subduing the Turks, Umayyad forces moved east, to the borders of China's T'ang dynasty. While the Turkish-speaking tribes originally followed Buddhism or an ancient form of shamanism (similar to Native American religions), in time they converted to Islam. As Muslims, they then moved into Persian and Arab lands, eventually establishing their own Islamic empires.

Despite many reforms and the expansion of Umayyad territory, trouble continued to brew within the house of Islam. Tensions were high among non-Arab Muslims and others who desired a pure Islamic state but experienced Arab Umayyad domination and greed. Through civil war, revolts, and tribal rivalries, the Umayyads faced violent opposition, especially in Kufa, Iraq, the heart of the Shi'ite movement.

Sufis and Separatists

In Kufa and the surrounding areas, an overall disgust for the increasing corruption and materialism of the Umayyad royal family inspired some to protest the caliphate through nonviolent means. Drawing from the ascetic and mystical examples of Muhammad, both Shi'ites and

Sunnis developed an early form of what has come to be known as Sufism. Many of these Islamic mystics adopted both monastic ideology and costume, living a life of contemplation and self-denial, shrouded in white wool garments. The Arabic word for wool, *suf,* was then used to describe this new brand of mystics, known as Sufis.

QUESTION?

Who are the Sufis?

The term "Sufi" can be used to describe Muslims from both Sunni and Shi'ite backgrounds who follow a mystical path and practice an esoteric form of Islam. With many different shades of Sufism, many Sufis interpret the Qur'an figuratively, distilling its words to a message of love and inner peace. In addition, most Sufis perform chants and repetitious movements meant to evoke supernatural experiences in their quest for oneness with God.

In Iraq, anti-Umayyad Sunnis rallied behind the Hashemite family of Muhammad, along with Shi'ites who revered the descendants of Ali and his wife Fatima (who was also Muhammad's daughter). In Kufa, a man named Abu Hashim gained many followers and was called "al-Suf," leading some scholars to believe he was the father of Sufi Islam. Though many dissident groups formed, the Abbasids (followers of Muhammad's uncle, Abu al-Abbas) offered a platform to unite the opposition.

Abbasids in Baghdad

Originally based in the Shi'ite stronghold of Kufa, Iraq, the Abbasids began their offensive with propaganda rather than force. By stationing propagandists at strategic locations throughout the Middle East, Abbasids were able to encourage widespread popular dissent, which eventually led to all-out revolt. In what turned out to be Islam's third civil war, Muslims and non-Muslims banded together in revolutionary fervor, bringing the Umayyads to their knees.

In A.D. 750, the Umayyads of Damascus were defeated and, except for one prince (who escaped to Spain), the entire royal family was executed, making the sons of Abbas the new leaders. Under the Abbasid dynasty, Arab and non-Arab Muslims were given equal rights. Imperial power and wealth reached new levels, and Islamic civilization enjoyed a "Golden Age."

A City from God

During the reign of the Abbasid caliph, Abu Ja'far al-Mansur (A.D. 754–775), the dynasty established itself by building a new capital city and separating from radical groups that had helped in the revolution. On the site of a small town near the ancient Mesopotamian city of Babylon, al-Mansur erected his new capital, the "City of Peace," Baghdad.

Built strategically between the Euphrates and Tigris Rivers, this unique circular city was surrounded by two walls, with four gates opening to the four corners of the empire. With nearly every major trade route crossing Abbasid lands, Baghdad's round walls formed a kind of axis for the spokes of global economics. African gold, Chinese silk, and Russian slaves were some of the exotic commodities brought to the Middle East through Baghdad's ports and markets. As Baghdad's business was booming, banking systems were established, immigrants flocked from far-off lands, and the world recognized the Abbasids as a new global power.

FACT

You can thank the Middle East for your algebra homework! From basic equations offered by ancient Egyptians and Mesopotamians, the Arab mathematician Al-Khwarizmi took mathematics to another level in the early ninth century A.D. Based on the Arabic word *al-jabr* (meaning "restoration"), algebra was known as the science of restoration and balancing.

With unheard-of riches pouring into the empire, Baghdad quickly grew in size and splendor, arguably becoming the most impressive city of its time. With nearly a million inhabitants, Baghdad's gardens, fountains, palaces, and mosques filled the city with divine beauty. From the sounds of merchants selling their goods, to the voice of the *mu'izzin* calling the faithful to prayer, Mesopotamia was revived with imperial power. Baghdad was the envy of the world, and Constantinople would settle for second.

Tolerance and Transformation

The Abbasids claimed legitimacy through their membership in Muhammad's Arab Hashemite clan, but with many of Iraq's inhabitants coming from Persian stock, they were greatly influenced by Iranian culture. In fact, over the centuries, Abbasid caliphs married Persian wives, making the royal family ethnically more Persian. Although non-Arab and non-Muslim peoples influenced the empire, the Abbasids ultimately identified themselves as Arab Muslims. Consequently, the Middle East was Arabized, with non-Arabs adopting Arab customs and language. Also, the region was Islamicized, as non-Muslims adapted to Islamic laws or converted to Islam.

One example of these changes comes from Alexandria, Egypt, in the early ninth century A.D. Here, some of the non-Arab Coptic (Egyptian) Christian population accepted Islam, while the majority simply learned the Arabic language and adapted to Arab culture. About the same time, the famous Muslim philosopher Yaqub al-Kindi recorded the emergence of a small group of Alexandrian mystics, called Sufis. Although these men considered themselves Muslims, they were said to have had uniquely Christian beliefs and practices.

The commingling of Islamic, Christian, Persian, and Greco-Roman philosophies created new ideas, and the mixing of Arabs and non-Arabs produced new peoples. In this case, Arab Muslims were the dominant force. Thus, new beliefs were interpreted as Islamic views and new bloodlines were considered Arab.

Distinctly Shi'ite

Shi'ites, who had been a part of the Abbasid revolution but were now shunned, opposed the emerging Abbasid Sunni dynasty, believing a descendant of Ali should rule the empire. The alienation of Shi'ite groups solidified distinct doctrines regarding leadership and theology. The most visible of these was their agreement on a definitive line of imams, or infallible leaders, descending from Ali to Hasan, Husayn, and so on. Although there have since been disagreements regarding the authority of certain later imams, to this day the vast majority of Shi'ite Muslims look to a succession of divinely inspired leaders. With various types of messianic expectancy, some Shi'ites even believe an imam (or one of his descendants) will return to earth as the Mahdi, establishing God's justice and peace around the world.

QUESTION?

Is the Mahdi the same as the Messiah?
Among both Sunni and Shi'ite Muslims, the Mahdi is seen as a powerful figure who will come to earth just before the Judgment Day. The Mahdi will rule the planet in much the same way Jews foresee the reign of the moshiach. The Mahdi's appearance is also similar to the Christian belief in Jesus Christ's second coming. (Many Muslims believe Jesus will be present in Mecca when the Mahdi is revealed.)

Umayyads in Spain

While the Abbasids were busy running their empire, the sole survivor of the Umayyad dynasty made his way to al-Andalus (Spain). Here, with the aid of Syrian troops (still present from the Umayyad conquests), prince Abd al-Rahman organized a new kingdom outside of Abbasid influence. Initially, in this revived Umayyad emirate (kingdom), Arabs ruled over the non-Arab and non-Muslim masses. In time, Spain was both Arabized and Islamicized, as many of its inhabitants learning to embrace Arabic and Islam. At the same time, many Christian and Jewish citizens chose to simply adapt to the language and culture of their new leaders.

In the Spanish capital of Cordoba, nearly half a million people enjoyed an age of scientific, philosophical, and artistic exploration. With hundreds of schools, mosques, libraries, and palaces, this Mediterranean city dwarfed all other European cities in size and splendor. By the early tenth century, the Umayyad dynasty and its subjects had developed a distinctly Andalusian culture that was known throughout the world. In an effort to establish al-Andalus (Spain) and the Umayyad monarchy, Abd al-Rahman III declared himself caliph. Although the kingdom would be dissolved in less than 100 years, various Islamic emirates continued to rule parts of Spain until 1492. Today, remnants of Arab and Muslim influence remain in Spain. This is especially true in the south, where you can see beautiful Islamic architecture, hear Arabic linguistic and musical influences, and taste the lingering flavors of North African cuisine.

Fractured Fraternities

In the Abbasid Empire and Umayyad Spain, religious and political factions threatened the power of Arab monarchs. From its inception, the Abbasid regime dealt with separatist groups across North Africa, including the Umayyads in Spain. In addition, Shi'ite movements in northern Iraq, Persia, and Arabia, combined with civil war at home, challenged the unity of the Islamic state.

The Mamluks

Fighting rebellion after rebellion, the Abbasids rarely enjoyed a significant period without conflict in some part of their domains. With the constant demand for skilled soldiers, the empire began training a warrior class of slave boys from Central Asian Turkish tribes, sub-Saharan African groups, and other ethnicities. Known as mamluks (meaning "those who are owned"), these boys from Christian, Buddhist, and other religious backgrounds were converted to Islam through intentional educational efforts. Soon, these young men grew to be powerful military leaders and strategists. While continuing to recruit new slave boys, mamluk generals established loyal family-like units of fierce non-Arab fighters.

In Egypt, a Turkish mamluk and Abbasid governor by the name of Ahmad ibn-Tulun separated himself from Baghdad's authority, establishing his own kingdom from al-Fustat (modern-day Cairo). Although the Abbasids temporarily regained control of Egypt in 905, Egypt was again taken by Turkish and African mamluks just thirty years later. Eventually, in 969, a Shi'ite group known as the Fatimids added Egypt to their growing

North African domains. Moving their capital from Tunisia to al-Fustat, the Fatimids renamed the city al-Qahirah (better known to Westerners as Cairo).

The Shi'ite Empire

This Fatimid dynasty was named after its founder, Ùbaydallah, who claimed to be a descendant of Fatima, the wife of Ali and daughter of Muhammad. In addition, Ùbaydallah also declared himself caliph of the Muslim world, above the Abbasid leader in Baghdad. Later he even took on the messianic title of Mahdi, bringing his followers to believe he would inspire an age of worldwide Islamic peace and justice.

The Fatimid state quickly established itself from its growing capital, Cairo. As an enthusiastic Shi'ite movement, in 972 the Fatimids completed building the famous al-Azhar mosque and university as a training center for their brand of Islam. To this day, al-Azhar is respected throughout the Muslim world as the premier Islamic university, though it is now a Sunni institution.

For the next century, the Shi'ite Fatimids surpassed the weakened Abbasid caliphate, even occupying the city of Baghdad for a short time around 1055. Eventually, the Fatimids lost power because of mamluk revolts and other opposition movements. The biggest threat came from the newly Islamicized Turkish tribes of Central Asia, who were moving southwest in the name of Sunni Islam. Over the next 200 years, Arab, Persian, and Byzantine territories were divided and conquered, changing the face of the Middle East forever.

When Turks Attack

From their ancestral homeland around the Altai Mountains (along the modern border of Kazakhstan and Mongolia), Turkish-speaking nomads moved south and west, finding new lands and religions. The Ghaznavids established the first Turkic kingdom in what is now part of Afghanistan. After conquering most of Central Asia, the Ghaznavids moved into modern-day Pakistan and northern India in A.D. 1001. In addition to taking massive amounts of gold and jewels from Hindu temples, they left their Islamic beliefs in what would become one of the most populous Muslim areas on the planet.

By 1040, the Turkish-speaking Seljuks rolled through Central Asia and Persia into Mesopotamia and Syria. Inspired by their new religion, Sunni Islam, the Seljuks proceeded to establish religious schools, hoping to "purify" their domains of Shi'ite thought. Although the Seljuk sultan (king) eventually captured Baghdad, the Abbasid caliph was allowed to remain as a symbol of Sunni supremacy.

FACT

Hashish, anyone? As the Seljuks rigidly enforced their brand of Sunni Islam, a minority of fanatical Shi'ites began killing prominent Sunni political and religious leaders. According to tradition, these men carried out their suicide missions aided by the drug hashish. Whether or not they actually used drugs, these terrorists came to be known as Hashishins, meaning "takers of hashish" (which later evolved into the word "assassins").

Seljuk Turks then turned their attention to the Byzantine Empire. For nearly thirty years, Turkic and Byzantine forces repeatedly met in bloody clashes, but the most important of these was waged in 1071 at Manzikert (in eastern Turkey). Here, the Seljuks defeated the Byzantines, capturing the emperor. From this victory, the Turks moved west into central Anatolia, to within 100 miles of Constantinople.

At this point, the Great Seljuk Sultanate was a vast empire, spanning east to west from Central Asia to central Anatolia and north to south from the Caucasus Mountains of Russia to the city of Mecca in Arabia. Although the Sunni Seljuks viewed the heretical Shi'ite Fatimid sultanate as their biggest enemy, Christian Europe would soon attack. To the Holy Roman Empire, the Turkish Muslims were a major threat. Not only had the Seljuks made short work of the Byzantines, but they also controlled the Holy Land. In the eyes of many European Christians (including the pope), the holy city of Jerusalem was calling for liberation.

Europe to the Rescue—Everyone Loses

Fresh from the Great Schism of 1054 (in which the pope's Western, Latin Catholic Church and the emperor's Eastern, Greek Orthodox Church severed all ties), the Byzantines found themselves on the brink of extinction. In a desperate attempt to save itself, Constantinople called for Western European assistance. Seizing the opportunity to expand Latin influence in the Middle East, Pope Urban II rallied Catholic Christians to wage a holy war, or Crusade, to reclaim the sacred city of Jerusalem.

By 1097, crusading knights from across Europe arrived in Constantinople, ready to reclaim the Holy Land. Moving quickly through the newly established Seljuk Sultanate of *Rum*, or Rome (the Arabic/Turkish term for Anatolia), Christian forces continued through Syria with victory after victory, taking the important city of Antioch by June 3, 1098. Almost a year after the capture of Antioch, the city of Jerusalem was taken as well. The liberation of Jerusalem was the stated objective of the Crusade, but after more than two years of fighting, and hundreds of thousands of lives, the Europeans occupied the entire eastern Mediterranean coast.

Although varying accounts of Crusader conduct exist, many sources tell of bloody massacres in which Jews, Muslims, and native Christians were slaughtered at the hands of Western warriors. Today, the savagery of the "Christian" Crusades lives on in the consciousness of the region, as many Middle Eastern peoples view modern military campaigns as further Crusades for Christ.

Colonial Kingdoms

In order to manage their newly acquired lands, knights established four colonial states, ruled from four major cities. The "Latin Kingdom of Jerusalem"—stretching from the Red Sea, through Palestine, to the present-day city of Beirut, Lebanon—was the largest and most powerful of the colonies. The other three states included the county of Tripoli (roughly contiguous with the modern-day country of Lebanon), the principality of Antioch (including contemporary northwestern Syria and the Hatay

Province of Turkey), and the Anatolian county of Edessa (centered on the modern Turkish city of Sanli Urfa).

During the turmoil of the Crusades, Sufism and orthodox Islam moved in opposite directions. At about this time, the Persian philosopher and theologian Al-Ghazali drafted a series of revolutionary works that married aspects of the two. Although his insightful writings legitimized mysticism, they also inspired many Muslims to reject rationalism.

New Alliances

Over the next two centuries, Europe launched a series of offensive and defensive Crusades, with Kurdish, Turkish, and Arab Muslims attempting to end European occupation. As the saying goes, politics makes strange bedfellows. Between Sunni and Shi'ite conflicts, Crusader and Muslim tensions, Orthodox and Catholic rivalries, and various tribal feuds, the bedfellows were strange indeed.

The most extraordinary of these alliances came as a result of a botched deal between a Kurdish general from Syria and the Fatimid caliph of Egypt. The resulting rift brought about an alliance in which Catholic Crusaders and Shi'ite Fatimids fought together against Sunni Syrians and their Kurdish commander. (That's a tongue twister!) This unlikely relationship eventually ended in 1169, as Syrian forces returned to Egypt with overwhelming force. Thanks to the Syrians, Egypt was free of Crusaders, the Fatimids were finished, and a new Sunni regime came to power.

Expulsion of the Infidels

The end of Shi'ite Fatimid rule in Egypt marked the beginning of a new era of Sunni resurgence in the Middle East. Under the leadership of Salah al-Din Yusuf ibn-Ayyub (also known as "Saladin"), the Ayyubid family would wage a two-pronged jihad against European occupation and Shi'ite heresy.

As sultan, Salah al-Din was just as much a diplomat as a warrior. Not only was he able to unite Damascus and Cairo under the banner of Sunni Islam, he also contributed to growing divisions between the "Latin" Crusaders and "Greek" Byzantines. The unification of Syria and Egypt meant Salah al-Din could squeeze Crusader forces from all directions. By 1187, the Europeans were expelled from Jerusalem and forced to retreat to a small area along the Mediterranean coast. For the next sixty years, Salah al-Din's Ayyubid sultanate extended its influence from Cairo across North Africa to a swath of land stretching from southeastern Anatolia in the north to Yemen in the south.

Between the Ayyubids in Cairo, the Abbasids in Baghdad, and the Seljuks in Konya (south-central Anatolia), the remaining coastal Crusader colony had little or no power. Nevertheless, many desired to see the European cancer completely removed. This wish was delayed, however, as both the Abbasids and Seljuks were plagued by a new group of infidels, the Mongol khans (rulers) and the Ayyubid dynasty was usurped by its own Turkish mamluks.

Under the leadership of Genghis Khan, the Mongols ravaged most of the world from Japan to Eastern Europe. Throughout the 1200s, the Mongols turned their attention to the Middle East, conquering the Seljuks in 1242 and eventually destroying Baghdad and the Abbasid dynasty in 1258. The Mamluks of Cairo remained as the only Muslim force able to repel the might of the Mongols, but only as far as Syria.

FACT

Jalal al-Din Muhammad Rumi, or "Mevlana" (*Mawlana* in Arabic) as he was later known, was a masterful poet whose works are renowned throughout the world for their lyrical luster and meaningful mysticism. After Rumi's death, his followers preserved his teachings, forming the Mevlevi Sufi order. Today, pilgrims from all corners of the globe visit Konya, Turkey, in hopes of gaining wisdom and blessings at Mevlana's grave.

By the late 1200s, Muslim forces decided once and for all to end the European occupation. Soon the cities of Jaffa (modern Tel Aviv, Israel),

Antioch, and Tripoli all fell to Muslim forces, leaving the coastal city of Acre (north of present-day Haifa, Israel) as the last Crusader outpost in the Middle East. Despite a last-ditch Crusade, in 1291, after nearly two centuries, the last bastion of European colonialism was removed from the Middle East. Although Muslim armies had finally succeeded in expelling the Europeans from Palestine, the Mongols remained in Iraq and Iran.

Eventually, just as monotheism transformed Judea's pagan Roman occupiers (via Christianity), it again changed the region's pagan Mongol conquerors, via Islam.

Known as the Il-Khans, these new Muslim converts continued to rule most of Iran and Central Asia for another 100 years.

The fall of Constantinople and the rise of the Turks, the revival of Islamic civilization and the decline of great empires—these are just a few of the monumental events that have shaped today's Middle East. In the following chapter, you will see the region transformed once again by conquest and confederation, as you travel from the medieval to the modern world.

Chapter 9

A New Empire Is Born

Crusader occupation, Mongol invasions, and internal conflicts left the Seljuk and Abbasid empires in ruins. In this power vacuum, nomadic Turkish tribesmen stepped up to try their hand at empire management. Within 200 years, three Turkish-speaking Muslim dynasties ruled an empire that stretched from Eastern Europe through the Middle East to India. Despite imperial power struggles and dynastic disputes, the Middle East led the world into a modern era of science, technology, and style.

The Aftermath of Defeat

Although European knights killed many Jews and Muslims during the Crusades, little lasting political or monetary damage was done to any of the Islamic empires. Ironically, the Byzantines suffered the most devastating blow. In what was originally promoted as a support effort, armies of the Latin Church actually weakened the protectors of Eastern Christian orthodoxy.

Despite random massacres of Eastern Christians, the Crusades were largely directed at non-Christians, until the sacking of Constantinople in 1204. During this series of raids, crusading knights pillaged Byzantium's ancient Roman wealth, taking massive amounts of gold, jewels, and priceless relics back to Europe as booty. With imperial treasuries emptied, the Byzantines would never fully recover, and Western Europe would never look back.

Powder Power

By the end of the 1200s, the great city of Baghdad lay in ruins, the caliph was dead, and Mongol khans ruled much of the Middle East. The mighty Arab dynasties were distant memories and, except for the Mamluks of Egypt, classical Islam's magnificent empires were extinct. From what could have been a deathblow to Islamic civilization, the Mongol hordes inadvertently provided an element that was more powerful than the pen or the sword—gunpowder.

Just as Chinese gunpowder revolutionized Middle Eastern warfare, European armies later found new strength as they borrowed powder power from the Middle East.

The newly Islamicized Il-Khan (Mongol) dynasty remained connected to its Asian roots, creating a type of cultural and technological exchange between Far Eastern and Middle Eastern peoples. Of the many shared ideas and practices, the introduction of Chinese gunpowder made the biggest impact. As certain Middle Eastern armies transitioned from the sword to the gun, an enormous technological gap was created, similar to that between an M-16 and a musket. In time, "gunpowder empires" emerged with the ability to exert overwhelming force on the powder-deficient masses.

Cairo's Conversion

In Egypt and Syria, the Shi'ite Fatimids were a distant memory as a series of slave warriors, known as Mamluks, ruled a distinctly Sunni empire. During the Fatimid period, most of Cairo's Muslim citizens remained Sunni despite their proselytizing Shi'ite leaders. Nevertheless, from al-Azhar University's role as a Shi'ite missionary training center, to those who had adopted Fatimid doctrines, Cairo was affected by the Shi'ite years.

Salah al-Din had made large strides in ridding the city of what he considered Shi'ite heresy, but in the case of al-Azhar University, he and his successors ignored its potential as a Sunni institution. With the rise of the Mamluks, al-Azhar was restored to its former greatness, but from that point forward it taught Sunni doctrines. In al-Azhar and other schools, some forms of scholarship were encouraged, but original ideas and philosophies were discouraged as students were taught to trust in the accomplishments of the past. From the vitality of classical Islamic intellectualism, the Mamluks inspired a long period of scholastic stagnation.

Slaves as Masters

Although the Mamluks were ethnically Turkish, Mongolian, and Circassian (a people from the Caucasus Mountains), they were not interested in their origins. Instead of ethnic pride, Islam guided the Mamluks as they ruled largely Arab lands. As a result, Arabic culture and language thrived, and Cairo emerged as the heart of the Arab world. In a political maneuver that pleased the Arab masses and satisfied Mamluk religious convictions, a series of Arab men from the fallen Abbasid dynasty were named "caliph." Although these men continued the centuries-old Arab caliphate, these caliphs were actually puppets of the Mamluks, nominally presiding over Sunni Islamic orthodoxy.

From the masterfully constructed Qait Bey Citadel in Alexandria, Egypt (possibly built in part from the rubble of the legendary lighthouse of Alexandria), to mosques, schools, hospitals, and fountains built in Cairo, Jerusalem, Damascus, and Mecca, Mamluk monuments peppered the Middle East. In addition to architectural achievements, the Mamluk era also produced beautiful textiles, ceramics, and poetry. Conservative views may have stifled new religious and philosophical exploration, but Arab scientific and mathematical innovations continued to lead the world. Eventually, Mamluk piety and fatalism would lead to their end, as plague and famine were met with little response.

In most of the Islamic world, the late thirteenth century saw conflict and upheaval. But from Cairo, the Mamluks protected their lands from foreign invaders. As a result, Cairo's greatness rallied Arab pride within the Mamluk territories, as well as Mongol and Turkish controlled areas. Eventually, the city was even given the title "Mother of the World."

Osman's Empire

As you read in the previous chapter, Turkish-speaking tribes moved southwest from their Asian homeland to establish Islamic empires as early as A.D. 1001. Due to volatile situations in Asia, new Turkic tribes moved into the Indian subcontinent, Persia, Mesopotamia, and Anatolia. By the 1100s, the Seljuks were the ruling Turkic power, with most other tribes recognizing Seljuk supremacy. As the Mongols decimated the Seljuks, Turkic tribes proceeded even farther west into Byzantine lands.

Less than 100 miles from Constantinople, a man named Osman led his *ghazis,* or "warriors of the faith," into Byzantine territories. Called Osmanli, meaning "followers of Osman" (or Ottomans), this Turkish-speaking tribe established its own kingdom under the banner of Sunni Islam. As it turns out, the Ottomans were in the right place at the right time, with the Byzantine Empire barely alive and the Mongols unconcerned with affairs in western Anatolia.

By the mid-1300s, the Ottoman Turks expanded their rule from Anatolia into Eastern Europe. After conquering most of the Balkans, the sultan (meaning "ruler") moved his capital from the Anatolian city of Bursa to the eastern European city of Edirne (Adrianople). With the Byzantine Empire whittled down to the walls of Constantinople, and most of Anatolia under the sultan's control, the Ottomans were well on their way to building an empire. From their simple Turkish and Muslim origins, conquest had transformed the Ottomans into a powerful multiethnic and multireligious empire.

FACT

Claiming descent from the dreaded Genghis Khan, Timur the Lame (Tamerlane) spent most of his adult life conquering distant lands. From his Central Asian base, Timur eventually controlled an empire stretching from southern Russia and Anatolia to parts of China and India. Timur is even reported to have been planning to invade China, but his death in 1405 ended what could have become the world's largest empire.

With the Ottoman war machine winning victory after victory in Europe and Anatolia, a Turkic warlord from Samarqand (in present-day Uzbekistan) established his own kingdom in Central Asia. Despite several physical disabilities, Timur the Lame (also known as Tamerlane) led a massive army through Iran and Iraq into Anatolia, conquering most of the Ottoman territories and capturing the Sultan. With the Ottomans subdued, Timur and his descendants after him controlled the eastern half of the Middle East for another fifty years.

Constantinople and Cairo Fall

Based largely in the Balkans, the defeated Ottomans regrouped from Timur's conquests to defend against ongoing European attacks. After many defeats, the Ottomans finally won a decisive victory at Kossova (Kosovo) in 1448. Under the leadership of the new sultan Murad II, the

Ottomans expanded their territories in Eastern Europe and Anatolia, with their eyes fixed on Constantinople.

The next Ottoman leader, Sultan Mehmed II, moved the empire to another level as he completed Muhammad's belated 800-year-old mission and captured Constantinople. In A.D. 330, Constantine established Constantinople as the new Rome, the eternal city of Christ and the protector of Christendom. Through centuries of domination, decline, and revival, the Byzantine Empire lived on—at the very least inside Constantinople's thick walls—with the notion that God was on their side.

On May 29, 1453, God's perceived favor turned to judgment as Ottoman forces used new technology to blast cannonballs through Byzantium's previously impregnable walls. With the emperor dead, Sultan Mehmed (known in Turkish as *Fatih,* meaning "the Conqueror") established the city as his new capital, renaming it Istanbul. The fall of Constantinople and the rise of the Ottomans marked the end of one era and the beginning of another, as ancient swords were replaced by modern firepower and the world moved into modernity.

As emperor of Islamic Byzantium, Mehmed the Conqueror quickly shifted his focus from conquest to construction and control. Although the Byzantine emperor and most of his Latin soldiers were killed in the battle for Constantinople, most of the city's Greek population survived the occupation/liberation. Under Ottoman rule, Greek and Armenian Christians, as well as Jews, remained the predominant business class in Istanbul and were even given limited autonomy within their own religious communities. However, as in other Islamic empires, non-Muslims were subject to special taxes, and many churches (including the central Hagia Sophia) were converted into mosques.

Earthly Expansion and Ethnic Evolution

With news of Mehmed's victory, both European and Mamluk leaders recognized the threat of Ottoman growth. Soon, their fears were realized as Mehmed's troops spread out in all directions. In Europe, Ottomans attacked from land and sea, conquering most of Greece and the remainder of the Balkan Peninsula (including at least some parts of modern-day Croatia, Serbia, Hungary, and Romania). Eventually,

Ottoman naval forces even moved across the Adriatic, taking the heel of the "boot" in Italy.

FACT

The English word "maraud" is defined as "the act of raiding or invading in order to gain booty." The exact origins of this term are uncertain, though some believe it was coined by Eastern Europeans who experienced the plundering Ottoman war parties led by sultans and commanders named Murad.

Having subjugated most of the Balkans, the Ottomans proceeded to take Eastern European children from their Christian families. Similar to the Mamluk slave-warriors of other Muslim empires, non-Turkic boys were instructed in the art of war and the ways of Islam, while the girls were utilized as slaves or concubines. From these non-Turkic boys, the most skilled soldiers were chosen to join the elite Janissary Corps. The most gifted of the janissaries were allowed to take positions of power within the empire, though the Ottomans never experienced a mamluk-style slave takeover.

Although the sultanate was never usurped by one of the janissaries, the Ottoman administration did become less Turkic as other ethnic groups joined their ranks. In addition, Ottoman officials (including the sultan) often married the most beautiful Eastern European slave girls. These and other mixed marriages produced an empire in which many of its subjects and sultans were not Turkic but Ottoman.

From Eastern Europe, the Ottomans continued around the north shores of the Black Sea, taking the region of Crimea and parts of what are now Ukraine and Russia. In time, Mehmed's navy not only controlled the Black Sea but most of its coastal regions as well. As they moved deeper into Anatolia, the Ottomans subdued unruly Turkic tribes, eventually clashing with soldiers from the Mamluk Empire.

Mastering the Mamluks

From the late 1300s to the early 1500s Egypt was basically in a state of emergency as major economic problems, food shortages, and the

Black Plague magnified existing dissatisfaction with the Mamluk sultans. Because of fatalistic religious ideas, little was done to contain the plague, resulting in the decimation of Cairo's population—with as many as 7,000 deaths per day during its worst period.

With Cairo in disarray, Ottoman armies moved as far south as Mamluk-controlled Syria. Hoping to repel the Ottomans, cavalrymen raced from Egypt to Syria, but Ottoman cannons overpowered the prideful Mamluks, who rejected gunpowder as a "weak man's weapon." Continuing south into Egypt, Ottoman firepower dealt the final deathblow, as the Mamluks were overrun outside Cairo in 1517.

After this great defeat, Mamluk commanders continued to hold great influence in Ottoman-controlled Egypt, eventually creating serious tensions with Istanbul. With the Ottomans on top, the Arab caliph was stripped of his honorary title, leaving the caliphate to gather dust until the 1800s, when Ottoman sultans again revived its symbolic power.

With the acquisition of Mamluk lands, the Ottoman Empire stretched from the borders of Austria and Russia to the deserts of Egypt and Arabia. With these lands under their influence, the Ottomans were well on their way to becoming the most powerful regime in the history of Islam. With momentum on their side, a strong leader was all that was needed to move the empire to another level.

FACT

In the Middle East, the year 1517 brought an end to the Mamluk Empire, moving the Ottomans toward becoming the world's most powerful Islamic empire. In Europe, 1517 saw the German theologian Martin Luther announcing his ninety-five disagreements with the Catholic Church, beginning a Christian movement known as the Protestant Reformation.

Sultan Süleyman and Ottoman Expansion

In 1520, a new sultan holding the name Süleyman (Solomon) rose to the Ottoman throne. Just like his namesake, the ancient Hebrew King Solomon, Süleyman used his wisdom to expand the kingdom's territory, wealth, and global influence. Because of his foreign policy and conquests, Europeans came to know him as Süleyman "the Magnificent," while his domestic improvements inspired his subjects to call him "the Lawgiver."

In 1529, Süleyman advanced Ottoman muscle deep into Europe, sending troops as far as Germany while at the same time besieging the Austrian city of Vienna. Although Vienna was not conquered, people across Western Europe developed a fear of the "Turks." Over the next thirty years, Ottoman territories expanded to include Mesopotamia, parts of Persia and present-day Sudan, and most of North Africa. The rein of Sultan Süleyman marked the Ottoman Empire's golden age, as it was the largest and most powerful force in the Middle East and Europe.

ALERT!

Sorry, coffee fans, but your caffe ain't so Italiano! According to tradition, European coffee and the crescent roll both made their début after the Ottoman siege of Vienna. As Muslim forces returned to Istanbul, the citizens of Vienna emerged from their city to discover coffee beans in abandoned Ottoman camps, and thus coffee was introduced to Europe.

The size of the Ottoman territories alone was enough to make the empire one of the most impressive of all time, but Süleyman's diplomatic, administrative, and architectural achievements were also extraordinary. From his alliances with France and other European powers, to the building of uniquely Ottoman style mosques throughout the Middle East and Balkans, Sultan Süleyman's majesty was so well known, that even Shakespeare makes reference to him in the comedy *The Merchant of Venice*.

As Süleyman the Lawgiver, this sultan ran a tight ship, implementing many reforms and holding tightly to *Sharià* (Islamic law), which was deduced from the Qur'an and Hadith. The grand vizier and members of the imperial council listened to the opinions of respected clerics as they determined Ottoman law. Ultimately, Süleyman was the final authority, although officials were given considerable power, and Islamic law was held in the highest regard.

Turkic Rivalries

In Iran, the Turkish-speaking Safavids emerged in the tradition of ancient Persian kings and their Sassanian successors. After starting as a religious movement, rather than a tribal unit, the Safavids manipulated Iranian tribal politics to become an influential force. By the early 1500s, a Safavid leader named Isma'il assumed the Persian title *shah an-shah*, or "king of kings," leading many of his followers to believe he was the messiah-like Muslim figure known as the Mahdi. With a fiercely loyal Shi'ite army behind him, the shah declared Iran and Iraq as his realm. Thus the Safavid dynasty was born.

Neighbors

To the east, Turkish and Mongol warriors, claiming descent from Genghis Khan and Timur the Lame, established themselves as the Islamic Mughal ("Mongol" in Persian) Empire. With distinctly Sunni beliefs, the Mughals ruled most of present-day India, Pakistan, and Bangladesh, as well as parts of modern-day Afghanistan, from the mid-1500s to 1857. Of the Mughals's many lasting influences in India, the tomb of Mumtaz Mahal (known as the Taj Mahal) is the most impressive and well known. For the most part, the Mughals were not involved in the Turkic rivalries. Instead, they focused on domestic issues—especially conflicts with Hindus, Sikhs, and other religious groups.

FACT

The English word "mogul," meaning a wealthy or powerful person, was inspired by the mighty Muslim sultans of India's Mughal (Mongol) Empire.

To the north and east, another Turkish-speaking dynasty established the Uzbek kingdom in what is now northern Turkmenistan, Uzbekistan, and southern Kazakhstan. As strong Sunni Muslims, the Uzbeks were a constant threat to the Shi'ite Safavids, but they never made significant advances into Safavid territories. To the west, fellow Turkish-speaking Ottomans unimposingly practiced Sunni Islam, while the Safavids unabashedly promoted Shi'ite views. In fact, the Safavids imposed their particular brand of Islam on the Persian population, transforming this historically Sunni area into the world's first large-scale popular Shi'ite state. Nevertheless, the Ottoman Empire was the biggest rival of the Safavids, who desired to expand westward into the Islamic holy lands of Iraq, Palestine, and Arabia.

A House Divided

For the next 200 years, the Ottoman and Safavid Empires remained bitter enemies, with jihad after jihad being waged on the "infidel" shah or sultan. Initially, the Ottomans held a major advantage with their black-powder–propelled cannons, allowing the Ottoman Sultan Süleyman to conquer Mesopotamia and other Persian territories in 1534. After continued conflict, the Safavids were forced to recognize Ottoman superiority by signing a peace treaty in 1555.

After the death of Sultan Süleyman the Magnificent in 1566, Shi'ite Ottoman subjects joined forces with their Safavid coreligionists to fight the Sunni sultan of Istanbul. Despite their desire to fight honorably and without that sissy gunpowder, the Safavids begrudgingly accepted this new explosive technology under the leadership of Shah Abbas "the Great." With both empires possessing the powder, a relative balance of power was achieved, leading to the Safavid Empire's greatest age.

Military power allowed Persia to develop institutionally and economically, despite their Ottoman neighbors. From 1588, until his death in 1629, Shah Abbas created a mighty empire by moving his capital to the economically strategic city of Isfahan (located on the Silk Road), reorganizing the government, revamping taxation systems, and utilizing the skills of both Muslim and non-Muslim subjects. Most notably, Armenian Christians were moved to his new capital because of their expertise in the silk trade.

Ultimately, the city and the empire prospered until Shah Abbas' death signaled a downturn in the dynasty's power. Most of the eighteenth century was marred by instability, but in 1795, a new Turkic dynasty, the Qajars, came to rule Iran. Moving their capital to the northern city of Tehran, the Qajar-dynasty–controlled Persia into the twentieth century.

Euro Power

From 1400 to 1800, various Turkic dynasties battled to control the ancestral homelands of Arabs, Persians, Kurds, Armenians, and so on. Meanwhile, the offspring of the once archaic European Crusaders experienced a Renaissance, a Reformation, and several revolutions. As Middle Eastern peoples continued to make important contributions to world civilization, the glory of their governments consistently faded. Eventually, European powers used their new technologies and power to profit from the wealth of natural resources found in Africa, the Middle East, Southeast Asia, and the Americas, and thus an age of European conquest and colonialism was born.

Throughout the 1400s, European kingdoms developed economic ties with Muslim governments in order to procure coveted spices, silks, and textiles. By the end of that century, Middle Eastern trade networks had become a vital part of the European business with Southeast Asia. As a result, European explorers such as Christopher Columbus risked their lives in order to find new ways to bypass the Middle Eastern middlemen and their high taxes. Although Columbus never reached India by going west, in 1498, the Portuguese explorer Vasco da Gama successfully reached India by sailing south around the southern tip of Africa. This successful voyage opened the way for the Portuguese and other European powers to trade directly with India, leaving the Middle East out of the equation.

ALERT!

Checkmate! This term comes from the Persian phrase *shah-mât*, "The king is dead!" Although chess is believed to have started in India, the game was introduced to Europe via the Middle East.

Although the 1500s saw continued trade between Southeast Asia and Europe, the Americas provided the biggest boost to European economies, with massive loads of gold and silver being taken back across the Atlantic. After a century of distant exploitation, the 1600s began a new era of colonialism, in which Spanish, Dutch, English, and French colonialists established long-term settlements in the Americas, Africa, and Southeast Asia.

By the 1700s, European navies controlled the world's oceans and with them the global economy. Ancient land-based Middle Eastern trade routes quickly became obsolete, causing huge economic problems for the Muslim empires. By the end of that century, the British had emerged as the world's most powerful military force, with the industrial revolution giving them an even greater advantage over other world markets. Despite troubles in the North American colonies, the British managed to effectively control the largest empire the world had yet seen.

Throughout the 1800s, the French, British, Spanish, and Italians extended their power into North Africa, while at the same time Russian and British governments vied for control of Persia and Central Asia. With the loss of its North African territories and a strong European presence in Persia and India, the Ottoman Empire was surrounded. Perceiving a squeeze play, the sultan moved quickly to protect his crumbling empire.

Division and Decay

By the early 1900s, the Ottoman Empire was a mere shadow of its former greatness; nevertheless, it remained the world's only independent Islamic empire. Despite nearly 200 years of internal revolts and external attacks, Istanbul managed to retain all of Anatolia, Syria, Palestine, most of Arabia and Mesopotamia, and a small piece of Eastern Europe. At the same time, Greek and Slavic independence movements whittled away at the former Ottoman Balkans (a region that would eventually spark the world's first world war), while British troops occupied the nominally Ottoman province of Egypt.

Which came first, the ottoman footstool or the Ottoman Empire?

While the French were the first to call their footstools "ottomans," this doesn't necessarily mean they were referring to their Middle Eastern rivals. Correctly pronounced *Osmanli* (followers of Osman), "Ottoman" may have been a French wordplay used to insult this Muslim empire. Either way, it appears the French desired to bring their enemies underfoot.

Following the example of European nationalistic revolutions, Arab and Armenian areas organized resistance movements, hoping to attain independence from the ailing Ottomans. With the aide of eastern Anatolia's Kurdish militiamen, the Ottomans managed to put down Armenian rebellions with overwhelming brutality. Over the next two decades, over a million Armenian men, women, and children were either killed or displaced from their ancient Anatolian homeland, in what some call the Armenian genocide. (For more information, see Chapter 11.)

Like a cornered wolf, the Ottomans unleashed their wrath on any that would threaten their failing empire. The rapid growth of European empires, and the rivalries that developed between them, created a combative climate that somehow ended up involving most of the world. From Europe's exploitation of Indian, Persian, and African lands, to alliances formed between European powers and others, like the Ottomans, or the distant and relatively young United States of America, a global powder keg was ready for a spark.

In the following chapter, the global stage is set, as empires will choose sides, ethnic groups will polarize, and the powder keg will explode with monumental consequences. In the end, imperialism will be replaced by nation-states, and the Middle East will be reshaped according to European and American interests. Why are some Kurds fighting for their own country? What started the Israeli/Palestinian conflict? How were the Middle East's modern borders determined? Find out in the next chapter as you witness the twentieth century's violent birth. Ⓔ

Chapter 10

World War and Change

As political tensions in Europe grew, the world's most powerful governments divided into two camps and went to war. As history would have it, the Ottomans chose the losing side, resulting in the dismantling of their empire. From the ashes of war, the Middle East was reshaped into Western style nation-states. Today, empires are a distant memory, as modern political boundaries divide the map. With most Middle Eastern governments less than eighty years old, national lines are fresh and, in some cases, unsettled.

Choosing Sides

Throughout the 1800s, a series of independence movements dramatically altered the face of Europe and eventually the Middle East. Based on ideals from the French Revolution of the late 1700s, Europeans of similar ethnic, linguistic, and cultural backgrounds sought to determine their own affairs. In the midst of this nationalist fervor, France, Britain, Russia, Austria-Hungary, Germany, and Italy vied for supremacy. As a result, economic rivalries and political alliances set the stage for a colossal war.

Zionism on the Horizon

Of the many European nationalist groups that emerged in the late 1800s, Jewish nationalism (the movement known as Zionism) was the only movement that desired a non-European homeland. In 1896, Theodor Herzl, a Jewish journalist from Vienna, published a book entitled *The Jewish State*. Just as Serbian, German, and other nationalist leaders desired to carve out independent states, Herzl's writings articulated the need for an ethnically Jewish nation.

Although Zionism did not attract large numbers during Herzl's lifetime, over the following decades persecutions inspired many to take up the cause while fleeing from Europe. In search of a homeland, some considered establishing a Jewish colony in East Africa, while others looked to Palestine as a long-lost motherland. Ultimately, they decided to colonize Palestine, but because Herzl and many other Zionists were atheists, the new "Land of Israel" would not be focused on the God of Abraham but on secularism and Jewish heritage.

ALERT!

The term "Zionism" is derived from Zion, the hill on which Israel's King Solomon built the first Jewish temple. Although this name has religious connotations, modern Zionism was not established as a religious movement. Quite the opposite; it began in the late 1800s as a secular political movement focused on celebrating Jewish culture and history and providing a national refuge from anti-Jewish forces.

Trouble Brewing

During the first ten years of the twentieth century, alliances were formed along political and ethnic lines, which polarized Europe. With Germany and France clashing over issues in Morocco, Austria-Hungary and Russia trading insults over tensions in the Balkans, and Italy rousing German disdain by attacking Ottoman territories in North Africa, large-scale war was narrowly averted several times. Nevertheless, war was unavoidable, and the powder keg exploded in the Balkans.

On June 28, 1914, Serbian nationalists assassinated the Austrian Archduke Francis Ferdinand in Bosnia. In response, Austria-Hungary declared war on Serbia, which in turn brought Russia to the aid of their fellow Slavs, the Serbians. With Russia threatening Austria, Germany declared war on Russia. Eventually, Germany also declared war on France, prompting Britain to do the same to Germany. Finally Italy announced its hostilities toward Austria-Hungary, and Europe was embroiled in battle.

Because of Europe's global influence, what would have been a major continental war turned into the first world war. With Britain, France, Italy, and Russia as the original Allied Powers and Austria-Hungary and Germany as the initial Central Powers, Japan, China, Brazil, Liberia, the United States, and many others joined the Allies' cause, while the Ottomans and Bulgarians chose to side with the Austrians and Germans. With the Ottomans in the mix, the Middle East was sucked into Europe's ever-growing conflict.

FACT

World War I (1914 to 1918) saw the combined use of revolutionary technologies and firepower. Chemical weapons, machine guns, landmines, tanks, armored gunships, submarines, and bomber and fighter planes were used in concert to create more than 37 million casualties. By comparison, the entire Vietnam War saw a total of about 3.5 million casualties.

In Anatolia, the Allies attempted to take the Dardanelles (a narrow waterway connecting the Mediterranean to the Black Sea) in 1915. With control of these important straits, the Allies could use the Black Sea to squeeze the Central Powers from all sides. Because of British planning blunders, lightly armed ANZAC (Australia New Zealand Army Corps) forces, along with limited British and French troops, were sent into a hopeless battle. Unexpectedly meeting powerful Ottoman machine guns and well-fortified positions, thousands of ANZACs were gunned down day after day on the beaches of Gallipoli.

In what was supposed to be the first of many victories in Anatolia, the Allies were soundly defeated. From this overwhelming victory, an Ottoman military leader named Mustafa Kemal rose to prominence, eventually becoming the founding father of the modern Republic of Turkey. With Turkish leaders in Istanbul breathing easier at home, their control of Arab lands remained uncertain.

In Mesopotamia, British troops from India used Persian outposts to attack Ottoman positions. Hoping to take the great city of Baghdad, the British were turned back repeatedly by Ottoman resistance. In Egypt, the British officially made the region a protectorate, having occupied the area since 1882. From Cairo, the British set up their chief command center for all campaigns against the Ottoman Empire.

Lawrence or Arabia?

The most famous British support missions included the eccentric Thomas Edward Lawrence (Lawrence of Arabia), who was sent to western Arabia to aid Arab separatists. While most British soldiers viewed Arabs as uncivilized "wogs" (a derogatory term for non-whites), T. E. Lawrence respected Arab culture, even adopting Arab clothing and mannerisms. While Lawrence of Arabia fascinated curious European crowds, most Arabs were not as impressed.

Although Lawrence is said to have unified the Arab tribes, this seems to be a bit of an exaggeration. Lawrence did develop a special relationship with a charismatic Hashemite named Faysal, but he never directly led any of the Arab tribes. Instead of T. E. Lawrence, the protectors of Mecca and Medina, Sharif Husayn (governor of western Arabia) and his sons Àli, Àbdullah, and Faysal, were the most influential leaders in Arabia. Due to their Hashemite family's reported descent from Muhammad and their relationship with Istanbul, Husayn's family held great sway in the Hijaz region of western Arabia. In addition, the Saùdi family of eastern Arabia used their power to fight the pro-Ottoman Rashidi dynasty of northern Arabia. Nevertheless, the Hashemites led the fight for Arab independence.

Everyone Wants a Piece

In a type of symbiotic relationship, Arab nationalists viewed British firepower as their meal-ticket to independence, while the British in turn used Arab nationalism to undermine Ottoman calls for global Islamic revolt. With Arab and British leaders united in their disdain for Istanbul, an alliance was struck in which Arab leaders were guaranteed certain territories in return for their cooperation in the war effort.

With the combination of Arab tactical superiority and British technological advantages, Arabia, Palestine, Syria, and southern Mesopotamia had fallen from Ottoman hands by October 1918. With the Ottomans defeated in most of their Arab lands, Anatolia was their only remaining territory. In hopes of salvaging some part of their once-great empire, Istanbul chose to withdraw from the ailing Central Powers. Less than two weeks later, the Central Powers surrendered in Eurasia, ending the first global war.

ESSENTIAL

"A land without a people for a people without a land." This Zionist motto was used to convince the world that Palestine should become the Jewish homeland. In reality, by 1914, the land was occupied by more than 500,000 Arabs, whose families had lived there for more than 1,000 years. In contrast, less than 100,000 Jews lived in Palestine in 1914, the majority of whom had emigrated from Europe since the late 1800s.

Throughout the war, the British and French offered various portions of the Ottoman territories to other governments as incentives for their alliance. For instance, the Greeks and Italians were offered parts of western Anatolia for their partnership with the Allies. In the early years of the war, other secret arrangements were made with Russia, including the partitioning of Persian lands and the 1916 Sykes-Picot Agreement—named after its authors, Englishman Sir Mark Sykes and Frenchman Georges-Picot. The Sykes-Picot plan agreed on the distribution of Ottoman territories, giving the Russians much of Ottoman Anatolia, while the British and French claimed Syria, Palestine, and Mesopotamia.

In addition, European Jews were promised territory in Palestine, despite previous promises to Palestine's Arab inhabitants. In a letter known as the Balfour Declaration, the British foreign secretary, James Balfour, assured the prominent Jewish tycoon Lord Rothschild that London would support the establishment of a Jewish homeland in Palestine. As a result, European Zionists (Jewish nationalists) continued to purchase plots of land in the hope that their scattered Palestinian settlements would one day be united in a viable Jewish state.

True Intentions?

As Arab leaders caught wind of the Sykes-Picot and Balfour plans, many began to question the true intentions of the West. In particular, King Husayn recognized serious contradictions between these new documents and his previous correspondence with Sir Henry McMahon, the British high commissioner in Egypt. In response, French and British delegates traveled to the Hijaz (western Arabia) to assure the Hashemite king of their postwar plans for the region.

By promising the same pieces of land to multiple peoples and governments, the Allies had managed to secure war partners for the short term. However, in the long term, Western double-talk created bitter enemies. After fighting alongside British soldiers, Arab warriors found their allegiance unappreciated. In their eyes, the West had defamed Arab honor, creating feelings of betrayal and resentment that remain to this day.

Settling Dust and Changing Maps

U.S. President Woodrow Wilson was a strong advocate of self-determination and democracy, believing all peoples should have the right to decide their own future. With the end of hostilities, Wilson sent a team to the Middle East to see what type of government the people of the region desired. The information from this fact-finding mission was then presented at the 1919 Paris Peace Conference, but it was largely ignored in favor of predetermined British and French plans. Nevertheless, Wilson remained a vocal proponent of self-determination for all peoples—including non-Westerners.

FACT

U.S. President Woodrow Wilson received the 1919 Nobel Peace Prize for his attempts to broker peace during World War I and his effort to establish stable democratic nations in all parts of the world. As an advocate of the little guy, Wilson took a personal interest in the future of Arabs, Armenians, and Kurds after the fall of the Ottoman Empire.

Getting a Piece, or Making the Peace?

The Paris Peace Conference led to anything but peace for the Middle East, especially the Arab world. In closed-door meetings, promises were betrayed as the British and French turned the Middle East into their chessboard. Without considering ethnic, religious, political, or historical realities, the European powers partitioned the region according to their own interests. In addition, aspirations for Arab independence were crushed as Faysal was forced to relinquish his position only four months after having been elected king of greater Syria. Throughout the 1920s, British and French actions seriously wounded Arab nationalism, but in time the movement would rise again.

In what was at best a well-meaning support effort, and at worst a deceptive imperialist plot, the Allies created the "mandate system." In this arrangement, Western governments would provide direct administration of areas deemed unfit for immediate self-rule. After the Paris Conference and several other meetings, the Allies determined that the "peace" of the Middle East would be assured by establishing "spheres of influence," in which varying degrees of Western oversight would be implemented.

For the first time since the establishment of Ottoman provincial boundaries hundreds of years earlier, the region was defined by new political boundaries, many of which would become today's national borders. However, for the first years of their existence, these artificial lines were more for the benefit of Western governments than Middle Eastern people.

The French sphere of influence included these territories:

- Syria and Lebanon—Under direct administration, a form of governance known as a "mandate"
- Eastern Anatolia—Loosely monitored
- Independent Armenian region—In northeastern Anatolia
- Autonomous Kurdish region—In southeastern Anatolia

The British sphere of influence included the following territories:

- Palestine, Transjordan (Jordan), and Iraq—Under mandate (direct administration)
- Egypt, Kuwait, southeast Arabia, and Persia—"Protectorates" under partial administration
- Northwest Arabia, Sudan, and the Horn of Africa—Loosely monitored

The Italian sphere of influence included these territories:

- Western Anatolia—Including the Greek-administered region of Smyrna
- Dodecanesus Islands—About fifty islands in the Aegean Sea (including Rhodes, Kos, etc.)
- Thrace—At the extreme southeastern tip of the Balkan Peninsula (annexed by Greece)

With the West controlling most of the Middle East politically, and with limited military action continuing throughout the region, Arab, Turkish, and Persian nationalists rallied their peoples against the "occupiers." Broken promises, gun-toting foreign soldiers, and memories of Crusaders and colonialists created resentment and suspicion among most Middle Eastern peoples. As Ottoman imperialism had come to a close, no one wanted British or French leaders to replace the sultan. At the same time, Ottoman

Anatolia was not ready for Italian or Greek rule, either. As a result, a period of nationalistic fervor swept through the region, producing wars, revolts, and, in the end, fully independent Middle Eastern nations.

Winds of Nationalism

After the Paris Conference and several other key meetings, it became clear to people across the Middle East that the West had betrayed their trust. The Arab world was determined to see their promised independence realized at any cost. In Anatolia, Turkish nationalism would allow Ottomans to avoid territorial extinction. Finally, Persia would resist British and Russian occupation by ejecting the weak Qajar dynasty for the nationalistic regime of Reza Khan.

The Bold and the Betrayed

In Egypt, forty years of colonialism and four years of obligatory support for the British war effort created great resentment. With Egyptian and Arab pride as their war cry, the Wafd Party provided a platform through which frustrated Egyptians could vent their anger and find hope for the future. As result of widespread civil disobedience, the British protectorate was terminated in 1922, but only on paper. In reality, British troops lingered in Egypt, and the Egyptian-born King Fu'ad (formerly the Ottoman governor of Egypt) was London's puppet.

In other parts of the Arab world, the call of nationalism was also stirring people to action. In Iraq and Transjordan tensions were rising daily, especially among Iraq's Shi'ite population, whose leaders declared a jihad on all British troops. Also, the French ejection of Faysal from Syria inspired Faysal's brother, Àbdullah, to lead Arabs from the Hijaz into Transjordan to attack the French. With Faysal and Àbdullah gathering supporters across the Fertile Crescent, the British decided to use the Hashemite brothers to regain some semblance of control.

In 1921, Faysal was named king of Iraq, and Àbdullah was given the throne in Transjordan. With Arab monarchies established, nationalist movements were temporarily appeased, but a continued British presence in these areas undermined each king's credibility. In fact, in each region, Arabs began to view their king as London's yes-man. Nevertheless, Faysal's descendants continued to rule Iraq until 1958; in Transjordan, now Jordan, Àbdullah's great-grandson Àbdullah II remains the Hashemite king.

Father and Savior

In Anatolia, the Allies were in the process of implementing the Treaty of Sèvres. As a way to punish the defeated empire, the treaty divided most of the non-Arab Ottoman territories between Greeks, Armenians, and Kurds, while the remaining areas were placed under British, French, Italian, or international rule. With the Ottoman homeland in danger of being dissolved, war hero Mustafa Kemal used his clout from the Gallipoli victory, along with his powerful persona and political panache, to unite the Ottomans under a banner of Turkish nationalism.

After centuries of intermarriage between Central Asian Turks, Eastern Europeans, Caucasians, Arabs, Persians, and other groups, Anatolia's Ottomans were not ethnically Turkic (with characteristically Asian features). Instead, they were a mix of the empires' diverse subjects. With Turkish as its root, the unique Osmanli language borrowed many words from Arabic and Persian and was written in Arabic script. Nevertheless, Ottomans were distinct from Arabs, Persians, and other neighboring ethnic and linguistic groups.

FACT

On October 29, 1923, Mustafa Kemal Atatürk established the modern Republic of Turkey. He then moved to modernize and secularize his new nation by abolishing many Islamic institutions (including the caliphate), implementing Western laws, introducing European clothing styles, adopting the Latin alphabet (in place of Arabic script), and eventually removing Islam from its position as the official state religion.

Despite Anatolia's lack of Turkic blood, a Turkish identity (similar to the multiethnic American identity) gave rise to fierce nationalism and resistance. By 1920, Kemal mobilized his people to rid Anatolia of foreign occupiers—especially Greeks—and free the region of the sultan's tyranny. After intense fighting and skilled negotiations, Kemalists managed to remove European forces, overthrow the sultan, and carve out a national homeland—declaring the independent Republic of Turkey on October 29, 1923.

Over the following fifteen years, Mustafa Kemal instituted massive reforms across his new nation, patterning most of his changes after the West. In addition, he sought to modernize the haggard Ottoman homeland at all costs, including tradition. After abolishing the office of the caliph, outlawing certain traditional clothing styles, and making other direct attacks on conservative Islamic constructs, Kemal intentionally ejected religion from the Turkish state. In the end, Kemalism emerged as a type of religion, with Turkey's masses passionately devoted to their great leader. Mustafa Kemal not only saved Ottoman Anatolia from being carved into multiple states, he also became *Atatürk* (meaning "Father of the Turks"), the founding father of modern Turkey.

Reza Rising

In Persia, an unlikely figure emerged from the military to overthrow the aging Qajar dynasty. In 1921, Reza Khan realized his revolutionary dreams by taking the city of Tehran and seizing control of the nation. As king, Reza Shah Pahlavi associated himself with the ancient Aryan kings of Persia, even renaming his country Iran, meaning "land of the Aryans."

In addition, Reza built his new dynasty on the pillars of nationalism and modernization. From the example of his Turkish neighbor, Mustafa Kemal Atatürk, Reza Shah moved to implement Western-style reforms in Iran. Although many resisted his efforts, especially his moves to separate mosque and state, the Pahlavi dynasty managed to improve Iran's infrastructure, school systems, and civil laws. Despite opposition, revolt, and a short period of foreign occupation, Reza's monarchy continued for another generation, as his son Muhammad Reza Shah ruled from 1941 until the Islamic Revolution of 1979.

FACT

Since Iran's 1979 Islamic Revolution, Shi'ite clerics have ruled the nation according to their interpretation of Islamic Law. At the same time, the deposed Pahlavi family has moved to establish a more free and democratic Iran. Today, the former shah's son, the thirty-two-year-old Reza Pahlavi II, lives in the state of Maryland working as an advocate for his country.

Memories of Imperialism

Throughout the 1920s, nationalist movements brought new hope to Middle Eastern peoples who had long been subjects of foreign and local empires. However, with British and French oversight continuing into the 1930s, many began to see the West as imperialists in disguise. Memories of Ottoman and Crusader conquerors, coupled with fresh resentment from the Allies' betrayal, inspired some Arabs to reject all Western political influences. In contrast, many of these same people embrace Western cultures, technologies, and economies.

In Palestine, local Arabs watched as European Jews continued to purchase land and build settlements. The message of the Balfour Declaration had clarified Britain's support for a Jewish homeland, and for many Palestinian Arabs this "homeland" would be nothing more than a European colony. At the same time, increasing anti-Jewish sentiments in Germany and other Eastern European countries made Palestine an attractive refuge. Increased immigration through the 1930s caused even greater tensions between Jewish newcomers and the indigenous Arab population.

As a result of Britain's conflicting promises, two peoples believed they would be given the same small region. For European Zionists, Palestine's Arab population would simply need to move to any of the surrounding Arab states to make way for the Jewish state. On the other hand, local Arab leaders believed they would control Palestine upon British retreat.

In their view, Jewish settlers would either accept Arab rule or return to Europe with the British.

In an attempt to rectify the situation, British officials tried to broker a compromise, but it was too little too late. Jewish settlers and Arab citizens both wanted an end to the British occupation of Palestine. In 1939, a document known as the White Paper officially ended London's support for Zionism, promising an Arab Palestinian state. One year later, however, Palestine remained under direct British control as a triangle of violence raged between British troops, Jewish immigrants, and the Arab inhabitants of Palestine.

ALERT!

Although today's circumstances have seen Palestinians using "terrorist" measures, the situation in the 1940s saw Jewish "freedom fighters" using these same methods. Among groups such as the Stern Gang and Irgun, acts of terror and sabotage took civilian and military lives from both the British and the Arabs. Of these Jewish terrorist activities, the 1946 bombing of Jerusalem's King David Hotel killed more than 100 people.

Birth of the Nations

From the ashes of Word War I, the Middle East was reshaped by the victorious European powers, but it was ultimately the tides of nationalism that brought the region back to life. Although Egypt was the first to officially receive its independence in 1922, British strings were still attached until 1952, when Gamal Abdel Nasser declared the Arab Republic of Egypt. That said, Turkey was actually the first truly independent Middle Eastern nation, as the shrewd nationalist Mustafa Kemal announced the independent Turkish republic in 1923.

In the mid-1920s, King Husayn of the Hijaz and his son, Alí, were deposed by Ibn Saùd of eastern Arabia's Saùdi kingdom. Nevertheless, the Hashemite family's honor was partially restored as Husayn's son, Faysal, assumed full control of an independent Iraq in 1932. Meanwhile,

Àbdullah (another of Husayn's sons) held limited power over the region of Transjordan.

Two years later, in 1932, the Saùdi family announced the united kingdom of "Saùdi" Arabia. While the British directly controlled Egypt, and Iraq for a time, most of Arabia had never been under organized European authority. As a result, the formation of Saudi Arabia was not related to any British or French decisions. In fact, the Arab kingdom remained free of any Western influence until oil was discovered in 1935.

Today the Persian Gulf region is known around the world for its massive oil reserves, but before World War I this area saw only limited production.

In the northern half of the Levant (present-day Syria and Lebanon), the French continued their strict control through the 1930s and until just after World War II. During their mandate, the French expanded the largely Christian area of Mount Lebanon to include surrounding lands, which were mostly inhabited by non-Christians. As a result, ancient ethnic and religious balances were disturbed, leading to a major civil war several decades later. Only after Britain and the United States pressured France to leave the region did Syria and Lebanon finally became independent nations in 1946. In that same year, the British mandate of Transjordan was terminated, and Àbdullah became monarch of the Hashemite Kingdom of Jordan.

Seeds of Conflict

With Palestine as the only remaining British-administered area, it was clear that both Jewish and Arab leaders were planning to establish their authority. In response, the United Nations proposed a plan to partition Palestine, with independent Jewish and Arab states and an international zone in Jerusalem and areas surrounding the city. Zionist leaders, desiring different borders and a much larger state, hesitantly accepted the plan as a temporary setback. However, Arab leaders rejected the plan outright, citing that it gave over half of Palestine to Jewish immigrants, who accounted for less than one-third of the region's population.

Finally, on May 13, 1948, the British gave up, and the mandate of Palestine was terminated. The next day, the independent state of Israel was established, followed hours later by an Arab declaration of war. To Palestinians and their fellow Arab neighbors, the State of Israel was simply another Western imperialist plot. Just as their ancestors had resisted Crusaders, they would repel the Zionists.

For more than fifty-five years this conflict has continued, with each side giving and receiving the sentence of death. Why do they hate each other? What are the Occupied Territories? Can there be peace between Israelis and Palestinians? The Arab-Israeli conflict has produced some of the most complex questions of this century, questions that cannot be answered with fatalistic or simplistic answers. In Chapter 12 you will find crucial background information, which will help you to understand this mind-boggling conflict. But first, Chapter 11 will introduce you to the modern Middle East and its diverse peoples.

Chapter 11

Modern Middle East Mosaic

When many Americans think of the Middle East, they envision devout Muslims, Arabs in traditional dress, and barren deserts. But just as the ancient Middle East was a crossroads of peoples and cultures, today's Middle East is more of the same. With diverse clothing styles (including Western apparel), modern technologies, sprawling mega cities, and a wide range of religious perspectives, the spectrum of facial features, skin tones, and languages is as wide in this region as any other part of the world.

Urban and Eclectic

Although most countries in the Middle East have retained parts of their traditional cultures, they have also been injected with new technologies and ideologies. The result is a unique coexistence of old and new, which can be seen in nearly all areas of daily life. In the streets of major cities like Cairo, donkey carts drive alongside new cars, while in small villages, radios simultaneously play the music of Western pop stars like Eminem and traditional Arabian singers such as Ibrahim Tatlises.

In addition to technology and pop culture, economies and lifestyles have changed drastically over the past forty years. In many nations, small family-run farms are no longer able to compete with more efficient high-tech farms. As a result, farmers are forced to leave their rural homelands for the possibility of work in the city. Because of this shift, huge urban centers have developed in once average-sized cities. In Istanbul, for example, the city's population has swelled from less than 2 million in 1960 to more than 11 million in 2000, and is estimated to reach 18 million in 2010.

FACT

With a population of more than 20 million, Cairo, Egypt, is the largest city in the Middle East and is one of the planet's ten biggest cities.

Technology and Traditions

As opposed to the lightly armed soldiers of the early twentieth century, most Middle Eastern governments are now equipped with tanks, fighter jets, radar systems, and other high-tech weaponry. Since 1990, Saudi Arabia has been the United States' biggest arms customer, paying more than $40 billion for weapons and the latest surveillance equipment. In addition, the Saudis have received expert antiterrorist training from the United Kingdom's elite Special Air Services (SAS) unit. Even in Taliban-ruled Afghanistan, where certain elements of modernity were banned, armored vehicles, heavy artillery, and wireless communications were used to combat coalition forces.

You will find varying levels of development in each nation. For the most part, however, cell phones, satellite televisions, computers, movie theaters, and automobiles are just as prevalent in the Middle East as they are in Middle America. From skyscrapers and electronic billboards to shopping malls, amusement parks, and bowling allies, there is more than enough modern in the Middle East.

The Middle East is not only a land of external contrasts, but of internal differences as well. With the rapid introduction of new technologies most people adapted functionally to modern life while retaining traditional values, social structures, beliefs, and superstitions. The point is that technology does not produce modernity in the way many Westerners might envision. The peoples of the Middle East have their own unique ways of doing things, which are not necessarily going to be changed by highways and high-tech gadgets.

Distinctions of Diversity

In the first chapter you read about the region's three largest ethnic groups, which divide the Middle East into Arab, Turkic, and Persian worlds. You also learned that these distinctions are by no means exact, as there are Turkic populations in Persian regions, Arab groups living in predominately Turkic areas, and so on. If that isn't confusing enough, there are other distinct minority groups throughout the Middle East whose bloodlines and/or languages are vastly different from the majority of their neighbors.

Kurds

The largest of these minority groups is the Kurds. With more than 30 million Kurdish people in the Middle East, they are hardly a minority when taken as a whole, but because they are a people without a national homeland, they live as minorities in more than seven nations. The most significant Kurdish populations are in the mountainous regions of eastern Turkey, northern Iraq, and western Iran, where they are actually the majority.

In Turkey, there are about 15 million Kurds (20 percent of the nation's citizens). In Iraq there are more than 5 million (20 percent of the population), and in Iran there are another 5 million (10 percent of the republic's people). While Kurds also live in parts of Syria, Lebanon, and the former Soviet Union, these groups account for less than 5 percent of the global Kurdish population. Of all the world's Kurds, the vast majority are Sunni Muslims, though some are Shi'ite Muslims or Christians and still others practice various forms of Zoroastrianism.

ESSENTIAL

After being promised an independent Kurdish state in 1920, the Kurds watched Western governments divide their homeland between the newborn nations of Turkey, Syria, Iraq, and Iran.

By now, you know there are millions of Kurds in the Middle East, but who are the Kurds? Let's start by determining who they are not. Kurds are not ethnically Arabs, Turks, or Persians, nor is Arabic, Turkish, or Farsi their mother tongue. These highlanders come from the same Indo-European stock as many Iranian tribes, but their distinct Kurmanji and Sorani languages set Kurds apart. In addition, unique Kurdish clothing styles, music, and so on have developed among these mountain people.

While some believe the Kurds are descendants of the ancient Medes, their exact origins remain uncertain. As with most modern questions of ethnicity, the concept of Kurdishness has become politically charged. For some Kurds, having their traditional homeland divided between Arab, Turkish, and Iranian nations is unacceptable. In their estimation, an independent Kurdish state should be formed in the region they call Kurdistan. At the same time, many Kurds are content with life under a non-Kurdish government, as long as they are not victims of discrimination.

In response to Kurdish nationalism, the governments of Turkey and Iraq have tried to suppress any possibility of rebellion. Over the past fifteen years, thousands of Kurdish guerillas and civilians have been shot, gassed, or tortured, while the living have been prevented from speaking their language or celebrating their heritage. Whatever their ancient roots or nationalistic aspirations, today more than 30 million people proudly consider themselves Kurds.

Armenians

North of the Kurdish region, a people known as the Armenians once inhabited a large area from Mount Urartu (Ararat) to central Anatolia (present-day Turkey). According to tradition, a man named Haik established the first Armenian kingdom around 2100 B.C. As a result, contemporary Armenians call themselves "Hay" and their nation Hayastan. Whether or not this tradition is completely accurate, most experts believe the Armenian people are a combination of ancient peoples, including the Urartians (Araratians), Hurrians, and possibly even Greek immigrants. Linguistically, Armenian is one of many in the Indo-European family, to which Persian, Kurdish, and Greek are also connected.

After adopting Christianity in A.D. 301, the Armenian people found themselves subject to a series of foreign rulers, including the Christian Byzantines and the Muslim Ottomans. In World War I, fearing the Christian Armenians would side with their Russian coreligionists, the Ottomans joined with Kurdish forces in a pre-emptive strike. As a result, more than a million Armenians were killed in what has come to be known as the Armenian Holocaust or Genocide.

FACT

One of the world's best-known Armenians is an American billionaire named Kirk Kerkorian. Known as the "Quiet Lion," Kerkorian was raised in a middle-class home but became one of Las Vegas's most famous hotel and casino moguls. Today, Kerkorian's net worth is estimated at a whopping $5.8 billion.

With the defeat of the Ottoman Empire, the Armenians (along with the Kurds) were promised an independent Armenian state, but (just as the Kurds) their land was divided between the newly formed Republic of

Turkey and the Soviet Union. In addition, another round of violence ensued, in which most of Anatolia's Armenians were forced to evacuate or die. In what is called the Armenian Diaspora, citizens of this ancient nation were scattered from their homeland into the Soviet Union, United States, and various parts of the Middle East.

Since 1991, nearly 4 million of the world's 6 million Armenians live on the eastern edge of their Middle Eastern homeland, in the newly independent Republic of Armenia. Most of the other 2 million Armenians have made their homes in the countries of Iran, Iraq, Syria, Jordan, Israel/Palestine, Egypt, and Sudan, while about 500,000 have settled in the United States.

Proud of their ancient Christian heritage, diasporic Armenians have found a source of identity and solidarity in the church. From liturgy written and recited in the Armenian language, to special cultural events and holiday celebrations, the church is a meeting point for the displaced. Because most Armenians are proud of their roots, local churches have been established around the world as a vital link to the mother church in Armenia.

Circassians

To the north of the Armenians, a people known as the Circassians (also called the Adyge or Cherkess) once inhabited a region in the Caucasus Mountains stretching from the Black Sea to the Caspian Sea. From time immemorial, these stately mountaineers have protected their honor and their homeland. By the 1200s A.D., pressure from the Byzantine Empire moved the Circassians to reject ancient tribal beliefs for Christianity. With the rise of the Ottoman Empire, the Circassians eventually adopted Islam in the late 1600s.

By the late 1700s, the Russian Empire expanded into Circassian lands, spurring a major war between these Christian and Muslim peoples. Despite fierce resistance, the Circassians were eventually overpowered by Russia in 1864. As a result, nearly 1.5 million Circassians fled their ancient homeland for the protection of their Ottoman coreligionists. In this mass exodus, more than 90 percent of the world's Circassian population found new homes throughout the Middle East.

FACT

Circassians around the world recognize May 21 as a day of mourning for those who died or were displaced during the 1864 Circassian diaspora.

As the native tongue of the indigenous people of Northwest Caucasia, the Circassian language is completely different from the Turkic, Semitic, or Indo-European groups. With its unusually large number of consonants and infrequent use of vowels, the Circassian language is one of the world's most unique. Although they are related to other Caucasian mountain peoples (such as the Georgians and Chechens), the Circassians are their own distinct group.

Today, more than 1.5 million Circassians live in fifty-six countries around the world. With about 500,000 living in southwestern Russia, most of the other million Circassians live as minorities in the Middle East. Turkey is home to the region's largest population, with more than 200,000 Circassians, followed by Libya, Jordan, and Syria. There are also significant communities in Iraq, Lebanon, and Israel/Palestine. Due to recent wars in the Middle East, some Circassians have come to the United States as well.

Assyrians

In northern Iraq, northwestern Iran, and northeastern Syria (south of the mountainous Kurdish homeland and to some degree overlapping Kurdistan), nearly 3 million Assyrian Christians live as a minority in what they believe to be their ancestral homeland. Geneticists from Stanford University have determined that modern Assyrians do have a distinct genetic profile, although definitive proof of their ancient bloodlines are unavailable. Still, the Assyrians' genetics distinguish them from their Arab, Kurdish, Turkic, and Persian neighbors.

Another difference between Assyrians and other Middle Eastern populations is their language. Known as Aramaic or Syriac, the language of the Assyrians is a Semitic tongue related to Hebrew and Arabic. Due to centuries of Arabization, some Assyrians now speak Arabic as their first language, though their Aramaic mother tongue continues to be used in liturgical church services.

In addition to their ethno-linguistic distinctiveness, Assyrians are also proud of their ancient Christian heritage. As some of the first gentile followers of Jesus Christ, Assyrian missionaries were responsible for spreading the new faith into Persia, China, and other parts of Asia. Over the centuries, church politics and doctrinal differences have produced four main Assyrian denominations: the Apostolic Assyrian Church of the East; the Catholic Assyrian Church of the East; the Chaldean Catholic Church; and the Assyrian Orthodox Church of Antioch.

ALERT!

Don't mistake Assyrians and Syrians. Citizens of the Arab Republic of Syria are known as Syrians, while Assyrians are a distinct ethnic group. Though nearly 1 million Assyrians live in Syria, another 3 million live in other nations.

Just as their Armenian coreligionists, Assyrian Christians experienced death and dispersion during and after World War I. Known as the Assyrian Holocaust, hundreds of thousands of civilians were forced from their lands and killed by Ottoman armies. Like their Kurdish and Armenian neighbors, the Assyrians received a promise of an independent state, only to see their lands parceled out into Arab, Turkish, and Persian states.

Today, there are nearly 4 million Assyrians around the globe, with more than 1 million in Iraq, just under 1 million in Syria, and more than 200,000 in Armenia. In addition, Assyrian communities can be found in Turkey, Iran, Lebanon, Jordan, other parts of the Middle East, and the United States, where nearly 500,000 Assyrians have made their homes.

Copts

The term *Copt* comes from the Greek *Aigyptos,* which comes from the ancient title *Hikaptah*, which was given to Egypt's capital, Memphis. From the late 100s to the early 300s A.D., after millennia of polytheism, most Egyptians accepted Christianity. By the mid-600s, Arab Muslim armies had conquered Egypt, setting up military installations among the indigenous non-Arab peoples. After several hundred years of Arab occupation, Egyptian Christians began converting to Islam. As Muslims, they adopted the Arabic language and began calling themselves Arabs. Those who remained Christian continued to identify themselves as non-Arab Egyptians or Copts.

The Copts are not Arabs, nor are they of the Semitic family; instead, they are their own subdivision within the Eastern Hamitic (Afro-Asiatic) group. Strictly speaking, Copts are a mixture of the ancient Egyptian peoples, African Nubians, Greeks, Jews, and Romans. Because Copts look much like their Arab Muslim neighbors, a cross worn around a person's neck or tattooed on the wrists is the most likely identifying factor.

The Coptic language used today in most Egyptian church services is largely the same tongue spoken by the ancient pharaohs (just as modern English is largely the same tongue as Old English).

Today, there are an estimated 7 million Copts who make up about 10 percent of Egypt's total population. While the vast majority of Egyptian Christians are part of the Coptic (Egyptian Orthodox) Church, others are members of various Eastern Orthodox, Catholic, and Protestant churches. The biggest distinction between members of the Coptic Church and other Egyptian Christians is their adherence to Monophysitism, an understanding of Christ's nature which most other churches view as heresy.

As late as 1600, Arabic surpassed Coptic as Egypt's spoken language. As a result, the ancient Egyptian (Coptic) language is only used in ceremonial church services, just as Latin is recited in Roman Catholic mass. Since priests and a select few laymen are the only people who can understand the language of the pharaohs, Greek and Arabic are also used in Coptic churches.

Berbers

From the western Egyptian oasis town of Siwa to the High Atlas Mountains of Morocco and Algeria, an ancient people known as the Berbers struggle to keep their identity and language alive. "Berber" is a broad term for the indigenous tribes of North Africa who have lived in this region for thousands of years. Referenced in Egyptian texts as early as 3000 B.C., about 50 million of these diverse non-Arab peoples continue to live in the mountains and rural areas of their African homeland.

As a whole, Berbers are the ethnic majority in North Africa, but because of continued Arabization, many ethnic Berbers have adopted the Arabic language and cultural identity. In some countries, if you call someone a Berber, you are calling him or her a backward country bumpkin. Because of this stigma, and the perceived superiority of Arab civilization, many ethnic Berbers now consider themselves Arabs. Nevertheless, some are strongly resisting Arabization and have launched Berber identity movements.

Nearly 80 percent of Moroccans and Algerians are ethnically Berber, while less than half of these people identify themselves as Berbers. Though more than half of Tunisians are descendants of Berber-speaking parents, only 5 percent admit they are Berbers. The same is true in Libya and Egypt, where Arabic has replaced ancient Berber dialects. Nevertheless, some Berbers remain proud of their heritage and, in Algeria, many Berbers have refused to learn Arabic.

FACT

The famous Christian theologian Augustine of Hippo was a Berber. Born in 354 A.D., and raised in a part of North Africa that is now Algeria, Augustine is revered by the Roman Catholic Church as a saint. Within his many writings, this blessed Berber clarified such doctrines as original sin, free will, divine grace, and predestination.

In addition to the ongoing Arabization of Berbers, these aboriginal peoples have also come to embrace Islam. Today, most Berbers consider themselves Muslims, but the process of Islamicization was slow, starting in the late 600s and continuing into the 1500s. Because of this gradual change, most Berbers have retained pre-Islamic beliefs and ceremonies. The intermingling of Islamic and pagan traditions has produced unique "folk Islamic" practices across North Africa. With Berber language and identity on the verge of extinction, these traces of ancient religion may be the only thing Berber to survive the twenty-first century.

Jews

As you read in Chapter 4, the Hebrews (Egyptian for "wanderers") are an ancient people who are said to have come from the Semitic family of Abraham, Isaac, and Jacob (also known as "Israel"). In about 1400 B.C., after more than 400 years of slavery and wandering, these sons and daughters of Israel settled in the land of Canaan, just inland from the eastern Mediterranean coast. In Canaan, they established a Hebrew kingdom, which eventually divided into a northern kingdom of Israel and a southern kingdom of Judah.

By the late 700s B.C., Judah was the only surviving Hebrew kingdom. Thus, the descendants of Israel came to be known as Jews, while their land was called Judea. Throughout the first century A.D., the people of Judea faced increasing persecution from Roman occupation forces, which had killed hundreds of thousands and destroyed the sacred temple of Jerusalem. After more than 1,500 years in Canaan, the Romans "cleansed" Judea of all Jews and renamed it Palestine (after the long-extinct Philistine people). Because of this event, known as the Diaspora, ethnically Jewish people were scattered around the globe.

Taking their monotheistic religion with them, ethnic Jews continued to practice their ancient traditions in foreign lands. Captivated by Jewish culture and faith, ethnically non-Jewish locals adopted the Jewish religion. With their conversions, people from many different ethnic backgrounds began calling themselves Jews. Thus, the distinction between ethnically Jewish people and those practicing Judaism must be made.

Nearly 2,000 years after the Diaspora, people who consider themselves Jewish are divided into two groups. European Jews, who tend to have lighter skin, are known as the Ashkenazim. In addition to their European appearance, the Ashkenazim are politically and culturally Western. In contrast, those who have lived in the Middle East, North Africa, and Spain for the past millennia usually have darker skin, making it difficult to distinguish them from other Middle Eastern peoples. Known as the Sephardim, these people have been shaped by centuries of life in the Arab and Muslim worlds.

QUESTION?

Are Jews a religious group or an ethnic group?
It depends! One who is born ethnically Jewish may or may not also practice the Jewish religion. At the same time, someone who is not born a Jew can choose to formally convert and practice the Jewish religion.

Since the creation of Israel in 1948, Eastern and Western Jews have lived together in one land for more than fifty years. Although these groups share a common religion, cultural differences have been a source of ongoing tension between the Ashkenazim and Sephardim. In addition, many darker-skinned Sephardic Jews feel they are being discriminated against by European Jews. The most striking example of this is seen in the controversy over the "Jewishness" of more than 80,000 Ethiopian Jews. Despite their ancient Jewish traditions and clearly Jewish beliefs, the dark skin and African features of Ethiopia's Jewish community almost kept them from receiving Israeli citizenship. Nevertheless, it was finally decided that these Ethiopians were in fact "real" Jews.

Despite internal differences, about 5 million Jews live as a majority in the state of Israel, while another 50,000 live as minorities in Turkey, Lebanon, Morocco, and other parts of the Middle East.

Islamic Offshoots—Reformers or Heretics?

Since the death of Muhammad in A.D. 632, Muslims have been faced with the fate of all major world religions—division. For Islam, this began as Muslims tried to choose a leader after the untimely death of their prophet. With some believing their leader should be the most qualified man, and others contending for Muhammad's closest male relative, the newly formed brotherhood was split. Over the centuries, this rift has inspired more than 1 billion Muslims to call themselves Sunni, while about 300 million consider themselves Shi'ites.

Though many non-Muslims view Islam as a monolithic religion, Islamic beliefs are as diverse and divided as any other religious movement.

As Islam was introduced to other populations, another shade emerged, known as Sufism. These mystical Muslim converts attempted to distill the words of the Qur'an to a simple message of love and oneness with God. In addition, they sought supernatural encounters through singing and dancing. While some Sunnis and Shi'ites were drawn to this new approach, others viewed Sufis as misguided heretics.

Today, after fourteen centuries of Islamic history, many orthodox and heterodox movements have appeared. While most of these groups continue to celebrate their Islamic roots, some conservative Muslims view them as apostates and infidels. The following are a few of these controversial factions.

Alawites (a.k.a. Nusayri)

Found primarily in the mountains that line the northwest Mediterranean coast, today about 2 million Arabs call themselves Alawites. Inspired by the teachings of the ninth-century Shi'ite theologian Muhammad bin Nusayr, Alawites have unique beliefs and practices, which some Muslims view as blasphemy.

An almost Trinitarian concept of Ali, Muhammad, and God being one in essence is the most striking Alawite belief. This sect is also criticized for not observing Islam's five pillars, not meeting in mosques, and for celebrating traditionally Christian and Zoroastrian holidays. Despite opposition from some Muslim leaders, Alawites believe they are Shi'ite Muslims.

Like his father before him, Syria's president Bashar Asad is an Alawite. Though less than 10 percent of all Syrians are Alawites, this minority has ruled the nation since 1963.

Alevi-Bektashis

As a unique synthesis of Sufism, Shi'ism, and pre-Islamic religious beliefs, Alevi-Bektashism is a flexible and complex movement. Inspired by the teachings of a twelfth-century mystic named Haji Bektash Veli, nearly 15 million Turkish and Eastern European people have combined aspects of all the major world religions with a view that holds humanity and divinity as one and the same.

Like the Arab Alawites of south-central Turkey, eastern Syria, and northeastern Lebanon, Alevi-Bektashis do not observe Islam's five pillars, though Muhammad and the Qur'an are held in high regard. If you ask an Alevi-Bektashi if he or she is Muslim, most will reply, "I am Muslim, Jewish, Christian, Buddhist, and atheist, but most importantly I am human."

Druze (a.k.a. Mowahhidoon)

Though the exact origins of this movement are unclear, the *Mowahhidoon* (Arabic for "Monotheists") emerged in the 800s, believing they were a new interpretation of Judaism, Christianity, and Islam. In their view, the other three had lost the true meaning of religion by focusing on rituals and laws. In contrast, the Mowahhidoon sought the "pure path," which incorporated aspects of Greek philosophy and Hindu spirituality with traditional monotheism.

In the late 900s, a Mowahhidoon leader named Darazi announced that the Fatimid Caliph al-Hakim was the incarnation of God. Although many initially accepted this teaching, his followers eventually rejected Darazi. Because of Darazi's spectacular claims, outsiders used the name "Druze" when referring to the Mowahhidoon.

Because members of this sect have kept the details of their religion secret, many non-Mowahhidoon have speculated about their beliefs and practices. Apart from fruitless speculation, the Mowahhidoon are by definition strict monotheists. Unlike most monotheists, the Mowahhidoon believe each soul is reincarnated from life to life and that heaven and hell are states of mind rather than destinations. Just as other offshoot groups, the Mowahhidoon have rejected the five pillars of Islam, causing many Muslims to reject them.

Today, there are about a million Mowahhidoon living around the world, with nearly 300,000 living in Lebanon, Syria, and northern Israel. The Mowahhidoon are ethnically Arabs, yet because they do not accept converts or marry outside of the faith, they have developed a distinct, almost ethnic identity.

With a clearer picture of the Middle East's history, peoples, and cultures, you can dive into the current history and politics of this massive region with confidence. From today's Arab-Israeli conflict to the contemporary Arab world, this book will move on to explore state-run religion in Iran, secular struggles in Turkey, and other issues that must be addressed in this new century.

Chapter 12

Israel/Palestine—All Eyes on Jerusalem

Welcome to the contemporary Middle East! To better understand today's Middle East, you will jump right into the most complicated place in the region. Take a moment to prepare yourself for heartache produced by more than fifty years of war and injustice. Set aside your preconceived notions, and allow the stories of these two peoples to move you. Try to understand their history, their hopes, and their dreams.

Aryanism, Zionism, and Exodus

While Britain was bouncing back and forth on its plan for Palestine, National Socialism (better known as Nazism) inspired the people of Germany as they rebuilt their war-torn country. Under the banner of Nazism, Adolph Hitler began a program of nationalistic conquest. Based on a corrupted understanding of the Aryan identity, Germany seized surrounding nations seen as Aryan homelands. In addition, Nazis attempted to rid their state of all non-Aryan peoples.

Although Gypsies, Slavs, and other groups were targets of Nazi racism, Jewish populations were their primary focus. After confiscating Jewish possessions, humiliating Jews with special identification symbols, and displacing Jewish families into ghettos, Aryan nationalists decided to exterminate all non-Aryans. By establishing death camps (concentration camps), Hitler's henchmen gassed, shot, raped, and starved millions.

British, American, and Soviet forces eventually defeated Germany and liberated those still living in death camps. If not for the Allied intervention, millions more would have been massacred, and most of Europe's Jewish population could have been annihilated. Nevertheless, the Holocaust stole the lives of more than 5 million Jews and another 5 million non-Jewish civilians.

ESSENTIAL

The term Palestinian is translated *Filastin* in Arabic, but this does not mean they are the descendants of the ancient Philistines! About 2,000 years ago, the Romans expelled all Jews from the province of Judea, renaming it Palestine after the ancient Philistines. Over the following centuries, those living in this region were known as Palestinians regardless of their ethnicity. Nevertheless, from about A.D. 700, most of Palestine's inhabitants were ethnically Arabs.

At the end of World War II, European and American populations felt partially responsible for the Holocaust, leading many politicians to look for ways to make amends. At the same time, Jewish nationalists were calling for a refuge in Palestine. For most Western leaders, the idea of creating a Jewish homeland was just what the doctor ordered. A Jewish state in Palestine would provide a new start for Holocaust survivors, but what about the Arab peoples who had made their start in Palestine centuries before? Was Palestine really a "land without a people," as Zionists were saying? The next fifty years answered these questions with catastrophic clarity.

Declaration of State and War

Three years after Nazi Aryanism's greatest defeat, Jewish Zionism gained its greatest victory. European immigration had increased the Jewish population in Palestine from less than 175,000 in the 1931 census, to more than 650,000 in 1948. With key members of the United Nations voicing their support for a Jewish state and Britain abandoning its thirty-year mandate of Palestine, Russian-born David Ben-Gurion announced the Jewish State of Israel on May 14, 1948. The next day, Arab armies made their own declaration of resistance, and the first Arab-Israeli war began.

The subsequent battle saw Ben-Gurion uniting Jewish terrorist groups, lightly armed farmers, and emboldened Holocaust survivors against Jordanian, Iraqi, Egyptian, and Lebanese regular armies. With both sides focused on Jerusalem, heavy fighting plagued the holy city and its surrounding areas. After one month of intense conflict, U.N. mediator Count Bernadotte organized a cease-fire, but only a month later, Jewish terrorists from the notorious Stern Gang assassinated the U.N. mediator, and fighting resumed.

On April 9, 1948 (more than a month before the Arab-Israeli war began), future Israeli Prime Ministers Menachem Begin and Yitzaq Shamir led a group of armed Jewish radicals into the Palestinian village of Dayr Yasin. When the dust settled, the bodies of 245 Palestinian men, women, and children were found, with many stuffed in wells and tied to automobiles.

Bolstered by new weaponry from Czechoslovakia, the Israeli army moved with fresh vigor on Arab positions, pushing them all the way to Jerusalem. After six months of renewed fighting, Arab armies were ready to throw in the towel. By July 27, 1949, the war was officially over, as Jordan and Egypt signed cease-fire agreements with the Jewish state.

As a result of the 1948 war, Israel's borders increased to include 78 percent of the land formerly known as Palestine. The remaining 22 percent was then divided between the Hashemite Kingdom of Jordan, which annexed the exclusively Arab area known today as the West Bank (once called Judea and Samaria), and Egypt, which assumed control of a strip of land along the southeastern Mediterranean coast, known as the Gaza Strip. Meanwhile, the coveted city of Jerusalem was divided between the Jewish state and the Kingdom of Jordan.

Displaced Peoples

To escape the raging war of 1948, 70 percent of Palestine's Arab population fled their homes and farms. Hoping to return when things cooled down, most moved to the safety of uncontested areas in the West Bank and Gaza Strip. In addition, Arabs in the north of Palestine escaped to nearby Lebanon and Syria, while many from Jerusalem and the Galilee region found refuge in Jordan. As things settled down, many families attempted to return to their homes, businesses, and farmlands, only to be told they were not welcome. Those who were able to make their way past Israeli soldiers found Jewish families living in their homes, using their furniture, and farming their lands.

FACT

In the aftermath of war, about 750,000 Palestinian Arabs found themselves homeless, while another 150,000 retained their property within the new Jewish state.

As most families had fled with only the clothes on their backs, they were unable to produce land deeds for Jewish officials. The only evidence most could provide was a simple skeleton key. Over the following years, the key became a common symbol for those who had lost everything to the new state. With no money to purchase property or pay for temporary housing, thousands of homeless families were exposed to the elements. This large-scale humanitarian crisis led the United Nations Relief and Works Agency (UNRWA) to move quickly, and the agency established "temporary" refugee camps.

Viewing the camps as a demeaning yet temporary necessity, most Palestinian Arabs believed they would return to their homes after a few months. As the months turned into years, shacks and eventually simple cement structures replaced the original U.N.–issued tents. After being displaced by the State of Israel, over 1 million people continue to live as refugees in impoverished Arab ghettos.

Today, refugee camps are home to more than 1 million people in the West Bank, Gaza Strip, and surrounding Arab nations, while another 2 million Palestinians live outside the camps under Israeli control.

Freedom Fighters or Terrorists

Throughout the early 1950s, many displaced Palestinian Arabs decided they would rather die fighting than rot in filthy refugee camps. Known as the *fida'yin* ("men of sacrifice"), these men mimicked Jewish groups like the Irgun, who had employed terror in their efforts to free Palestine from British occupation just a few years before.

The *fida'yin*, known to the West as "fedayeen," understood they were no match for the Israeli army. But just as the lightly armed Stern Gang had tormented the British, the fedayeen believed they could make their homeland undesirable for Jewish immigrants. Despite their killing of hundreds of Israeli soldiers, the fedayeen attacks actually emboldened the Jewish newcomers, inspiring them to launch counterattacks into refugee camps, killing their share of Arab fighters and civilians.

The Fix of '56

In 1956, Egypt nationalized the Suez Canal, nullifying London's claims to the important waterway. In response, the British and French combined forces with the Israelis, who also had a bone to pick with Egypt because of fedayeen attacks staged from the Sinai. After bombing Egyptian air bases and occupying the Sinai Peninsula, the Europeans allowed Israel to manage the newly acquired Egyptian lands and destroy the fedayeen rebel camps. However, within a year, pressure from the United States and other nations forced Israel to leave the Gaza Strip and Sinai Peninsula. Although the Sinai was back in Egyptian hands, Israeli operations had dealt a major blow to the fedayeen guerillas in the region.

Hello PLO

Throughout the late 1950s and early 1960s, a period of relative peace allowed Israel to grow economically, politically, and militarily. Meanwhile, Arab nations were caught in the middle of American-Soviet rivalries. As some countries sided with the West and others looked to the USSR, the Arab world was quickly divided along Cold War lines. In addition, ideas of Arab nationalism and Islamic revolution created new movements across the Arab world.

In the midst of these changing times, Palestinians sought to regain their dignity and homeland by attacking Israel. Arab governments also desired to rid the Middle East of the Jewish state, which in their estimation was a Western colonial outpost. In 1964, thirteen Arab nations met in Cairo to discuss their response to the Zionist state. The Arab governments agreed that Palestinian fedayeen should be mobilized to deal with Israel. In addition, the governments decided to train and supply Palestinian guerillas in their quest for liberation.

Yasser Arafat's movement, known as al-Fatah, translates to "conquest," but the name is also derived from the reversed first letters of its full name, *Harakat al-Tahrir al-Filastini*, meaning "Movement for the Liberation of Palestine."

In order to determine an official governing body for the Palestinians, Jordan's King Husayn gathered 400 prominent Palestinians in Jordanian-controlled East Jerusalem. Through this inaugural Palestinian National Council meeting, the Palestinian Liberation Organization (PLO) and Palestinian Liberation Army (PLA) were confirmed as the official channels for Palestinian nationalism. Although the PLO was meant to be an umbrella organization for all Palestinians, a separate group calling itself al-Fatah emerged as the most influential resistance movement.

Yasser Arafat

With support from Syria, an influential Palestinian engineer named Yasser Arafat organized al-Fatah's members to attack Israeli positions. Because of the group's great success and Arafat's charisma, al-Fatah's popularity grew exponentially among downtrodden refugees. Realizing Arafat's popular strength, the chairman of the PLO moved to combine forces with al-Fatah.

Six Days in '67

During the mid-1960s, intense fighting erupted between Israeli and Syrian forces, bringing instability to the Soviet-backed Syrian regime. To deal with this situation, the Russians employed another of their patron states, Egypt, to defend Syria in the event of an Israeli invasion. After learning of this pact, Israel decided to direct its reprisals against Jordan, which was not part of the Soviet deal.

By spring of 1967, the Russians were anxiously watching Israeli-American relations. Jordan was writhing under recent Israeli attacks, and the United States was scrambling to dissuade Israel from making any rash moves. In the midst of this, the Soviets sent bad intelligence to the Egyptians, warning them of a massive Israeli buildup on the Syrian border. With this information, Egyptian forces rolled through the Sinai Desert toward the Israeli border, reoccupying border positions held by the United Nations since 1949. In addition, Syrian, Jordanian, and Iraqi troops moved to Israel's borders to deflect possible strikes. Depending on whom you talk to, Israel's next move was either part of a calculated plan of expansion or a pre-emptive strike of desperation. Either way, on June 5, 1967, the Israeli air force made the first move, destroying most of Egypt's air force before they could leave the ground. With no air cover, the Egyptians were soundly defeated on the ground, as Israeli troops quickly took the entire Gaza Strip and most of Egypt's Sinai Peninsula. In addition, Jordanian advances were quickly repelled, as the Israeli army took East Jerusalem and all of the West Bank. Finally, the full force of the Israeli military moved north to secure a mountainous region in southern Syria known as the Golan Heights.

The Cease-Fire

After only six days of fighting, the war was officially over. As part of the cease-fire, the United Nations drafted a set of principles meant to bring lasting peace to the region. The main points of this foundational document, known as U.N. Resolution 242, are as follows:

- The international community will not recognize territories acquired (occupied) through conquest.
- Israel's armed forces should withdraw from occupied territories (such as the West Bank and Gaza Strip).
- All states will recognize and respect the borders of all other states (that is, Arab states will recognize Israel's right to exist).
- The refugee problem is to be resolved in a just manner (meaning the more than 400,000 newly displaced Palestinians as well as those uprooted since 1948).
- All states must cooperate with the U.N.–designated special representative and adhere to the principles found in this resolution.

While Israel, Egypt, and Jordan agreed to these principles, Syria refused to accept them. In their minds, any recognition of Israel's right to exist would legitimatize colonialism and ignore the displaced Palestinian people. Nevertheless, this document's vague declarations did little to bring lasting peace. Instead, finger-pointing and inaction left Israeli occupation forces in control of Egyptian, Syrian, and Palestinian peoples, while Palestinian fighters continued their resistance efforts in Israel.

Domination and Terror

Before 1967, Arabs living in the West Bank and Gaza Strip recognized themselves as Palestinian Arabs, but because they were living under other Arab governments, many were not moved by Palestinian nationalism. However, after the '67 War, Palestinian Arabs found their homeland occupied by a non-Arab government whose laws and language were unfamiliar. Because of this, Palestinians looked to their unique heritage while resisting the expanding Zionist state.

In the midst of this nationalist upsurge, several groups organized Palestinians to fight for their independence. Believing the international community was unaware of their suffering, the PLO (headed since 1969 by Yasser Arafat), along with other guerilla groups, decided to bring their cause to the world stage. By hijacking airplanes, taking hostages, and choosing high-visibility targets—such as Israeli athletes at the 1972 Munich Olympics—Palestinian leaders believed they could make their plight known.

Although the PLO did succeed in securing the world's attention, images of "crazed Muslim hijackers" overshadowed any recognition of Israeli injustice. In fact, for many Europeans and Americans, this period of international terror actually served to create a lasting image of Palestinians as bloodthirsty fanatics. In many people's estimation, Israel's occupation was justified as a necessary "security" measure.

War of Atonement

After unsuccessful attempts to take back the Sinai in the early 1970s, the Egyptians were anxious to use newly acquired Soviet weaponry and training. On October 6, 1973, Egypt and Syria launched a surprise two-front offensive against Israel, with Egypt hoping to regain the Sinai and Syria desiring to reclaim the Golan Heights. Because the attack was launched on the Jewish Day of Atonement (*Yom Kippur* in Hebrew), many Israeli soldiers were unprepared for battle, giving Egyptian and Syrian forces a great advantage.

Despite Israeli resistance in the Sinai and Golan, Egyptian and Syrian armies conducted successful operations, pushing the Israeli Defense Forces (IDF) out of the occupied lands and threatening the State of Israel proper (sometimes distinguished as "Green Line Israel"). After a week of fighting, it appeared Israel might be overrun, but the United States came to the rescue, resupplying the embattled nation with superior weaponry. From near defeat, Israel managed to push the Syrians back through the Golan, advancing to within twenty-five miles of Damascus. In addition, the IDF moved Egyptian troops back through the Sinai, over the Suez Canal, to within sixty miles of Cairo.

With the Soviet Union and United States supplying opposing sides, the real threat of nuclear war led the two superpowers to draft a cease-fire just eighteen days into the battle. As part of the agreement, the United Nations drafted Resolution 338, which called for the complete implementation of U.N. Resolution 242. Despite the influential role of the United States in the region, the peace process once again stalled, as Israel continued its occupation of the Sinai, Golan, and Palestinian territories, and the PLO remained violently opposed to the Zionist state.

Peace Camps and Refugee Camps

In 1977, Israel elected Menachem Begin as its prime minister. With a hawkish view toward all Arabs, Begin's tough stance did little to bring peace in the region. Since their initial occupation of the West Bank and Gaza Strip in 1967, some Israeli extremists began constructing heavily fortified Jewish settlements in the occupied Arab areas. Although most Israelis were happy with the pre-1967 borders, Begin set out to claim the Arab West Bank, Gaza Strip, and Sinai Peninsula by populating them with Jewish citizens.

As these areas were outside of Israel's internationally recognized borders (Green Line Israel), it was illegal to build Israeli settlements on them. Concerning these Israeli-controlled Arab areas, Prime Minister Begin declared, "What do you mean 'Occupied Territories'? If you mean Judea and Samaria, they are 'Liberated Territories.'" With statements like these, Palestinians had little reason to believe they would ever find freedom.

Camp David

Despite Begin's harsh attitude toward the Palestinians, Egypt's President Anwar Sadat shocked the world by visiting the Jewish state. While addressing the Israeli parliament, Sadat insisted that Israel relinquish the occupied territories in exchange for peace. Impressed by Sadat's risky first move toward peace, U.S. President Jimmy Carter invited the Egyptian and Israeli leaders to his Camp David retreat in September 1979. After days of deliberation, a historic agreement was made between the two nations. Israel returned the occupied Sinai Peninsula and dismantled all its settlements there, and Egypt recognized Israel's right to exist. Although this peace agreement was a monumental achievement, it failed to deal with the Palestinian territories, causing many Arabs to see Sadat as a sellout.

Lethal Lebanon

At about the same time, Yasser Arafat and the PLO found a home in Lebanon, where they became entangled in the Lebanese civil war. As a result, Israel supplied the Lebanese Phalange Party's militia with weapons to fight their Lebanese Muslim rivals, who had welcomed the PLO. At the request of the Phalange and their leader Bashir Gemayel, Israel invaded Lebanon in 1982, hoping to rid the region of PLO forces once and for all.

Under the leadership of General Ariel Sharon, Israeli forces moved through Lebanon, encircling the capital city, Beirut. Understanding that the IDF wanted to remove the PLO, Lebanese Muslim leaders asked Arafat to leave the city. Gathering about 15,000 PLO and Syrian fighters, Arafat evacuated Lebanon, moving his operations to the North African nation of Tunisia. In retaliation for the Christian Phalange Party's role in expelling the PLO, their leader Bashir Gemayel was assassinated. Holding the Palestinians responsible, enraged Phalange militiamen sought swift retribution.

In circumstances that remain unclear, it seems Ariel Sharon ordered Israeli troops to encircle two Palestinian refugee camps while the Lebanese Phalange took their revenge. As it turns out, the Sabra and Shatila refugee camps were not full of PLO fighters, and instead, about 800 women, children, and elderly people were ruthlessly massacred. The extent of Israeli involvement in these killings remains unclear, but in 1983 upon investigation of the situation, Ariel Sharon was forced to step down from his position as Israel's Defense Minister.

After the expulsion of PLO troops, U.S., French, and Italian peacekeepers attempted to bring stability to the splintered nation. In 1983, just months after arriving in Beirut, a massive truck bomb rocked the U.S. marine barracks, killing more than 300. As a result of this bombing, the peacekeepers left Lebanon, and the war raged on. By 1985, the Israeli army pulled most of its forces out of Lebanon, leaving a small force in the south to fight the Syrian/Iranian-supported *Hizbullah* guerillas.

FACT

The 2001 movie *Spy Game,* starring Brad Pitt and Robert Redford, shows the ugly realities of everyday life during Lebanon's civil war. With Christian and Muslim militias fighting for control of Beirut, Syrian troops occupying parts of the country, and Israeli soldiers battling *Hizbullah* ("Party of God") forces in southern Lebanon, Palestinian refugees and Lebanese citizens were caught in the bloody middle.

With Israel and the PLO out of Lebanon, Syrian troops remained, while domestic militias continued to decimate the nation. Lebanon was once a unique concoction of French and Middle Eastern cultures, with beautiful ski resorts, lavish nightclubs, and the like that created a legendary playground for the world's rich and famous. After fifteen years of war, little beauty or glamour remained, and the Lebanese people were left with more than 300,000 casualties and a country in ruins.

Desperation and Uprising

In 1982, the Golan Heights were annexed into the State of Israel, and the Arab inhabitants of these lands were encouraged to accept Israeli citizenship. On the other hand, the West Bank and Gaza Strip remained occupied territories, and the Arab inhabitants of these lands remained nationless. By occupying the West Bank and Gaza, Israel created a "manageable buffer zone" to the Arab states. By not annexing these areas, Israel would not be required to give citizenship to hundreds of thousands of Arabs. Thus, occupation avoided the creation of an Arab majority within the Jewish state while offering temporary and synthetic territorial security. Meanwhile, day-to-day life for Palestinians went from bad to worse.

The term "Arab Israeli" refers to indigenous Palestinians who have been given Israeli citizenship. Today, there are more than 1 million Arab Israelis, with about 75 percent calling themselves Muslims and most of the remaining 25 percent considering themselves Christians.

By 1987, Palestinians in the West Bank and Gaza had been without many basic human rights for more than twenty years, while many refugees had lived in Arab ghettos for nearly forty years. Since 1948, Israel had grown to become one of the wealthiest nations in the Middle East, yet the occupied territories remained isolated and impoverished. Cut off economically from the rest of the world, Palestinians were forced to become day laborers in Israel.

For most Palestinian workers, the daily trip from their poverty-stricken lands to Israel's luxury created mounting resentment. If only they could be freed from Israel's clutches, they too might improve their lands and enjoy prosperity. Like a master of a plantation, the Israeli government determined the fate of the Palestinians, until one day the slaves revolted.

During a period known as the intifada ("the shaking off"), the occupied peoples vented their frustration in a massive and spontaneous popular uprising. With scores of youth taking to the streets, workers going on strike, and various other forms of civil disobedience, the Palestinians were ready for change. Aware of Israel's vastly superior weaponry, stones were used to deliver their message of exasperation. In addition, the Palestinian flag (illegal under the Israeli occupation) was flown proudly as a symbol of their desired independence. With the PLO on the sidelines in North Africa, the Palestinian people were ready to liberate themselves.

Instead of recognizing the intifada as a serious warning sign, the Israeli government decided to continue the occupation and suppress the uprising. With Palestinians desperately wanting freedom, the IDF sought to break their will by making mass arrests, beating protestors, demolishing homes, and torturing prisoners. Despite Israel's use of psychological warfare, the Palestinians continued to shake off the occupation for another six years.

ALERT!

The Islamic group Hamas was formed by the Muslim cleric Shaykh Ahmad Yasin in 1987, at the start of the intifada. Although Hamas is a Palestinian movement, its members desire an Islamic state in the occupied territories and all of historic Palestine. While other Palestinian groups, such as Islamic Jihad, also have religious goals, most Palestinian liberation movements are strictly secular.

Suicides, Strikes, and Settlements

The passion of the intifada fighters awakened many Israelis to the injustices caused by their government. In addition, forty years of life under Israeli rule brought many Palestinians to realize the Jewish state was not going to go away. With each side wanting a normal life, compromises were made in which Israeli "doves," or peacemakers, pushed for a withdrawal from the West Bank and Gaza, while Palestinian doves called for the recognition of Israel according to its pre-1967 borders.

After several years of unproductive peace talks in Madrid and Washington, D.C., secret back-channel negotiations in Oslo, Norway, produced a major breakthrough in 1993. In order to formally recognize this achievement, U.S. President Bill Clinton invited Israeli Prime Minister Yitzak Rabin and PLO Chairman Yasser Arafat to Washington for a treaty-signing ceremony.

According to the principles of the Oslo Accords, Israel and the PLO were to mutually recognize one another. Israel was to withdraw from the occupied territories, and the PLO was to take specific steps toward ensuring Israel's security. In the face of this monumental victory for moderates on both sides, Israeli and Palestinian hawks violently opposed the arrangement. For Israel's minority of extremists, any loss of territory was unacceptable. At the same time, some fanatical Palestinian groups viewed the recognition of Israel as cowardly submission to Zionism.

Struggle and Peace

In the city of Hebron, on February 25, 1994, an Israeli settler responded to Rabin's concessions by killing twenty-nine Palestinians as they prayed at the Mosque of Abraham inside the Tomb of the Patriarchs complex. The Islamic group Hamas answered the Hebron massacre with several bombings, yet both Arafat and Rabin continued their march toward peace. As part of the Oslo Accords, Arafat was allowed to return from exile in Tunisia to establish a provisional Palestinian government known as the Palestinian Authority (PA). With the West Bank town of Jericho and most of the Gaza Strip under PA administration, it appeared the Palestinian people were on the road to liberation.

In 1994, Yitzak Rabin continued his dovish efforts, signing a peace treaty with the Kingdom of Jordan. In addition, a second agreement was made between the PA and Israel, known as Oslo II or the Taba Accords. As part of this "interim agreement," Israeli forces would pull out of certain West Bank towns and villages in several phases. Then, at the final status talks (scheduled for May 1996), tough issues like the fate of Jewish settlements, the nature of a Palestinian state, and control of Jerusalem would be decided.

By 1995, Egypt, the PLO, and Jordan were in the peace camp, leaving Syria (and its client state, Lebanon) as Israel's only adversarial neighbor. In hopes of completing the peace train, Rabin approached Syrian

President Hafez Asad with a deal, in which the Golan Heights would be returned to Syria in exchange for peaceful relations. But before the train could leave the station, it was derailed: On November 4, 1995, an Israeli extremist assassinated his own prime minister.

QUESTION?

Isn't the Israeli-Palestinian conflict about religion?
Although religion is a factor, it is not the main issue for most Israelis and Palestinians. Most Israelis see the Jewish state as a secular haven in which Jewish people should be able to celebrate their culture and heritage in safety and security. At the same time, the vast majority of Muslim and Christian Palestinians desire basic freedoms and human rights, unavailable to them under Israeli occupation. In the end, the conflict can be summarized as a struggle for Israeli security and Palestinian liberation.

Polarization and Pain

After Rabin's assassination, two large Palestinian suicide bombings rocked the nation, creating a drastic shift in Israeli public opinion. From the euphoria of Rabin's peace victories, the region spiraled into a pit of desperation and fear. More concerned with security than peace, the Israeli people elected the hawkish Benjamin Netanyahu as their leader. Reluctantly, the new prime minister continued with the principles of the Oslo Accords, allowing increased Palestinian autonomy in the West Bank and Gaza. At the same time, Netanyahu showed his true colors by lifting the four-year ban on settlement construction and refusing to meet with Yasser Arafat for scheduled final status talks.

Over the next two years, clashes between Palestinians and the IDF, followed by a series of bombings in Jerusalem and Tel Aviv, left the peace process at a standstill. In 1998, U.S. President Bill Clinton convinced Netanyahu to restart the peace process by signing the U.S.–sponsored Wye River Memorandum, which guaranteed Israeli withdrawal from another 40 percent of the West Bank. Like a political car bomb, implementation of the agreement divided the Israeli government, and within a year the Wye deal was suspended. That same year, a dissatisfied Israeli public replaced Netanyahu with a new leader— Ehud Barak.

Signs of Hope

As prime minister, Barak revived the Wye agreement, called for the long-awaited final status negotiations, and put a freeze on all settlement construction in occupied lands. Despite periods of disagreement and several stalemates, Barak agreed to make concessions, which allowed final status negotiations to move forward. In July 2000, Israeli and Palestinian leaders met at Camp David, hoping to produce a historic agreement, just as Israeli and Egyptian leaders had done in 1979. As it turned out, the summit was fruitless, as neither side would compromise on having Jerusalem as its capital.

By September 2000, after months of gridlock, Barak was showing signs of conciliation regarding the fate of Jerusalem. With tensions running high among frightened Israelis and frustrated Palestinians, this type of meaningful concession could have ensured lasting peace. Instead, Barak's goodwill was undermined by the right-wing Israeli hawk, Ariel Sharon.

The Bully and Bang

In an attempt to show the Palestinians who was boss, Sharon and a small group of his cronies paraded across the Temple Mount, known to Muslims as *Haram al-Sharif* ("Noble Sanctuary"). Not only was Sharon's act against his own Jewish religious regulation, it was also a slap in the face to the Palestinian people, and for that matter the entire Muslim world. As a result of Sharon's calculated actions, Palestinians erupted in protest and the second intifada (known as the al-Aqsa Intifada) was born.

Although infuriated Palestinians had utilized the strategy of minimal force in the first intifada (by throwing rocks instead of firing guns), the second uprising was characterized by Palestinians who were so far beyond exasperation that they were ready to kill themselves. After more than thirty years of daily road closures, never-ending curfews, and time-consuming checkpoints, Palestinians longed for an unimpeded life.

Decades of home demolitions, early morning arrests, torture sessions, random interrogations, and "accidental" deaths had left people more than angry. Poverty, humiliation, and pain, plus years of shattered dreams, produced mind-numbing hopelessness and unimaginable rage. For many, suicide was seen as freedom, and the death of even one Israeli was viewed as a victory.

Over the following year, men and women of varying ages killed themselves and others in the name of liberation, turning many Israeli peaceniks into protective hawks. Despite U.S. efforts to foster peace, suicide bombers and Israeli reprisals eventually killed more than 700 Israelis and 1,900 Palestinians. The evaporation of the peace process, and the chaos that ensued, moved Barak to resign from his position as prime minister. Ironically, in February 2001, Ariel Sharon—the man whose actions sparked the al-Aqsa uprising—was elected prime minister on a platform of strict security and decisive retaliation.

In the wake of September 11, Sharon's hard-line attitude gained support from many Americans, who saw Palestinian attacks as part of Al-Qaeda's global terror network. In the following two years, the cycle of violence worsened, as Israel's harsh reprisals only intensified Palestinian resentment and rage.

ALERT!

Although nearly all Palestinians want the occupation to end, most are not willing to blow themselves up for this liberation. At the same time, you will find that most Israelis want to live in a secure nation but are not willing to wipe out the Palestinians in the process. Despite the horrible actions of Palestinian and Israeli extremists, most are willing to live in peace if it is just.

Probable Peace

In the face of ongoing violence, the hawkish leader Ariel Sharon has shown uncharacteristic moderation by acknowledging the West Bank and Gaza as occupied territories and speaking of a future Palestinian state. For Palestinians living under the thumb of Israel, words are cheap, and only tangible freedom will give them relief. At the same time, fearful Israeli citizens desire a secure nation without the threat of terrorism, and only the cessation of Palestinian attacks will suffice.

After years of empty promises and failed peace plans, most Israelis and Palestinians have grown extremely cynical. Is there any hope for peace in this land? Only time will tell, but one thing is certain. The status quo will only produce more death, more pain, and more injustice.

Chapter 13

Egypt—Heart of the Arab World

While Israel/Palestine has been the center of regional conflict for more than half a century, Egypt has been the hub of Arab nationalism. As the most populous Arabic-speaking nation, Egypt has led the way, becoming the first independent Arab nation and the first Middle Eastern state to make peace with Israel. But with a swelling population of more than 75 million, increasing poverty, and widespread distrust of the government, militant Islamic groups have found fertile ground.

Remnants of Imperialism

After World War I, the Egyptian people were ready to shake off forty years of British control. In the spirit of Europe's nationalist movements, the Wafd Party was established to coordinate popular impetus for change. Wafd (meaning "delegation") was named after the Egyptian delegation that pled for independence from Britain at the postwar Paris Peace Conference. Run by educated professionals and wealthy elites, the Wafd Party harnessed the power of the people, channeling it into an effective nationalist movement.

FACT

While English speakers use the name Egypt, the country is called *Misr* (meaning "country") by Arabic-speaking peoples. Although there are various explanations of the origins of this name, it is likely Arab invaders were influenced by one of this region's ancient names—*Mizraim*.

To appease Egyptian nationalist desires, the British ended Egypt's protectorate status in 1922. Although Egypt was officially independent, the British continued to control the profitable Suez Canal and the nation through their puppet, King Fuad. By 1924, members of the Wafd Party formed most of the Egyptian government, though Fuad remained the ruling monarch and British forces remained on the ground.

Frustrated by Turkey's abolishment of the pan-Islamic office of caliph, as well as by the secular nature of Middle Eastern nationalist movements and perceived corruption in Egypt's government, Hassan al-Banna formed a youth movement known as the Muslim Brotherhood (*Al-Ikhwan*, "the Brotherhood") in 1928. Originally focused on promoting moral and social reforms, the organization became more political throughout the 1930s, eventually promoting militant action against the Egyptian government.

Sacred or Sick

In what some call an Islamic revival and others see as the rebirth of Islamic militancy, the Muslim Brotherhood rallied dissatisfied Egyptians behind the utopian vision of an Islamic state. Teaching his followers, "Islam is creed and state, book and sword," Banna gathered more than 500,000 who were ready to fight for their faith.

After King Fuad's death in 1936, his son Farouk became monarch. Soon the new king's playboy lifestyle enraged conservative Egyptians and members of the Muslim Brotherhood, who responded with intentional efforts to destabilize the kingdom. Because of their militant actions, the Egyptian government banned the Muslim Brotherhood, forcing them to go underground.

United They Stand

Meanwhile, as World War II erupted in Europe, the Allies attempted to gain support from the newly established Arab nations by promoting the idea of a unified and prosperous Arab world. Although Egypt and other Arab states remained neutral during the war, the Allies managed to plant the seeds of pan-Arabism. On March 22, 1945, these seeds bore fruit, as Egypt, Iraq, Lebanon, North Yemen, Saudi Arabia, Transjordan, and Arab representatives from Palestine formed the League of Arab States (or the Arab League).

ALERT!

Today, the Muslim Brotherhood movement (*al-Ikwan al-Muslimin* in Arabic) has members in more than seventy countries around the globe and holds seventeen seats in the Egyptian parliament. The organization desires to see individual Muslims develop their faith, practice, and community, but it also states one of its primary goals as "mastering the world with Islam."

With Cairo established as the Arab League's headquarters, the Arab member states turned their attention to the region of Palestine. Because Jewish immigrants to Palestine were preparing to establish a Zionist state, Arab nations looked for ways to prevent the birth of what they viewed as a European colony. In response, King Farouk committed Egyptian troops and weaponry to a massive Arab coalition against the emerging Jewish nation. Viewing the Zionist state as an insult to the Arab people and Islam, irregulars from the Muslim Brotherhood joined the war as well.

As you read in Chapter 13, the Arab resistance of 1948 was soundly defeated, and Israel was able to maintain the Jewish state. Nevertheless, the Arab world continued to reject the new nation as a Crusader-type colony. While most Arabs resented Western governments for meddling in their domestic affairs, they vehemently opposed the Jewish state as an unmistakable arm of Western imperialism.

Nationalism and Revolution

Blaming King Farouk for their poor training and shoddy equipment, Egyptian soldiers turned their anger toward the government. One of these dissatisfied soldiers, Gamal Abdel Nasser, organized a revolutionary movement within the Egyptian Army. Known as the Free Officers' Movement, their ultimate goal was the removal of Farouk and his government. For the Free Officers, total independence from European powers was the only way Egypt could revive its former glory.

Assassination

With the Free Officers growing in strength, the illegal Muslim Brotherhood also expanded as an underground religious and political movement. Since Egypt's defeat in the '48 War with Israel, members of the Muslim Brotherhood turned their power against the Egyptian government, organizing demonstrations, riots, and acts of terror. In response to the group's violent acts, King Farouk is said to have ordered the death of its leader, Hassan al-Banna.

Whether or not the king put out a hit, Banna was assassinated on February 12, 1949, giving him the title *al-Shaheed*, meaning "the martyr." Despite the death of their supreme leader, the Muslim Brotherhood continued in their efforts to overthrow Farouk and establish an Islamic state in Egypt. At the same time, the Free Officers sought to inspire their own brand of revolution, based on secular nationalism.

The Officers' Uprising

On July 22, 1952, Gamal Abdel Nasser and several other high-ranking Free Officers gathered for a late-night meeting at El-Fishawi's, Cairo's oldest and most enchanting coffeehouse. With the sweet smell of smoldering apple tobacco emanating from an army of Middle Eastern water pipes (*nargilas* or *shishas*) and the rich flavor of thick Arabic coffee emboldening each man's palate, Nasser and his companions prepared for one of Egypt's most significant days. Believing King Farouk was ready to move against them, the Free Officers' leadership decided a pre-emptive strike was their only option.

FACT

Traditional coffee and tea houses are an integral part of Middle Eastern society. From Istanbul to Casablanca, water pipes bubble and delicious black teas and coffees simmer, as men enjoy watching football games, playing board games, and talking politics. Of Egypt's numerous coffee shops, El-Fishawi's is the oldest, with a continuous flow of smoke and joe since 1773.

The following morning the Free Officers staged a coup d'état. After three days, King Farouk was deposed and on his way to a life of exile in Italy. The Free Officers then formed the Revolutionary Command Council (RCC), which would be the governing body for the new republic. With a desire to see their impoverished nation revitalized and freed from all British influence, the RCC implemented strict reforms based on secular and nationalistic ideals. Among the many changes was the requirement that all political parties dissolve, including the once-powerful Wafd Party.

Nasser's Pan-Arabism

By 1954, Gamal Abdel Nasser was the leader of an independent Arab Republic of Egypt. Over the following years, Nasser continued to rally Egyptians under the banner of Arab nationalism. In keeping with his original goals, Nasser wanted to remove Britain's influence over his nation, while providing prosperity to his impoverished citizens. As a result, the Egyptian president looked to the British-controlled Suez Canal, which ran directly through his country.

Although Europeans had paid for the canal's construction and King Farouk had agreed to British administration of this lucrative waterway, Nasser and many other Egyptians saw the British as exploiters. In addition, the Egyptian president recognized the canal as an important source of revenue, which could fund his massive Aswan High Dam Project. As a logical extension of his nationalistic goals, Nasser declared the Suez Zone part of Egypt and ordered all non-Egyptians out of the area. As you read in Chapter 13, Britain and France responded by joining forces with Israel and attacking Egypt. This conflict, known as the '56 War (or Sinai Campaign), not only served to drive Arabs further away from the west (and toward the Soviets), it also popularized Nasser as the Arab world's hero against Crusader-type, Zionist aggression.

FACT

Today, revenues from the Suez Canal provide Egypt with about $2 billion each year.

Though most Arabs respected Nasser for his defiance and nationalism, conservative members of the Muslim Brotherhood were infuriated by the secular nature of the new republic. They thought the revolution should have been followed by an Islamic state, governed by Islamic law. Instead, Nasser and the RCC established a secular government and on top of that, they were dealing with the atheist Soviets. Because of this, members of the Muslim Brotherhood attempted to kill Nasser. In response, Nasser's regime put down the rebellion. The five perpetrators were executed, and more than 4,000 Muslim Brotherhood members were arrested, causing thousands of others to flee to other Arab states.

United Arab States

With the Arab League headquartered on Egyptian soil, Nasser used the organization as a staging ground for his pan-Arab agendas. In 1958, Nasser realized part of his dream, as Syria agreed to come under his leadership in a pan-Arab state known as the United Arab Republic (UAR). Nasser then looked to Yemen as a possible partner state, but before he could go any further, a coup in Syria caused the breakup of the UAR in 1961.

The following year, civil war erupted in the Arabian kingdom of North Yemen. In the spirit of Nasser's independent Arab republic, a group of Yemeni separatists attempted to wrest power from the royal family of a Muslim cleric named Imam Muhammad al-Badr. In what was originally a civil war, Egypt and the Soviet Union soon came to the aid of their like-minded republican fighters, while the kingdoms of Saudi Arabia, Iran, and Jordan supported the royal family of Imam al-Badr.

Despite the UAR's failure, Nasser continued to use the term United Arab Republic for the remainder of his presidency. While Egypt and Syria ceased to be a unified state, the idea of pan-Arab strength continued to unify Arabic speaking nations. Throughout the 1950s and 1960s, nearly every Arab nation joined the Arab League. Though the assembly was plagued with division, member states proudly declared their unity. With Nasser guiding a body of independent Arab nations, a sense of dignity was restored in the region, which had withered during centuries of non-Arab imperialism and Western colonization.

In addition to being an Arab state, Egypt recognized itself as an African nation. In 1963, the concept of pan-Africanism inspired Egypt and thirty-one other states to form the Organization for African Unity (OAU). Similar to the Arab League, the OAU sought to unify the continent under a banner of African pride. Emerging from years of Western colonization, the OAU hoped to bring stability to nations attempting to agree upon borders and form their own governments.

As part of the Arab world and of Africa, the countries of Egypt, Libya, Tunisia, Algeria, Morocco, and Mauritania enjoy a unique mix of Afro-Arabic culture and history. This distinct character empowered Nasser and other North African leaders to rally their citizens behind the concepts of Arab and African nationalistic pride.

War and Withering

By 1967, Egypt was receiving substantial military aid from the USSR, but the war in Yemen had drained the nation, costing many Egyptian lives and resources. In addition, Egyptian support of the anti-royalists in Yemen moved Saudi Arabia to cut off all financial aid to Nasser's regime. About this time, the Soviets sent bad intelligence regarding Israeli troop movements. As a result, the Egyptian government ordered all U.N. peacekeepers to evacuate its border with Israel, closed the Red Sea to all Israeli ships, and moved several divisions toward the Israeli border. The outcome of all this was six days of war, in which Israel defeated the Egyptian forces and took all of Egypt's Sinai Peninsula.

Because of the massive losses sustained in the war with Israel, Nasser was forced to pull his troops from Yemen as well. After this great humiliation, the Egyptian leader announced his resignation but, in an overwhelming show of popular support, Egypt's people encouraged him to remain as their president. Although Nasser chose to continue his presidency, he never held the same regional influence that he had enjoyed through the late 1950s and early 1960s. Under the stresses of his failing nation, Nasser suffered a fatal heart attack on September 28, 1970, ending more than twenty years of inspiration and action.

Sadat's Peace

Known as a key leader in the 1956 Revolution and as Egypt's vice-president, Anwar al-Sadat assumed the presidency following Nasser's death. Influenced greatly by the social reforms and anti-colonialist nature of Turkey's founder, Mustafa Kemal Atatürk, Sadat sought to lead Egypt into an age of strict nationalism and prosperity.

Hoping to usher in a new era of independence and economic might, Sadat dedicated Nasser's brainchild, the Aswan High Dam, in 1970. After ten years of construction, this miracle of engineering produced a structure two miles long and more than 360 feet tall. Today, the dam retains part of the Nile in Lake Nasser, a 500-mile-long lake that stretches from southern Egypt to northern Sudan. Because of this project, the amount of arable land in Egypt has increased by 30 percent and its production of electricity has doubled.

The Quest for Honor

Despite the improvements offered by the Aswan project, most Egyptians continued to deal with increasing poverty and sickness, as well as the strains of rapid urbanization. While Egypt continued to boast the Arab world's most powerful military, they were also licking their wounds from the Six-Day War of '67, as well as the humiliation caused by their withdrawal from the civil war in Yemen. In an effort to restore Egyptian pride and sovereignty, Sadat decided it was time to reclaim the Sinai Peninsula by force.

As you read in Chapter 13, the 1973 conflict, known to Egyptians as the 6th of October War and Israelis as the Yom Kippur War, was a joint effort between Syria and Egypt, aimed at reclaiming lands occupied by Israel in 1967. Viewed by most Egyptians as a major victory, the '73 War united Egyptians in a revived spirit of nationalism. Although they failed to reclaim their lands, Egypt and Syria did manage to awaken Israelis to the real threat of Arab invasion. As a result, the Israeli government began to soften its grip on the Sinai.

By 1977, however, that sparkle was gone, and most Egyptians were again frustrated by their country's apparent weakness, Israel's defiance, and the continued deterioration of their urban living conditions. Viewing peace with Israel and the West as a necessary move toward prosperity, Sadat went against popular opinion and the political mainstream, announcing his willingness to visit Israel for peace. After receiving a formal invitation, Sadat became the first leader of an Arab nation to visit the Zionist state.

Peacemaker and Pariah

For many Egyptians and people throughout the Muslim World, Sadat's trip was not a positive step toward peace but an irresponsible action that gave credibility to the illegitimate Jewish state. Despite great opposition in the Middle East and elsewhere, U.S. President Jimmy Carter saw Sadat's action as a brave step toward peace. Inspired by Sadat's gesture, President Carter organized the Camp David peace summit of 1978. From the Camp David talks, Israel agreed to return the Sinai Peninsula to Egypt and Sadat and Israeli Prime Minister Menachem Begin signed a historic peace treaty.

Although both Sadat and Begin received the Nobel Peace Prize for their efforts, most people in the Arab and Muslim worlds viewed Sadat as a traitor. Signing the treaty returned the Sinai to Egypt and assured the nation of substantial aid from the United States, but in the minds of most Middle Eastern people, it ignored the plight of nearly 3 million Palestinians. Not only that, it ensured that the Arab world's most powerful nation would not be involved in resisting the Zionists. In response to Sadat's deal, the Arab League suspended Egypt from membership and moved the organization's headquarters from Cairo to Tunis, Tunisia. In the face of this shame, Egyptians violently protested their leader's actions, with some even calling for his death.

Assassination

Despite Sadat's efforts to pacify disgruntled citizens, many remained opposed to their government's domestic efforts and its attitude toward the Palestinian crisis. Capitalizing on popular frustration, extremist groups rallied the masses in large-scale protests. Sadat answered this unrest with overwhelming force, which was met with condemnation from the international community. Incensed by their government's perceived acts of injustice and lack of piety, Islamic extremists decided they would forcefully remove Sadat.

On October 6, 1981, assassins opened fire on the Egyptian president at a ceremony commemorating the 1973 war with Israel. Ironically, Sadat spent his last moments battling for life because of his struggle for peace, while this peacemaker's mortal defeat arrived during a celebration of his most successful war. With Sadat's passing, Vice President Hosni Mubarak became president of an unstable nation threatened by militants calling for Islamic revolution and moderates demanding equity and reform.

Radicals Reborn

Throughout the 1980s and 1990s, a new round of assassinations, car bombings, and other attacks threatened the secular nature of the state. As the masterminds of Sadat's assassination, the Egyptian Islamic Jihad group worked alongside another cadre of militants by the name of Gamaat al-Islamiyya (meaning "the Islamic Group"). With separate leadership and distinct modes of operation, both movements desired to overthrow Egypt's secular government and replace it with a "pure" Islamic regime. While these Egyptian extremists were made up almost entirely of Sunnis, they were inspired by Iran's Shi'ite revolutionaries, who had ousted the shah and his secular government in 1979 and established an Islamic state.

Both the Egyptian Islamic Jihad group and Gamaat al-Islamiyya were the result of a rift between the members of the Muslim Brotherhood who wanted to continue their armed resistance and the brotherhood's leadership, which agreed to work peacefully within the Egyptian political system. Under the leadership of a medical doctor named Ayman al-Zawahiri, the Egyptian Islamic Jihad group waged war on the state by targeting high-level Egyptian officials and other political interests. Guided by a blind cleric by the name of Sheik Omar Abdel Rahman, Gamaat al-Islamiyya staged attacks on anyone and everyone, including tourists, hoping to destabilize the economy and, in turn, the government of Egypt.

E ALERT!

Contrary to popular belief, most terrorists are not dimwitted psychopaths. Although their actions are deplorable and horrific, many are sane, highly educated individuals who justify their violent actions as the only response to perceived injustices, immorality, and state-sponsored terrorism.

Since 1993, the Egyptian Islamic Jihad group has not carried out attacks on Egyptian soil. Instead, it has joined forces with Al-Qaeda and other groups to wage a global war against nations they view as a threat to Islam. While the Egyptian Islamic Jihad group has turned its attention away from Egypt, Gamaat al-Islamiyya has continued its struggle in North Africa, as well as other parts of the world. In 1993, members of the organization bombed New York's World Trade Center, while in 1997 they carried out several attacks in Egypt, including the massacre of fifty-eight tourists near the southern city of Luxor.

As planned, these attacks dissuaded travelers from visiting Egypt, bringing the nation's vital tourist industry to a standstill. While extremists wanted to undermine the secular government by crippling its economy, their plan backfired. With hundreds of thousands out of work, Egyptians didn't turn their anger toward the government; instead, they blamed the militants. Due to this outcry, Gamaat al-Islamiyya signed a cease-fire with the Egyptian government in 1999. Since this agreement, they have not carried out major attacks within Egypt, though Gamaat al-Islamiyya remains a threat to President Mubarak and others around the world.

FACT

Egyptian Islamic Jihad leader Ayman al-Zawahiri partnered with Osama bin Laden throughout the 1990s and is now Al-Qaeda's number-two man, while Gamaat al-Islamiyya leader Sheik Omar Abdel Rahman is serving a life sentence in the United States for his involvement in the 1993 attack on New York's World Trade Center.

President Mubarak—Stayin' Alive

Under the circumstances of Hosni Mubarak's rise to the presidency, his number-one goal was to see Islamic militancy removed from Egypt. Mubarak was shot in the hand during the October 6 assassination, making him a victim of Sadat's killers as well. Although he vowed to continue Sadat's policies toward the West and Israel, Mubarak knew he would have to make drastic changes if he was going to survive.

After an initial crackdown on members of Egypt's Islamic Jihad—the organization responsible for the assassination of Sadat—Mubarak looked for ways to stop Islamic extremism at the root. By instituting economic reforms the new president hoped to remedy the hopelessness that turned many of Egypt's unemployed and impoverished toward the promises of radical Islamic groups. In addition, he attempted to remove certain policies that excluded religiously based political groups from the Egyptian government. By allowing the Muslim Brotherhood to hold seats in the parliament, Mubarak hoped to give controlled representation to frustrated Muslims who had been rallying outside of the political arena.

Finally, Mubarak made it his mission to improve relations with the rest of the Arab world, which had virtually excommunicated the nation because of Sadat's treaty with Israel. Throughout the 1980s, various Arab states decided to renew diplomatic ties with Egypt, and in 1989, Mubarak's state was readmitted into the Arab League. With Egypt again part of the fold, the League of Arab States moved its headquarters from Tunis back to its birthplace, Cairo.

Conflict Inside and Out

The following year, Egypt and eleven other Arab states voiced their condemnation of Iraq's invasion of Kuwait. Over the next year, President Mubarak responded by sending more than 38,000 Egyptian troops to support U.S.–led operations Desert Shield and Desert Storm. Fighting alongside American, British, Saudi Arabian, Syrian, and other forces, Egyptian troops aided in pushing Iraq from Kuwait.

Despite his efforts to improve Egypt's standard of living, rejuvenate ties with the Arab world, and liberate the fellow Arab Muslim nation of Kuwait, Mubarak was repeatedly targeted by radical Islamists who viewed his secular laws, ties to the West, and friendship with Israel as an abomination. Of the many plots to assassinate the president, in 1995 Egyptian gunmen almost succeeded in hitting Mubarak as he visited Ethiopia's capital city for a meeting of the Organization for African Unity.

In response to repeated threats and attacks, the Egyptian government again cracked down on Islamic organizations believed to be involved in militant actions. Walking a fine line, the Egyptian president tried to stabilize his country by offering more freedoms to opposition groups while still holding extremist organizations accountable for their deeds. This has led some to feel Mubarak is too soft on terrorism and others to believe he is a ruthless anti-Islamic dictator.

Each year, about one-third of all U.S. foreign aid is sent to Egypt and Israel, with about $2 billion going to Egypt and $3 billion to Israel. By comparison, just over $1 billion is distributed among all the nations of sub-Saharan Africa.

Another sore spot for many Egyptians is their government's friendly relationship with Israel. In their estimation, partnership with Israel sends a message to the Palestinian people and the rest of the Arab world that Egypt condones the holding of more than 3 million Arabs under occupation. On the other hand, most Egyptians are also frustrated by their nation's poverty and huge unemployment rate, which would only worsen if the United States were to suspend the nearly $3 billion it gives Egypt in aid each year in return for Egypt's peaceful relations with Israel.

Colossal Constructs

By nationalizing the Suez Canal and implementing the gargantuan Aswan High Dam Project, Nasser attempted to bring self-sufficiency and prosperity to his people. With the completion of the high dam, Sadat realized Nasser's dream, but even this feat was not enough to move Egypt out of its financial funk. By improving relations with the West and making peace with Israel, Sadat hoped to move Egypt into the elite circle of developed nations, but even after the billions of dollars in aid the country has received, its average citizen remains below the poverty level.

After more than twenty years at the helm, Mubarak has benefited from his predecessors' accomplishments, but he is also dealing with their failures. Revenues from the Suez Canal, improved irrigation and energy production from the Aswan High Dam, and substantial foreign aid have helped Egypt's economy, but the resulting political problems, ecological devastation, and domestic unrest have arguably done more harm than good to the nation as a whole. In the face of uncertain times, the Egyptian government is looking for new ways to deal with its extreme poverty, exponential growth of unemployment, exploding population, and expanding extremist groups.

In the tradition of Nasser's and Sadat's mega-projects, Mubarak has begun his own monumental plan. Known as the Toshka Project, Mubarak's undertaking is meant to alleviate Egypt's population crunch, unemployment rate, and water problems by creating a new Nile river-valley and civilization. Beginning in 1997, a huge pumping station was built, which is now moving water northwest from Lake Nasser to the Toshka depression, where it has formed massive desert lakes. From these lakes, a network of canals has been built, moving the "New Nile" farther to the north and west.

At its projected completion date in 2017, a second Nile River will flow through Egypt's western desert all the way to the Mediterranean Sea. By doubling Egypt's arable and inhabitable land, proponents believe millions will move from the crowded and desperate conditions of Cairo to the open spaces and opportunity of new western cities. In addition, advocates argue that improved living conditions will eliminate one of the factors that drive many moderate Muslims to extremism. Whether or not the Toshka Project will solve Egypt's social problems, it will be a historic day if the waters of the Nile find another path to the Mediterranean.

Until Mubarak's dream is realized in 2017, he will need to keep his nation from slipping further into poverty and extremism. As you have seen, there are no simple answers or quick fixes for this nation. The Toshka Project is a bold new plan that will take decades to complete, but it could be the type of monumental undertaking that will bring monumental change. If the heart of the Arab world is made healthy, it will naturally pump its life to the rest of the body. Until then, the nearly eighty-year-old President Hosni Mubarak must keep himself, his vision, and his secular nation alive. Ⓔ

Chapter 14

**Saudi Arabia—
Crossroads of Islam**

Since Islam's birth, the cities of Mecca and Medina have attracted prayers and pilgrims from around the globe. Saudi Arabia's oil reserves have also drawn businessmen from all corners of the earth. Since the early 1900s, pious puritans and secular separatists throughout the Muslim world have scrutinized Saudi Arabia's oil-rich royals, but today, this critique has turned to explosive violence. From terror to trade, this chapter unveils the immeasurable importance of this international intersection of faith and finance.

Hashemite Protectors and the House of Saùd

Since the mid-600s A.D., individuals claiming descent from Muhammad's Hashemite tribe have ruled the Hijaz region of western Arabia as the custodians of the holy mosques in Mecca and Medina. After nearly 400 years of Ottoman administration, the people of the Hijaz appeared to be on their way to independence as the Hashemites joined with British forces during World War I. After defeating the Ottomans, the British rewarded their Arabian allies by recognizing the independent Hashemite Kingdom of the Hijaz.

Meanwhile, on the eastern side of the Arabian Peninsula, Abdul Aziz ibn Abdar-Rahman (better known as "Ibn Saùd"—meaning "son of Saùd") ruled the kingdom of Najd, a realm created by his forefathers in the early 1800s. From their capital city, Riyadh, the Saudi family gained control of most of Arabia through the 1920s, leaving the Hashemite Kingdom of the Hijaz as the only thing standing between them and regional domination.

In 1926, the Saudis conquered the Hijaz, ending more than 1,300 years of Hashemite rule. Although their administration of Islam's holy cities was terminated, two Hashemite princes were each named king in the newly established nations of Iraq and Transjordan (later Jordan). Ruling nearly all of the Arabian Peninsula, Ibn Saùd became King of Najd (East Arabia) and the Hijaz (West Arabia). In 1932, the Saudi king renamed his territory the Kingdom of Saudi Arabia, establishing his family and their unique interpretation of Islam in the heart of the Muslim world.

What's a Wahhabi?

If you've ever heard the term "Wahhabi" thrown around in the media, you were likely left scratching your head. Is it another religion, maybe an ethnic group, or even a cult? "Wahhabi" refers to a Muslim from the Sunni branch of Islam who has chosen to follow the conservative teachings and interpretations of an eighteenth-century theologian and teacher named Muhammad ibn Abd al-Wahhab.

The Beginnings

As a Sunni Muslim raised in Arabia, al-Wahhab began his puritanical quest in Mesopotamia, where he confronted the region's mystical Sufi Muslims. After returning to Arabia, he turned his attention toward popular beliefs and practices in his homeland, which he saw as "un-Islamic."

Inspired by al-Wahhab's reforms, the Saudi family aligned themselves with his movement and proceeded to re-establish "pure" Islam in Arabia. With a policy of expansionism, the Saudis spread al-Wahhab's theology throughout the region. Today, Islam is the state religion in Saudi Arabia, and Wahhabism is the kingdom's official denomination. Although other schools of thought are tolerated, conversion from Wahhabism to another stream of Islam is viewed as a crime against the state.

Sometimes viewed as an Islamic equivalent to Martin Luther's Protestant Reformation, al-Wahhab's reforms were also a reaction to perceived corruption in the religious establishment. Just as Luther hoped to rid Catholicism of things he deemed unbiblical, al-Wahhab sought to purify Islam of beliefs and practices he viewed as un-Qur'anic. In his sermons, al-Wahhab forbade such things as gravestones (because they could lead to idolatry), minarets (as they were not believed to be used at the time of Muhammad), and smoking (due to the intoxicating effects of tobacco). In addition to his passionate sermons, al-Wahhab wrote the *Book of Unity,* a text his followers continue to use in their quest for the unaltered Islam of Muhammad's day.

"Wahhabism" is not synonymous with "terrorism." Although Wahhabis tend to be conservative in their religious views, most are not looking for holy war. While some believe Islamic law should be implemented throughout the world, even these apparent fanatics usually seek their dream through nonviolent proselytizing. Nevertheless, the passion and activism created by a few Wahhabi clerics has moved some to take up arms against any who might stand in the way of their plans.

Unitarian Uniformity

Calling themselves the *Muwahhidun*, or "unitarians," Wahhabis desire to see unity in issues of faith and conformity in areas of practice. In their view, outward appearances and expressions are directly connected to one's inward state. In other words, clothing styles, mannerisms, and specific actions prove whether or not one is a "true" Muslim.

One striking example of Wahhabism's outward influence on Saudi society is the widespread uniformity of men and women's apparel. In other parts of the Middle East, you will find a mix of traditional and modern clothing styles. You will also discover great variety among those who sport time-honored robes, headdresses, and veils. But in Wahhabist Saudi Arabia, nearly everyone dresses the same.

For women, a long black head covering (concealing all but the eyes) flows over a loose-fitting black outer garment that covers the entire body. This ensemble is usually accompanied by black gloves and sunglasses, covering any remaining skin. For men, a red-and-white checkered headdress (sometimes exchanged for an all-white head covering) is neatly creased at the front and held in place by two black camel-hair rings. With his face exposed, the average Saudi man keeps the hair on his head short but sports some type of facial hair, ranging from a long beard to a neatly trimmed mustache. From the neck down, what appears to be a tailored white cotton shirt flows down to the ankles and is accented by leather sandals or shoes.

FACT

While outsiders may feel this uniformity is oppressive or strange, most Saudis don't consider their country's monolithic fashions unusual. Most are not consciously trying to dress the same. In fact, most don't ask why they wear what they do; it is simply the way to dress as a Saudi citizen. These Saudi uniforms are born out of a much bigger cultural construct, which views conformity as righteousness and contrast as rebellion.

In order to maintain religious order, Saudi society is monitored by a type of morality police, known as the *muttawa*. If a man is not prostrated during one of the five daily prayer times, or a woman is not properly covered, the morality police are there to "encourage" holiness. In addition to their policing efforts, the *muttawa* are involved in missionary activities inside Saudi Arabia and around the world. In their understanding, the words of the Qur'an are not suggestions or subjects of debate but the only acceptable way to live.

The Young and the Passionate

As you read earlier, most Saudis are at least nominally Wahhabis, but not all are actively pursuing this "pure" Islam and its stringent rules. For idealistic Saudi youth and those able to evaluate religion on an academic level, Wahhabism is extremely attractive. In many of their minds, literal interpretation and active implementation of God's laws is the only acceptable way to exist as a Muslim. For these individuals, anything less than total devotion and submission to the dictates of Islamic texts would be hypocrisy.

Most Wahhabis believe they are following not a certain brand of Islam but the *only* brand of Islam. In addition, many Wahhabis see Islam not as one of many equally valid religions but as God's only true path. As a result, serious Wahhabis make a concerted effort to spread their message through personal purity and missionary endeavors, known as *dawah*. In their estimation, all humans are Muslims at birth, but some are pulled away from Islam as they are raised in non-Muslim societies. As evidence of this, when a non-Muslim accepts Islam, this person is not called a convert, but a "revert."

With an estimated 20 million Muslims adhering to Wahhabi ideologies, this movement accounts for less than 2 percent of the world's 1.3 billion Muslims.

God's Black Gold

Although the Saudis managed to establish themselves as the leaders of modern Arabia's first independent kingdom, most of the region's inhabited areas remained loyal to local tribal chiefs, just as they had been in Muhammad's day and before. In addition, the relatively poor nation was void of any real infrastructure or modern conveniences, much the same as it had been for thousands of years. Other than propagating Wahhabi ideologies, the Saudi regime didn't really change the nature of this ancient land—but all this was about to change.

Only six years after establishing the Kingdom of Saudi Arabia, the royal family received what many viewed as a gift from God. In 1938, oil was discovered along Arabia's eastern coast, beginning a new age of petroleum power and prosperity. With the discovery of massive oil reserves, four U.S. companies came together to form the Arabian-American Oil Company (Aramco) in Saudi Arabia. As revenues flowed to Aramco, the Saudis and their American friends realized huge profits. From this influx of Western funds and friends, the royal family began a program of modernization in which paved roadways, bridges, and sanitation systems were introduced. Also, the Saudi royal government decided to cultivate their new Western business relationships into new political alliances.

The first test of their partnership came at the outset of World War II. While the Allies were trying to muster support in the Middle East, Egypt and other Arab nations chose to remain neutral. In a bold move, the Saudis joined with the United States and Great Britain, declaring war on Germany and Japan and allowing the United States to build an airbase on their soil. In addition, Saudi Arabia was among the fifty-one nations that came together to establish the United Nations on October 24, 1945.

FACT

Throughout the early 1950s, King Ibn Saùd personally received more than $2 million per week from oil revenues.

Worldwide Wahhabism

In 1953, the Saudi throne was passed to Ibn Saùd's son Saùd. As the protectors of Islam's holiest cities and one-fourth of the world's petroleum, the Saudi family was in a unique situation. They could use their astronomical wealth to continue modernization projects, which in turn solidified their popularity in the kingdom, but they were also in a position to extend their influence beyond Arabia. Viewing their fortune as a direct result of their adherence to God's genuine laws, the Saudis looked to continue their obedience by using billions to establish "true" Islam throughout the Middle East and the world.

Within two years of becoming king, Saùd agreed to send millions to Nasser's flowering Egyptian nation. In turn, the leaders signed a mutual defense pact. The Saudis also promised large loans to Syria and other Arab states. Because of their agreement with Cairo, the Saudis severed all ties with Britain and France after they joined Israel in the 1956 attack on Egypt. With Britain and France cut off from Saudi oil, the United States remained the major purchaser of Saudi Arabian petroleum.

FACT

For the past thirty years, Saudi Arabia has given 4 percent of its gross national product to development projects in more than seventy predominately Muslim nations.

Fractured Fraternities

In the early 1960s, when civil war erupted in Arabia's southwestern kingdom of Yemen, the Saudi and Egyptian governments found themselves at odds. Whereas the Saudi royals sympathized with the family of Islamic clerics who had ruled the area for almost half a century, the Egyptian republic supported the revolutionary Yemeni nationalists. Because of this conflict, the Saudi-Egyptian agreement was scrapped, and King Saùd cut off all financial aid to Nasser's nation. In response, the Egyptian air force bombed several Saudi towns, causing the Saudis to mobilize for possible war with this North African neighbor. In the end, a regional war was averted, but Yemen's civil struggles continued into the 1970s.

In 1964, Saùd's brother, Prince Faisal, assumed the title of king. Under Faisal's authority, Saudi Arabia continued to lead the world in oil production and Wahhabist propagation. In 1967, as Egypt, Jordan, and

Syria entered the infamous Six-Day War with Israel, Saudi Arabia sent 20,000 troops to Jordan as reinforcements. Because the United States backed the Israelis, King Faisal stopped all oil exports to America. In addition, Saudi clerics called for a pan-Islamic jihad against the "Zionist aggressors."

After the disgrace of '67, Saudi Arabia gave only limited support to the Syrian-Egyptian–led Yom Kippur/6th of October War in 1973, though they did deny oil to all countries that supported Israel. Nevertheless, King Faisal was more concerned with his own kingdom than the plight of the Palestinians or the political problems of other Arab nations.

During the late 1960s and early 1970s, Arabia's oil-rich coastal states— Bahrain, Qatar, the United Arab Emirates, Oman, and Yemen—received complete independence from Great Britain. With their new autonomy, these nations gained full control of their natural resources. Inspired by these states, King Faisal decided to fully secure his oil fields by taking control of the Arabian-American Oil Company (Aramco, later to be known as Saudi Aramco). Just months later, King Faisal was assassinated, leading some conspiracy theorists to believe his killer was sponsored by the United States as a response to the Saudi monarch's takeover of Aramco.

In 1960, the Organization of Petroleum Exporting Countries (OPEC) was formed by the world's largest oil-producing nations. Today, Saudi Arabia is one of the organization's most influential member-states.

Bin Laden's Bucks

After Faisal's death, Prince Khalid inherited the Saudi throne. With untold fortunes at his fingertips and most of Aramco's shares in the Saudi family's hands, King Khalid began a five-year development plan. The equivalent of $150 billion (eventually $300 billion) was allocated to improving infrastructure, building petroleum and natural-gas plants, and producing steel and cement for these massive projects.

In the late 1960s, an immigrant from Yemen named Muhammad impressed the royal family with his exceptional building skills and honorable business practices. As a result, King Faisal issued a decree naming this man's family-run construction company as the kingdom's official builders. Because of this promise, the vast majority of King Khalid's monumental modernization plans were carried out by Muhammad bin Laden and his large family.

As an immigrant to Saudi Arabia, Muhammad bin Laden worked as a laborer from the 1930s on, making just enough money to feed his growing family. After landing this royal remodeling job in the 1970s, the bin Ladens were transformed into one of the most powerful families in the kingdom. As founder of the nation's largest construction company, worth more than $5 billion, Muhammad used his financial blessings to support a large family that included many wives and about fifty children. From one of his Syrian wives, in 1957 Muhammad bin Laden received his seventeenth son, whom he named Osama.

The Making of a Mastermind

As part of the bin Laden family business, Osama worked on many large projects, including the renovation of Islam's most sacred mosques in Mecca and Medina. While working on these holy places, Osama drew closer to his Islamic upbringing. In addition, Osama was influenced by the flow of Muslim pilgrims who visited his country each year from around the world. Inspired by the perspectives of those who were putting their lives on the line for Islam, Osama developed new relationships and ideologies that would shape the rest of his life.

ALERT!

Bin Laden wasn't always a "bad guy"! The United States gave about $3 billion to Afghani fighters during their decade-long war with the Soviet occupiers. Osama contributed to the same effort with financial and logistical support.

Osama's religious views moved to a new phase as he encountered the teachings of a professor named Sheik Àbdullah Azzam. After ingesting

Azzam's perspectives on the interconnectedness of politics and religion, bin Laden was inspired to take militant political action for the sake of Islam. Through his journey of faith, Osama came to a place where he felt compelled to fight those he deemed "enemies of Islam."

In 1982, Osama put his convictions to the test and traveled to the mountainous battlefields of Afghanistan, where he believed God would ensure victory over the powerful Soviet invaders. While bin Laden was actively involved in fighting the Russian infidels and financing the Afghan freedom fighters, his organizational efforts were by far the most memorable and effective contributions to the war. With many Arabs coming to the aid of their Central Asian coreligionists, Osama established a guesthouse where newcomers could stay until they were connected to a training facility or placed with a group of mujahedin ("holy warriors" in Arabic). This guesthouse came to be known as "The Base," *Al-Qaeda* in Arabic, a name that would later be attached to Osama's global organizational efforts.

With Osama at war in Afghanistan, the bin Ladens' construction company continued to thrive. In 1982, King Khalid died. The new king, Fahd, continued the traditional Saudi line of modernizing public works while attempting to preserve the conservative Islamic character of the Wahhabi kingdom. Nevertheless, radical elements questioned the king's piety and his family's friendship with the West. In order to offset these dissenting voices, in 1986, Fahd added the Islamic title "Custodian of the Two Holy Mosques" to his noble name.

FACT

Saudis in space? Yes! On June 24, 1985, Sultan ibn Salam ibn Abdul Aziz al Saùd traveled aboard NASA's shuttle *Discovery,* making him the first Saudi Arabian citizen in space.

Osama Is Back in Town

When the Soviet Union finally withdrew from Afghanistan in 1989, Osama bin Laden returned to Saudi Arabia as a war hero. He and many other Arab mujahedin had succeeded in repelling an invading superpower from a needy Muslim nation. Inspired by their victory, Osama organized veterans of the Soviet-Afghan War to continue their struggle against non-Muslim "oppressors" in Bosnia, Chechnya, Somalia, and the Philippines.

Fresh from the euphoria of jihad, Osama was angered by what he saw as a lack of religious enthusiasm coming from the Saudi leadership. As Iraq invaded Kuwait in 1990, bin Laden saw an opportunity to engage the backsliding leadership of Iraq with his holy warriors. Believing his men could protect Arabia from Saddam's schemes, bin Laden presented his plans to King Fahd. Instead of accepting Osama's offer, the king embraced President George Bush's plan, allowing the United States to protect the Islamic Holy Land.

Enraged by the presence of largely non-Muslim American troops on the sacred soil of Saudi Arabia, bin Laden publicly voiced his criticism of the royal family and their relations with the West. Because of his statements, Osama's Saudi citizenship was revoked, and he was forced to leave the kingdom. By 1992, the homeless millionaire found refuge in the East African nation of Sudan. Here he continued to speak out against the Saudi family and the 5,000-plus American military personnel remaining in the kingdom. In addition, bin Laden used his new position in Africa to partner with Egypt's Islamic Jihad group and other Islamist radicals in the area.

The Homeless Man's Horror

Within months of arriving in Sudan, Osama organized attacks on U.S. soldiers stationed in the Arabian nation of Yemen and the East African country of Somalia. By 1994, both the Saudi and American governments were pressuring Sudan to kick bin Laden out of their land. The following year Osama answered these calls by organizing the bombing of a U.S. training facility in the Saudi capital of Riyadh. Following this deadly attack, Sudan asked bin Laden to leave in 1996. Once again homeless, he returned to the country of Afghanistan, which had been embroiled in civil war since he and the Soviets left in 1989.

Protected by the familiar mountains of Central Asia, the Saudi dissident made his first public declaration of war against the United States, calling all "true" Muslims to kill American "occupation" forces in Arabia.

This bold statement was followed in June 1996 by a devastating truck bomb, in which nineteen American airmen were killed in eastern Saudi Arabia. Impressed by bin Laden's passion for jihad, Mullah Omar, spiritual leader of Afghanistan's ruling Taliban movement, voiced his support for the war against Western soldiers in Arabia. In addition, Osama's pan-Islamic propaganda encouraged Muslim extremists from around the world to join the fight from his base in the "pure" Islamic State of Afghanistan.

In 1998, Osama made several appearances in the media, broadening his previous declaration of war to include all Americans (including civilians, women, and children). Six months later, simultaneous bombs rocked U.S. embassies in Kenya and Tanzania, leaving 226 dead and many more wounded. The United States responded to these attacks by launching missiles at locations in Sudan and Afghanistan that were believed to be part of bin Laden's global terror network, Al-Qaeda.

Since targeting Osama bin Laden and his worldwide web of militants, the United States experienced the worst domestic attack in its history on September 11, 2001, when nineteen of Osama's associates used four commercial airliners to kill themselves and thousands of others.

Worldwide War

The aftermath of these catastrophic events revealed 2,998 dead and many injured men, women, and children. In order to punish Osama and his Taliban hosts, the United States led an international coalition into Afghanistan as Operation Enduring Freedom. In this action, coalition forces joined with Afghan separatists to remove the Islamist Taliban regime and their militant Al-Qaeda guests. After thousands of sorties and special forces operations, the fate of Osama bin Laden remains a mystery. However, many of his closest associates have been killed or captured. The ultraconservative Taliban government has been toppled, and a new representative government has been formed in Afghanistan.

As a pivotal point in American history, September 11 has also changed the way things are done across the globe. From Buenos Aires to Beijing, the world's governments are working to stop Islamic militants before they act. In addition, the threat of domestic terror has compelled the Saudi administration to spend billions of dollars on training and equipment for its antiterrorist units. As the protectors of Islam's most revered cities, the Saudi family is responsible not only for the safety of sojourners and Saudi citizens but also for the very reputation of Islam. With such great responsibilities, this wealthy Arab nation is criticized from all sides for its actions. Nevertheless, the royal family tries to retain honor, tradition, and stability in the Islamic Holy Land.

With fifteen of the September 11 hijackers believed to be Saudi citizens, and with other Saudis actively supporting bin Laden's efforts, the royal family has been forced to clear its name, defend its sovereignty, and uphold its religious views. In order to deal with its unsavory reputation as a "breeding ground for terrorists," the Saudi regime has implemented a global public-relations campaign.

All Roads Lead to Mecca

In all of Islamic history, no location has equaled Mecca's prestige. From Muhammad's first supernatural encounter to the Qur'anic sermons given in its ancient streets, this city is inseparably part of Islam. Today, Muslims' prayers from across the globe are physically directed toward Mecca, its Grand Mosque, and the sacred cube at its center (known as the Ka'ba). Looking to the future, most Muslims believe Mecca will play a major role in an Armageddon-type battle and the final Day of Judgment. For conservatives and liberals, Arabs and Malaysians, rich and poor, the city of Mecca holds an eternal place in the heart of each and every follower of Islam.

While Osama bin Laden and a fraction of other Saudis use the Qur'an and other Islamic texts to legitimize their militancy, not all Saudis are willing to kill for their faith. Though conservative Wahhabi practices and interpretations are popular in Saudi Arabia, there are also other shades of Islam within the kingdom. Worldwide, Islam is understood and observed in as many ways as any other major religion. Despite differences of opinion regarding faith and practice, nearly all Muslims look forward to a common experience—the pilgrimage to Mecca, known in Arabic as the Hajj.

In accordance with the specific directives of Muhammad, Sunnis and Shi'ites, "Twelvers" and Ismailis, literalist Wahhabis and mystical Sufis, conservative clerics and liberal librarians, moderate mailmen and militant mujahedin all travel to Arabia each year to complete the Hajj. While in the Saudi Kingdom, Muslims from around the globe visit the cities of Mecca and Medina to take part in prescribed rituals that date back to at least the seventh century. From the symbolic stoning of Satan, to the seven counterclockwise trips made round the Ka'ba, multitudes of men (all dressed in white) separate themselves from hordes of women (all dressed in black) as they re-enact rituals conducted by Muhammad and countless faithful after him.

Each year, about 2 million Muslims enter the Saudi kingdom during the month of pilgrimage to take part in the Hajj. Hailing from more than seventy countries, this annual pilgrimage injects the Arab Wahhabi nation with a mosaic of ethnic and theological diversity. Not only that, but this yearly event brings a steady flow of money to the Islamic Holy Land and its Wahhabi custodians. Though every "true" Muslim is called to visit Mecca at least once in his or her lifetime, some are excused from this duty for physical or financial reasons. Even those who cannot make the sacred trek find their faith intimately connected to this Saudi city.

Times, They Are a-Changin'

Because of growing domestic and international threats, the royal family has dramatically improved their aging military and security forces. Although Saudi Arabia has been purchasing weaponry and aircraft from the United States since the mid-1960s, by the late 1970s they had come to believe that it was necessary to take their defenses to another level.

With less than 20 million nationals living in the kingdom, the Saudi royals have compensated for their small population with big guns. From 1987 to 1997, the Saudis spent $262 billion to overhaul their army, air force, navy, national guard, and various police forces. Securing some of the world's most sophisticated weaponry, training, surveillance equipment, and defense systems, Saudi Arabia is now one of the best-defended nations in the region.

FACT

Saudi Arabia is the United States' number-one arms client. Since 1990, the Saudis have purchased nearly $40 billion in weaponry from the United States.

With billions continuing to flow toward modern security, infrastructure, and social services, much of Saudi Arabia's exterior has been transformed. However, on the inside, Saudi society has maintained many medieval practices and traditions. In the area of human rights, the international community has chastised the kingdom repeatedly. From the limitations put on women in the public sphere to the restrictions imposed upon its non-Muslim guests, the conservative laws of this Wahhabi state are far from modern.

Because of these strict regulations, some Saudis long for their society to evolve. One example of this can be seen in the vision of Riyadh's Faisaliah Center. The owners of this thirty-story complex opened their shopping mall/hotel/office/convention center with the idea that they would help their city progress beyond restrictive social norms. They had controversial plans to remain open during prayer times and provide an exciting and free environment, but the morality regulators stifled these "rebellious" ideas.

Swarming the mall's "mischievous" halls, the *muttawa* (religious police) found many ways to suppress this moral mutiny. Ordering women to cover their heads and barring single men from entering the center on weekends, zealous religious enforcers ensured the purity of those inside. Forcing Muslim men to evacuate shops and head to mosques during prayer times, while informing non-Muslims they would need to stop shopping until the prayers were finished, the *muttawa* secured the sacred prayers of the city's citizens.

Though this story reveals the extremes of Saudi society, even mainstream Saudis are subject to what many Westerners would call restrictive religious laws. For many Saudis these rules are considered positive in that they uphold traditional Islamic values. To others, however, these constructs are frustrating remnants of a long-lost age.

In the Middle East and the rest of the Muslim world, Saudi Arabia's conservative Islamic laws are not the norm. As one of a few nations to implement Islamic law, the Wahhabi kingdom's ways are viewed by many Muslims as old-fashioned and extremist.

In the 1960s Wahhabi clerics spoke against the evils of radio and television, but nearly fifty years later these apparent vices are employed to deliver Islamic teachings. Though these technologies were eventually embraced, it remains to be seen whether the pressures of postmodernism, women's liberation, and Western pop culture will change basic Wahhabi traditions. The times might be changing, but when it comes to Saudi society, don't expect an Arabian Woodstock.

Chapter 15

Iraq—British Colony to Ba'thist Beginnings

Since at least 3500 B.C., Mesopotamia has been a center of cultural and religious diversity. For hundreds of years the Ottoman Empire administered this region through three ethnically and religiously distinctive provinces. After World War I, the British combined these provinces into a single nation—Iraq. Apart from brutal dictatorships, Iraq has been the site of ongoing division and unrest. After reading this chapter, you will have a much clearer picture of the complicated nation Saddam Hussein came to rule.

Ousting Ottomans and Housing Hashemites

At the beginning of the twentieth century, the Ottoman Empire had been in control of most of the Arab world for about 400 years. In order to govern its vast Middle Eastern and European territories, Istanbul created administrative areas known as *vilayets*. The region of Mesopotamia consisted of the following territories:

- The northern *vilayet* of **Mosul,** inhabited by a majority of Kurdish and non-Arab peoples
- The central *vilayet* of **Baghdad**, predominately populated by Sunni Arabs
- The southern *vilayet* of **Basra**, almost entirely made up of Shi'ite Arabs

Although the Arabic word *al-Iraq*—meaning "the riverside slope"—was used as a general term for these river-rich lands, it was never used for a specific Ottoman administrative area or nation-state.

After defeating the Ottomans in World War I, British and French mandate areas replaced centuries-old *vilayet* boundaries throughout the Middle East. In the region of al-Iraq, the ethnically and religiously distinct *vilayets* of Mosul, Baghdad, and Basra were merged into a single British-controlled area. While leaders in London debated the nature of their nation-building efforts, some Iraqis began to question the intentions of their powerful European guests.

Born in the Hijaz region of western Arabia, Emir Faysal was the son of Sharif Husayn, protector of the sacred cities of Mecca and Medina. After receiving his education in Istanbul, Faysal returned to his family in Ottoman-controlled Arabia. During World War I, the Hashemites aligned themselves with the British (and T. E. Lawrence) as Faysal led the Arab revolt against Ottoman imperialism.

In March 1920, Prince Faysal of the Hashemite-ruled Hijaz (leader of the World War I Arab Revolt) established an Arab government in Damascus. Here, a council of Arab leaders named him king of Syria, while his older brother, Àbdullah, was declared king of Iraq. Inspired by the idea of an independent kingdom, Iraqi nationalists united in revolt but were quickly put down by British troops. Though Iraqi nationalists were defeated, their uprising convinced British leaders to end their direct administration of Iraq.

At about this time, France expelled Faysal from Damascus, citing his kingly claims as a challenge to their internationally recognized mandate of Syria. With Faysal and the Arab nationalists kicked out of French-controlled Syria, the British decided they could more effectively manage the region by offering Faysal the Iraqi throne. The Hashemite prince accepted this invitation, and on August 23, 1921, he was crowned king.

As part of Faysal's arrangement, the British mandate was to be replaced by a treaty of alliance, in which Great Britain would retain certain privileges within Iraq but would no longer directly control the domestic affairs of the kingdom. The new king proceeded to form Iraq's first national government and draft its first constitution, while Iraqi nationalists moved to form political parties. Unnerved by Iraq's independent actions, London drafted a second Anglo-Iraqi treaty, which revived many of the controls found under the post–World War I British mandate. Realizing they were not fully independent, Iraqi nationalists united to expel the lingering British colonialists.

Independence with Strings

Known to many Iraqis as the "perplexing predicament," the second Anglo-Iraqi treaty created a situation in which two governments guided the kingdom, one national and one foreign. Although London verbalized its desire to see Iraqi "self-rule," nationals recognized the impossibility of this end, given Britain's continued control of domestic affairs. Voicing their frustration with London's controls, Iraqis took to the streets in protest.

After more than a decade of broken promises and nationalist resistance, the British decided to end their administration of Iraq. By drafting a new treaty of independence, Great Britain relinquished control of Iraq, with the understanding that the two countries would maintain a close alliance. Britain would remain involved in Iraqi foreign affairs, and

British troops would stay at several key airbases within Iraq. After accepting the articles of this new treaty, the independent kingdom of Iraq was admitted to the League of Nations on October 3, 1932.

ALERT!

From 1921 to 2003, political power in Iraq remained in the hands of individuals who were both Arab and Sunni. In a region like Saudi Arabia, where the population is almost entirely Arab and Sunni, this type of leadership would be expected. In Iraq, however, where only 20 percent of the population is both Arab and Sunni, this balance of power is unusual, to say the least.

With their British coreligionists removed from domestic affairs, many Assyrian Christians in northern Iraq feared they would be mistreated by the kingdom's Arab Muslim government. Remembering the genocide carried out by the Ottomans just decades before, Assyrian leaders appealed to the League of Nations, asking for an autonomous region near the city of Mosul (once called Nineveh—capital of the ancient Assyrian Empire). On August 7, 1933, hardliners in the Iraqi administration decided to answer this "rebellious" minority with force, resulting in the death of several hundred Assyrian men, women, and children and the displacement of many others.

Just months after the Assyrian uprising/massacre, King Faysal died of a heart attack in Switzerland, making his son, Ghazi, king of Iraq. With Ghazi at the helm, the Iraqi cabinet developed a massive irrigation project in the south, a lucrative oil pipeline in the north, and a stretch of railway that connected Iraq's railroads to Europe. Despite these concrete improvements, the political situation in the Hashemite kingdom spiraled out of control, leading to a military coup in 1936. Though King Ghazi remained as the figurehead monarch, Iraq came under the direct rule of the army and its pan-Arab agendas.

Kingless Kingdom

Over the next few years, tribal disputes, political power plays, and violent protests plagued the nation as opposition groups gained new strength and military officials used their might to stay in power. In the midst of these turbulent times, King Ghazi was killed in a car crash, leaving his three-year-old son, Faysal II, as king of Iraq. In 1939, with an infant on the throne, a regent was appointed to oversee the king's duties. In the meantime, internal struggles continued among Iraq's military leaders, who were running the nation.

As the majority in northeastern Iraq, Kurds account for nearly 20 percent of the country's total population. While most Kurds are Sunni Muslims, less than 40 percent of Iraqis consider themselves Sunni.

Europe's Involvement

At the outset of World War II, some Arab leaders felt that an alliance with Germany and the Axis Powers would be better for the Arab world than its existing agreement with Britain and France, who continued to occupy the Arab lands of Syria and Palestine. This view spread to the popular level in the summer of 1940, as France fell to the Nazis and the future of Great Britain appeared uncertain. While some Iraqi leaders remained loyal to London, the majority decided to move away from the Anglo alliance.

To restore "stability," British troops invaded Iraq in 1941. Within thirty days, the anti-Anglo regime was defeated, and civilian politicians who were more sympathetic to British desires established a new government. By January 1942, the pro-British Iraqi administration affirmed its support for the Allies, declaring war on Germany and the other Axis Powers. Though London's intervention kept Iraq from joining the losing side during World War II, it did little to remedy Mesopotamia's fractured religious, ethnic, and political terrain.

A Nation Divided

In 1946, as Iraq joined the United Nations and helped to establish the Arab League, a Kurdish tribal leader named Massoud Bazrani formed the Kurdish Democratic Party (KDP). Hoping to secure autonomy in northern Iraq's predominately Kurdish region, thousands of *peshmerga* (translated "those who face death") followed Bazrani in opposition to Baghdad's administration of their homeland. Though Bazrami was forced to leave Iraq, the Kurdish *peshmerga* continued to resist Arab domination into the twenty-first century.

By 1946, ethnic fires were under control in the north, but internal political passions in Baghdad were ablaze. After forming yet another government, civilian politicians were once again usurped by a military commander. Within a year, this leader was pressured to resign, and the administration was again turned over to a civilian. Though Prime Minister Salih Jabr was not a military man, he was the first Shi'ite to rule the nation. With the country destabilized by violent clashes between young liberals and older members of the establishment, Jabr was forced to resign less than a year after taking office. With Jabr's resignation, a general once again gained control of the Iraqi government.

Instability and Revolutions

In 1953, King Faysal II turned eighteen, technically making him the ruler of Iraq. In reality, the former regent, military leaders, and powerful politicians continued to throw their weight around, making it difficult for the young leader to exercise his royal authority. With great political instability in his kingdom, King Faysal II entered Iraq into a controversial security agreement with Turkey, Iran, Pakistan, and Great Britain. Known as the Baghdad Pact, this arrangement was unacceptable to nationalists who opposed partnership with the colonialist powers. Inspired by Egyptian President Gamal Abdel Nasser's Pan-Arabism, Iraqi youth began to envision an Iraq free from the Hashemite monarch and his Western friends.

In February 1958, Syria came under the authority of Egypt in a federation known as the United Arab Republic (UAR). Only two weeks later, the Hashemite kings of Jordan and Iraq combined their territories to form the Arab Union of Jordan and Iraq. As a direct response to the UAR and its revolutionary ideologies, the pro-Western Hashemites hoped the Arab Union would appease those desiring pan-Arab unity while neutralizing calls for revolution. Reacting to this Hashemite union, voices from Nasser's UAR urged Iraqis to rise up against their "corrupt" king.

Inspired by Egypt's 1952 Revolution (led by Nasser and the Egyptian Free Officers' Movement), Iraqi soldiers calling themselves the Free Officers captured Baghdad. Led by Brigadier General Abd al-Karim Qasim and Colonel Abd al-Salam Arif, the Iraqi Free Officers established their regime by killing King Faysal II, the crown prince, and other members of the royal family, as well as the Arab Union's prime minister. The following day, on July 15, 1958, Iraq was declared a republic, ending more than thirty years of Hashemite rule and less than six months of federation with the Hashemite Kingdom of Jordan.

FACT

The Iraqi flag's three stars represent Iraq, Egypt, and Syria. Following the 1958 Revolution, some Iraqi leaders hoped to join Egypt and Syria in the United Arab Republic. Before this Pan-Arab plan could materialize, a coup in Syria caused the UAR to dissolve, but for many Arab nationalists this dream will never die.

Soon after Iraqi revolutionaries wrested power from King Faysal and family, the new republic's leadership was divided. While Colonel Arif and other pan-Arabists wanted to join Nasser's United Arab Republic, newly elected Prime Minister Qasim and his nationalist backers planned to focus on developing an independent Iraqi nation. Eventually, the government fragmented even further as disputes arose between Qasim and his former nationalist supporters.

Starting the Ba'th

By the early 1960s, ideological and ethnic differences once again divided Iraq, as socialist revolutionaries set their eyes on Baghdad and Kurdish *peshmerga* fighters struggled for independence in the north. On February 8, 1963, the Iraqi branch of the Arab Socialist Renaissance Party (*hizb al ba'th* in Arabic) joined forces with dissatisfied members of the Iraqi Army to topple Qasim's regime. Following the coup, popular pan-Arabist Abd al-Salam Arif was asked to be president, while Renaissance (Ba'th) Party leader Ahmad Hassan al-Bakr was given Iraq's premiership.

Seizing Power

After less than a year, al-Bakr's Ba'thist administration was overthrown, and President Arif took full control of the nation. Just two years later, Abd al-Salam Arif was killed in a helicopter crash and was replaced by his brother, Abd al-Rahman Arif. In the absence of popular support, Arif relied on the military to maintain his position, but the reorganized Ba'th Party had other plans for Iraq.

By convincing several powerful military officials to move against Arif, Ahmad Hassan al-Bakr, his cousin (Saddam Husayn al-Tikriti), and the Arab Socialist Ba'th Party seized control of Iraq on July 17, 1968. The Ba'thists proceeded to establish the Revolutionary Command Council as the new governing body, with al-Bakr as the republic's leader. Though the Ba'th Party planned to implement sweeping reforms, Iraq's ethnic diversity once again shook the nation's foundations.

Continued Kurdish Clashes

Backed by Iranian arms, Kurdish separatists effectively challenged the Iraqi army, forcing negotiations. After the Ba'thists agreed to recognize a semiautonomous Kurdish region in the north, a peace treaty was signed between Iraq's ruling Arab Ba'th Party and the Kurdish Democratic Party. However, because Baghdad did not include the oil-rich province of Kirkuk in the proposed Kurdish-controlled area, the treaty was scrapped, and civil war returned in 1974.

For al-Bakr and the Revolutionary Command Council, the Kurds and other opposition groups were an annoyance that could not be tolerated. Al-Bakr's younger cousin, Saddam Husayn (or Hussein) used his knack for brutality to gain respect within the Ba'th Party.

Through a matrix of ardent nationalism and calculated political maneuvering, Hussein created a network of loyal followers within his cousin's regime that would eventually become Iraq's dreaded secret service. Saddam Hussein's sadistic reputation precedes him, but for many this man remains a mystery. In the next chapter, you will follow this "madman" from his dysfunctional childhood to his humiliating capture at the hands of American soldiers.

Chapter 16

Iraq—The Rise and Fall of Saddam Hussein

After years of instability and division, Iraq was eventually subdued by the totalitarian rule of Saddam Hussein and the Ba'th Party. In this chapter, you will uncover the details of this oppressive period while examining the intricacies of a diverse nation teetering on the edge of an unknown and uncomfortable future.

The Boy from Tikrit

On April 28, 1937, the Tikriti clan of north central Iraq gained a new member. Husayn and Subha al-Majid became the proud parents of a son, whom they named Saddam. Raised in a largely Arab and Sunni Muslim region just north of Baghdad, Saddam lost his father at an early age. When his mother remarried, Saddam was forced to live with a violent man who taught him to lie, cheat, and steal. At age ten, Saddam left the abuse of his stepfather's house to live with his mother's brother in Baghdad. While under his uncle's care, the boy from Tikrit was introduced to anti-British and anti-Imperialist ideologies. From his uncle's teachings, this abused farm boy was transformed into a fiery young nationalist.

As the first expression of his passionate political views, the tenacious teen took part in an unsuccessful attempt to assassinate King Faysal II in 1956. The next year, Saddam found the Arab Socialist Renaissance (Ba'th) Party promoting the same pan-Arabist and anticolonialist ideologies he already believed in. Following the 1958 revolution, Saddam helped his older cousin (and Ba'th Party leader), Ahmad Hassan al-Bakr, with an assassination attempt on the new republic's leader, General Qasim. Failing to kill Qasim, Saddam was shot in the leg and forced to flee Iraq.

After a short stay in Syria, Hussein moved to Cairo, where he remained for four years, until his Ba'thist buddies successfully murdered General Qasim in 1963. With an apparent Ba'thist revolution on the horizon, Saddam returned to Baghdad. Less than a year after Saddam's return, Iraq's new leader, Colonel Abd al-Salam Arif, pushed the Ba'thists out of power. In 1964, while trying to oust Arif, Hussein and al-Bakr were thrown in prison. Two years later, Saddam escaped from his cell, where he had been plotting yet another takeover.

Tikriti Takeover

As secretary general of Iraq's Ba'th Party, Saddam was instrumental in organizing the 1968 bloodless coup that brought the Arab Socialist Renaissance (Ba'th) Party and the Tikriti clan to power. With his second cousin at the helm of Iraq's ruling Revolutionary Command Council,

Hussein was named deputy chairman of the RCC and vice president of the republic. Familiar with Iraq's turbulent history, the boys from Tikrit immediately purged the nation of ethnic, religious, and political opposition.

Through the late 1960s and early 1970s, ethnic Kurds and Turkomans, Assyrian Christians and Arab Shi'ites, conservative Sunnis and communist students were deported, arrested, tortured, and executed for their "disloyalty." Though these gruesome acts may appear to be the work of madmen, they were actually pre-emptive strikes organized by sane but paranoid politicians. No matter how inhumane these Ba'thist bad boys may have been, they were responding to issues that had violently divided their nation since its foundation. For this regime, fear was the glue that would keep Iraq in one piece.

FACT

After being kicked out of Iran in 1964, Ruhallah Khomeini (spiritual leader of Iran's 1979 Islamic Revolution) settled in the Shi'ite holy city of an-Najaf, Iraq. In 1978, Saddam Hussein banished Khomeini from Iraq. The following year, Khomeini's followers overthrew the shah, making the Ayatollah Khomeini supreme leader of the Shi'ite-led Islamic Republic of Iran.

Through the late 1970s, al-Bakr remained Iraq's leader in name, but in practice Hussein was running the show. On July 16, 1979, al-Bakr finally recognized his impotence by retiring and transferring his titles to Saddam Hussein al-Tikriti. As president of the republic, chairman of the RCC, and secretary general of Iraq's Ba'th Party, Saddam wasted no time exercising his powers and solidifying his totalitarian rule.

Cleaning the Ba'th

Five days after his inauguration, Hussein held an important meeting of the nation's top leaders. When all were assembled, Saddam read from a list of names, which included a high-ranking RCC official, the head of Iraq's labor unions, a leading Shi'ite member of the RCC, and twenty others. These individuals were accused of conspiring with the Syrian government in a plan that would have killed Saddam and brought Iraq into an Arab federation led by Syria's Ba'thist president Hafez al-Assad. For their "treason," each was executed, with Hussein personally killing many of the conspirators. Over the next week, as many as 450 others were put to death for their alleged involvement in the plot against Saddam.

Like many Arab states aiming to break away from capitalist colonial powers, the Ba'th Party looked to the USSR as their superpower of choice. Though Saddam and his cronies were fierce nationalists, working with the Soviets was acceptable, given Russian rivalries with the West. In addition to their communist connection, Ba'th Party officials were enjoying new wealth due to the nationalization of Iraq's oil fields. By the late 1970s, Saddam's Iraq was one of the region's most powerful nations. Though his iron-fisted domestic policies brought a type of stability to the republic, Saddam's next threat would come from the outside.

At War with Iran

Although Saddam's secular regime harassed Shi'ite leaders throughout the 1970s (for example, by deporting the exiled Iranian cleric Ayatollah Khomeini in 1978), the 1980s began a new era of calculated anti-Shi'ite efforts. After banning the Shi'ite-led Da'wa Party and executing leading Shi'ite clerics during the spring and summer of 1980, on September 21, Iraqi forces invaded the Ayatollah Khomeini's newly established Islamic Republic of Iran. Though this was primarily a territorial dispute, the ethnic and religious aspects of this war cannot be ignored.

While Saddam's Arab regime represented about 80 percent of Iraqis who were ethnically Arab, its largely Sunni Muslim makeup ignored the three out of four Iraqi Arabs who were Shi'ite Muslims.

Seeds of War

Since at least the early 1600s the border between "Persian" Iran and "Arab" Iraq has shifted according to the politics of the time, especially along the southern Shatt al-Arab (a waterway to the Persian Gulf, formed by the joining of the Euphrates and Tigris Rivers). In 1975, Iraq and Iran agreed to divide control of the river, but after the shah was overthrown in 1979, tensions between Saddam's secular state and Iran's revolutionary religious government revived longstanding disagreements.

Hoping to spread his revolution into the largely Shi'ite nation of Iraq, Iran's Ayatollah Khomeini denounced the Iraqi leadership as "backsliding" secularists. To undermine the Soviets and the Ayatollah, the United States courted Hussein, assuring him they would support Iraq in any military action taken against Iran. With the threat of Shi'ite revolution looming over his head, Saddam looked to the long-disputed Shatt al-Arab as a pretext for his pre-emptive strike. Knowing that Washington would back him, Saddam also planned to capture the oil-rich Iranian province of Khuzestan, which was inhabited almost entirely by Arabs.

FACT

In 1981, Israeli jets flew into the heart of Iraq, destroying the soon-to-be-activated Osirak nuclear reactor near Baghdad.

Over the next few months, border disputes led to small-scale fighting, moving Baghdad to withdraw from the 1975 Shatt al-Arab agreement. Four days later, on September 21, 1980, Iraqi troops crossed into Iranian territory, and Iraqi planes bombed Iranian airbases. After two months of successful operations in Iran, the Iraq army met stiff resistance, leading to a one-year stalemate. By the spring of 1982, a rejuvenated Iranian army pushed Iraqi forces out of their lands. After another year of intense fighting, Iran mounted its first offensive into Iraqi territory. Over the next few years, fighting spread into the Persian Gulf, with islands, oil platforms, tankers, and other ships being attacked. As a result, the Iran-Iraq War is also known as the first Gulf war.

International Conspirators

From 1983 to 1986, as fighting continued in the Persian Gulf, Iranian troops retained control of the Shatt al-Arab and part of southern Iraq's Basra province. In the north, Iranian forces joined Kurdish separatists, taking several Iraqi border towns and operating well into Iraq's Kurdish region. As part of the Iran-Contra Affair, it was discovered that the United States had sold more than $14 million worth of weaponry to Iran in exchange for American hostages. While Washington was technically neutral, after this double-dealing was uncovered, the Reagan administration decided to salvage its image in the Arab world by openly supporting Iraq.

By 1987, France and the Soviet Union were sending weapons to Iraq (including chemical and biological agents), while Washington was also supplying Baghdad with limited weaponry, logistical assistance, and intelligence. In addition, the U.S. Navy sent a huge naval armada to the Persian Gulf to "protect" the flow of oil from the region. In the process, U.S. forces carried out operations against Iranian ships, oil platforms, and tankers. On several occasions Americans mistakenly targeted civilians, as seen in the downing of an Iranian commercial airliner that resulted in nearly 300 civilian deaths.

After eight years of unthinkable carnage, the Ayatollah agreed to accept a cease-fire agreement on August 20, 1988, but not before the Iran-Iraq War had taken more than a million lives and left another 1.7 million people wounded. Despite these harsh lessons, the boundaries between Iraq and Iran returned to their prewar positions, and the leaders who orchestrated this bloody grudge match remained in power.

At War with the World

Just five days after signing the cease-fire with Iran, Saddam Hussein began a strategic campaign against the Kurds. As retribution for the Kurdish partnership with Iran, the Iraqi town of Halabjah was gassed, killing 5,000 Kurdish men, women, and children and injuring another 10,000. Over the next year, more than 180,000 Iraqi Kurds "disappeared," and about 4,000 non-Arab villages were demolished. With the distraction of war gone,

Saddam was determined to put out all opposition fires, no matter what the human cost.

During the eight-year struggle with Iran, Iraqi oil exports had come to a near standstill and millions had been spent on weaponry. Saddam therefore attempted to rebuild his nation's decimated economy. Between 1988 and 1990, the ruling Ba'th Party tried to revive its petroleum industry and began to accumulate large amounts of conventional and nonconventional arms. Though Washington supported Iraq during its long war with Iran, Saddam's stockpiling of weaponry, as well as his extreme anti-Israeli statements, prompted the United States to rethink its alliance with Baghdad.

QUESTION?

Why are so many Iraqis unhappy with the United States?
For many Iraqis, the United States is an arrogant superpower that uses smaller and weaker nations for its own purposes. In the words of Saddam Hussein, "You Americans, you treat the Third World in the way an Iraqi peasant treats his new bride. Three days of honeymoon, and then it's off to the fields."

With Iraq struggling to revive its economy, Saddam looked to its successful southern neighbor—Kuwait. Though this tiny Persian Gulf state had partnered with Saddam during the Iran-Iraq War, the Iraqi leader jealously set his eyes on its petroleum. As a pretext for invasion, Hussein accused Kuwait of intentionally hurting Iraq's economy by flooding the world markets with Kuwaiti oil. Looking to Iraq's long-standing claims to southern Mesopotamian (that is, Kuwait), Saddam invaded on August 2, 1990, declaring Kuwait as Iraq's nineteenth province.

Another War in the Gulf

The United Nations immediately condemned the Iraqi occupation of Kuwait, implemented an international trade embargo on Iraq, and set January 15, 1991, as a deadline for Iraqi forces to withdraw from Kuwaiti lands. With Iraqi troops in Kuwait believed to be moving toward Saudi Arabian oil fields, King Fahd accepted an American offer to protect his kingdom. Known as Operation Desert Shield, this effort to guard Saudi Arabia soon turned into a massive deployment of American troops throughout the Persian Gulf region. In response to Iraq's invasion of Kuwait, more than thirty nations, both Arab and Western, joined the U.S. buildup in the Gulf.

On January 17, 1991, with the U.N. deadline passed, Operation Desert Shield erupted into Operation Desert Storm. What began as an overwhelming air campaign expanded into a well-orchestrated ground assault, aimed at removing Saddam's soldiers from Kuwait. With armed forces from Egypt, Syria, Saudi Arabia, and other Arab nations and troops from the Afghanistan, Pakistan, Turkey, and other non-Arab Muslim nations fighting alongside soldiers from North and South America, Europe, and Asia, most of the world was united against Baghdad's bad boys.

While coalition forces were successful in their air and ground campaigns, Iraq was able to send several Scud missiles into Kuwait, Saudi Arabia, and Israel, killing many civilians and soldiers. In addition, retreating Iraqi troops set fire to about 700 Kuwaiti oil wells, which burned for months until special crews were able to contain them.

Only six weeks after the start of Desert Storm, Kuwait was cleared of Iraqi combatants. Tens of thousands of Iraqi soldiers were dead, and most of Iraq's heavy weaponry and defense systems were destroyed. Clearly defeated in Kuwait, Saddam was forced to sign a cease-fire agreement. With hostilities officially over, U.N. peacekeepers were stationed along the Kuwait/Iraq border, and most coalition forces returned to their home countries.

Suppression, Sanctions, and Suffering

During Desert Storm, coalition forces dropped leaflets and sent radio broadcasts encouraging Iraqi opposition groups to rise up against Saddam's oppressive Ba'thist regime. Believing they would have an international force behind them, Kurds in the north and Shi'ites in the south revolted. But because the war ended so quickly and coalition forces didn't continue their efforts inside Iraq, lightly armed opposition groups were left to fight the Iraqi army alone. Although Saddam's forces were substantially reduced, the remaining Iraqi military easily suppressed the Kurdish and Shi'ite revolts.

In northern Iraq, Saddam's soldiers killed thousands of Kurdish Iraqi citizens, while hundreds of thousands more escaped into Iran and Turkey. In response to these atrocities, American, British, and French troops entered the region, establishing a safe zone for the remaining 600,000 Iraqi Kurds who were threatened by Saddam's armies. In addition, a no-fly zone was enforced over the northern third of Iraq as a way of ensuring that Kurds would not be attacked from the air. In southern Iraq's Shi'ite area, Iraqi forces put down anti-Ba'thist demonstrations, killing thousands and forcing many others to flee to Iran, Jordan, and Syria. As with the north, a southern no-fly zone was set up to protect the Shi'ites from Saddam.

After the war, the United Nations continued to enforce its trade embargo, promising sanctions would be lifted if Iraq destroyed all its chemical/biological weapons, ended its nuclear program, and allowed U.N. inspectors to confirm the completion of these measures. Because Saddam refused to comply with these stipulations, the sanctions continued for more than a decade.

Punishment

In 1992, Saddam began a drainage program of southern Iraq's marshland. By destroying this important ecosystem, Baghdad hoped to punish the Shi'ite "Marsh Arabs," whose livelihood was intricately connected to the wetlands. In addition, removing the water from this soggy region enabled Iraqi soldiers to move more freely in search of Shi'ite rebels.

ALERT!

As a result of Saddam's systematic abuses of southern Iraq's "Marsh Arabs," many were killed, imprisoned, or forced to flee their ancient homeland, reducing the population of Iraqi Marsh Arabs from about 250,000 in 1991 to fewer than 40,000 in 2003.

In 1994, after two years of continuously draining southern Iraq's ancient wetlands, Saddam Hussein sent troops into the dry marshes to root out "terrorists" and any other Shi'ites who dared to oppose him. In the same year, Baghdad renewed its efforts against Kurdish Iraqis by establishing an economic embargo against the already impoverished northern region.

From Wealth to Want

Throughout the 1980s, Iraqis had grown accustomed to air conditioning, clean running water, and other modern conveniences. As capital of an oil-rich nation, Baghdad was a bustling metropolis, complete with modern highways, tall buildings, and new cars. By the mid-1990s, after five years of U.N. sanctions, Iraq's economy was in shambles. Luxuries such as reliable electricity and sanitation services were almost nonexistent. Skilled professionals were quitting their jobs for more lucrative forms of employment, such as selling cigarettes on the street. With Iraqi currency worth little more than the paper it was printed on, food and basic medicines in short supply, and Saddam's regime firmly in place, the international community began to question the effectiveness of the embargo.

During more than ten years of U.N. sanctions, Saddam and his Ba'th Party loyalists continued to enjoy luxurious lifestyles, while more than 5,000 children died from common illnesses and/or malnutrition.

After recognizing widespread malnutrition throughout Iraq, the U.N.–sponsored Oil-for-Food Program was implemented in 1996, allowing Iraq to sell limited amounts of oil to offset the cost of its growing humanitarian needs. In May 2002, the United Nations again tried to lessen the burden on Iraqi civilians by changing the embargo to focus on military goods.

Though more than $28 billion in humanitarian supplies and equipment were sent to Iraq between 1997 and 2003, the people of Iraq continued to suffer in many ways.

Between Iraq and a Hard Place

Since U.S. President Bill Clinton ordered strategic strikes throughout Iraq in the 1998 Operation Desert Fox, American and British planes limited their attacks to hostile targets within Iraq's northern and southern no-fly zones. After the tragedy of September 11, Washington once again turned up the heat on Saddam, naming Iraq, Iran, and North Korea as the Axis of Evil. With President George W. Bush and other U.S. officials convincing the United Nations to pass a new resolution concerned with Iraq's reported weapons of mass destruction (WMD), Baghdad's Ba'thist bad boys were once again in America's crosshairs.

Failing to obtain U.N. support for a pre-emptive strike on Iraq, the United States, Great Britain, and several other countries decided to deal with Saddam themselves. On March 19, 2003, the first of many powerful bombs rocked the Iraqi capital as Operation Iraqi Freedom was underway. Following another night of intense bombing, American and British troops camped in Kuwait moved into southern Iraq, bound for Baghdad. Over the next three weeks, some of the most powerful nonnuclear bombs known to man were guided to specific targets in a "shock and awe" air campaign. At the same time, ground troops battled their way toward Baghdad from the south, while others secured positions in western and northern Iraq.

FACT

In order to help coalition troops recognize important Ba'th Party officials, the U.S. Department of Defense issued the "Iraqi Most Wanted" set of playing cards. This dual-use deck pictured the fifty-five most important Ba'thist leaders, including Saddam Hussein as the ace of spades, his son Odai Hussein as the ace of hearts, and his other son Qusai Hussein as the ace of clubs.

Looting and Liberty

By April 14, coalition forces had gained control of Baghdad and Saddam's hometown of Tikrit, sending the toppled regime into hiding. Because most experts expected a long and bloody fight in the streets of

Baghdad, no one was prepared when the government gave up the city after a matter of days. The resulting security vacuum gave the city's impoverished people the opportunity to take back what Saddam had stolen from them. Though looting was initially limited to Ba'th Party offices, it soon spread to warehouses, banks, and even museums.

After coalition forces made the transition from the role of warrior to policeman, relative order was eventually restored, but not before millions of dollars in cash, property, and artifacts were taken. Less than two weeks after Saddam's government collapsed, widespread rioting erupted as outspoken ethnic and religious leaders rallied their people, calling foreign troops to leave their liberated lands as soon as possible. This development shocked many, but given Iraq's previous experiences with British occupation, their discomfort may be understandable. At the same time, with Saddam on the run, possible WMDs floating around, and the country devastated, coalition forces believed their continued presence was a necessity.

As American and British troops hunted for Hussein and company, many high-ranking Ba'thist officials were captured or killed, including Saddam's sons Odai and Qusai, who were slain in the northern city of Mosul (ancient Nineveh). Despite these successes, coalition forces experienced repeated attacks from suicide bombers, rocket-propelled grenades (RPGs), and snipers. Though some of these attacks were the work of Saddam loyalists, many were made by individuals with varied political, ethnic, and religious backgrounds, who wanted to repel another round of foreign occupation.

Quagmire of the Conquerors

On May 1, 2003, President George W. Bush announced the end of major battle operations in Iraq. But for coalition forces, the battlefield was still hot. Though no WMDs were found, Saddam's regime was toppled. Though the Iraqi army was no longer functioning, the "fida'yin Saddam" and other guerillas continued sporadic attacks. With heavily armed young adults forced to police the streets of a foreign land, mortal mistakes were made. At times, troops took the lives of innocent Iraqis suspected of hostile intent, while at other times soldiers and marines lost their own lives by giving attackers the benefit of the doubt.

With Iraqi civilians dying at the hands of confused coalition forces, and citizens concerned that their liberators were now occupiers, protests increased in frequency and intensity. Soon after the fall of the Ba'thists, tribal and religious leaders gathered with American representatives to discuss Iraq's post-Saddam government, but the average Iraqi did not see the fruits of these talks until the summer of 2003.

On July 13, a twenty-five-member interim administration known as the Governing Council met for its first official meeting. Because U.S. officials chose this temporary governing body, it was quickly criticized, but for the first time in Iraqi history the nation's administration was representative of the ethnically and religiously diverse populace. The twenty-two male and three female cabinet members constituted the following:

- 13 Shi'ite Muslims
- 5 ethnic Kurds
- 5 Sunni Muslims
- 1 ethnic Turkoman
- 1 Assyrian Christian

Though July saw the formation of Iraq's first indigenous representative government, August 2003 was the bloodiest month since Saddam Hussein was ejected from power. On August 7, a car bomb exploded at the Jordanian Embassy in Baghdad, killing ten. The following week, oil, water, and electrical lines were sabotaged, and on August 19, a large truck bomb ripped through U.N. headquarters in Baghdad, killing the chief U.N. envoy to Iraq and seventeen others, while injuring 100 more. To round out the month of terror, a massive car bomb rocked Friday prayers at the Imam Àli Mosque in an-Najaf (home of the tomb of Àli, spiritual founder of Shi'ite Islam). In this attack, the Ayatollah Muhammad Baqir al-Hakim (spiritual leader of Iraq's Supreme Council of Islamic Revolution) was killed along with 124 other worshipers, while another 142 were wounded.

Iraq's Future?

Are these attacks the organized efforts of a lingering underground government, or are they the work of frustrated Iraqis who want to avoid foreign occupation? There are colorful arguments on both sides, but as of yet it seems to be a combination of the two. Though no WMDs have been found, Iraqis are experiencing freedoms they haven't seen for decades.

With little or no restrictions on morality, pornographic videos and sex theaters have become commonplace. In response, religious leaders are using their new liberty to criticize these evils and the Western "occupation" forces believed to be importing them. Many Iraqis are also using their increased wages to buy satellite dishes, which were forbidden under Saddam's strict media controls. In addition, Iraqis are now free to tear down the numerous pictures of Saddam Hussein that have peppered the nation for decades.

While Saddam's capture and the removal of his regime have given the average Iraqi freedom to buy, sell, watch, and do many new things, it has also dissolved the glue of fear from this troubled and diverse nation. Will Iraq's many political, ethnic, and religious groups be pacified by a representative national government, or will they return to the familiar conflict of their forefathers? If American and British troops leave immediately, will there be chaos or can Iraqis keep the peace? Does Iraq need a dictator to stay together, or will democratic leaders develop separate Kurdish, Sunni, and Shi'ite states? Though every expert has an opinion, the future of Iraq now lies in the hearts and hands of the Iraqi people. Ⓔ

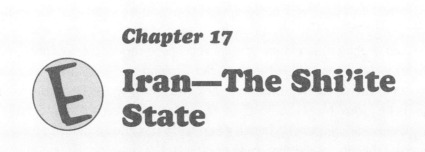

Chapter 17

Iran—The Shi'ite State

The Iranian plateau has produced some of the world's most colorful cultures and powerful politicians. Following World War II, America and Iran developed a strong friendship that lasted nearly forty years, until the Islamic Revolution of 1979. Today, the United States and Iran have been at odds for more than twenty years; but why? Find out as you uncover the complexities of this corner of the globe, known to many as a hotbed of Islamic extremism.

Dynasties and Divisions

Since at least 800 B.C., Aryan peoples from the Fars/Pars tribe have lived in the region now called Iran. Long known as Persia (because of its Fars population), this land was ruled by a succession of Aryan, Greek, Arab, Mongol, and Turkic families. After the Turkic Safavid dynasty was toppled in the mid-eighteenth century, several short-lived monarchies controlled parts of Persia. Meanwhile, the powerful Russian and Ottoman empires planned to divide the region and annex its territories. In 1795, the Turkic Qajar tribe, from the southern Caspian Sea region, saved Persia from foreign annexation. Moving Persia's capital to the city of Tehran, the Qajars established a dynasty that would last 130 years.

Through the 1800s, British-Russian rivalries inspired each empire to vie for supremacy in the region. As Russia conquered Persian provinces in Central Asia, and as London expanded its influence from British-controlled India into the Persian territory of Afghanistan, each empire secured economic concessions from Tehran. In a 1901 agreement, Great Britain was granted a sixty-year dispensation to exploit Persia's oil reserves, while the Qajars also promised most of Persia's customs proceeds to St. Petersburg in return for several large Russian loans.

Persia's Parliament and Predicament

In 1906, London was given concessions over Persia's tobacco industry. Believing the Qajars were jeopardizing Persia's independence, nationalists organized a constitutional revolution. As part of the new constitution, an elected consultative assembly (known as the Majlis) was given considerable authority over the kingdom's affairs. Though Persia's parliament desired to end foreign control over the country's markets, in 1907 Russia and Britain divided the kingdom into spheres of economic influence. Hoping to improve Persia's situation, the Majlis invited the successful American banker Morgan Shuster to put things in order. As treasurer-general, Shuster was given complete control of Persia's finances. Fearing Shuster's input would produce an economically empowered Persia, Russia forced the national assembly to fire the American expert.

As World War I erupted, Persia remained neutral, but because of its strategic importance and coveted petroleum reserves, Allied and Axis armies battled for position within this nonaligned nation. After the war, Persian delegations were excluded from the Paris Peace Conference. Instead of allowing Tehran to build an independent nation-state, British officials drafted the Anglo-Iranian Treaty, basically making the Qajar kingdom a protectorate.

ALERT!

Though Iran was long called Persia, just over half of the nation's people are ethnically Persian. The Turkic Azeri people make up about a quarter of Iran's population, while Kurds, Turkmen, Arabs, and other ethnic groups combine to form the other roughly 25 percent of the populace.

Embittered by Britain's persistent imperial presence, the Majlis and other nationalists looked to expel the weak Qajar monarchy. To avoid violence, London pulled back from the direct controls afforded by the Anglo-Iranian Treaty. In 1921, a military leader named Reza Khan conquered the Persian capital, establishing a new government with himself as war minister and, eventually, prime minister. In 1925, more than a century of Turkic Qajar rule came to a close as Shah Ahmad Mizra was deposed, and Reza Khan became Persia's new shah.

Aryans All over Again

Since the Mongols conquered Persia in the thirteenth century, non-Aryan dynasties dominated the region, but with the rise of Reza Khan, an Aryan was back on top. Associating himself with the ancient Achaemenian kings, the new shah adopted the name Pahlavi. Like other leaders of his time, Reza Shah worked to promote a clear national identity. As a way of celebrating the region's rich pre-Islamic and non-Arab heritage, Pahlavi changed Persia's name to Iran, in reference to its ancient Aryan peoples.

Reza Shah adopted the name Pahlavi (the name of an ancient form of the Persian language) in order to stress his nation's pre-Islamic Aryan history. He hoped to establish a nationalistic, secular, and modern state. The Pahlavi dynasty was Persia's first Aryan regime in more than 1,000 years.

Emulating Mustafa Kemal Atatürk, the charismatic founder of Turkey, Reza Shah Pahlavi began a controversial program of modernization in Iran. Just as the Republic of Turkey was established as a secular Turkish state, the new Iranian shah divorced the long-married mosque and state in his own nation. Since the Safavids declared Shi'a Islam the state religion in 1501 (transforming the largely Sunni region), Shi'ite clerics (leaders of the Shi'a brand of Islam) remained intimately involved in the kingdom's administrative affairs. Under the Pahlavi monarchy, preachers were expected to stay out of politics, and individual religious convictions were a private matter.

Modern, Independent, then Occupied

Like Atatürk, Pahlavi looked to Western civilization in his quest for modernization. Through the late 1920s and early 1930s, new French-inspired law codes were introduced, breaking the tradition of governance guided by *Sharià* (Islamic law). In the mid-1930s, Iranian women were forbidden to wear veils in public, and all citizens were encouraged to wear Western-style clothing. Inspired by Europe's wealthy industrialized nations, Reza Shah built new factories, roads, and railways (including the Trans-Iranian Railroad) and developed a modern European-style education system.

Though Pahlavi tried to emulate the West in his modernization efforts, his nationalist agendas brought Iran closer to true independence. Soon after becoming shah, Reza negotiated the withdrawal of Russian and British troops that had been stationed in Iran since the beginning of World War I. In addition, Pahlavi abolished the special economic rights that had allowed foreigners to exploit Iran for more than 100 years. As part of his anticolonialist efforts, Reza Shah established friendly relations with Nazi

Germany, which he saw as a shining example of modernity and nationalism. With the outbreak of World War II, Reza Shah sided with Hitler and the Axis Powers, provoking Britain and Russia to invade Iran in 1941.

Occupied by Allied troops, Reza was forced to turn the kingdom over to his son Muhammad Reza Pahlavi, who joined Iran to the Allied cause in 1943. That same year, Iran hosted the Tehran Conference, in which U.S. President Franklin D. Roosevelt, Soviet Premier Joseph Stalin, and British Prime Minister Winston Churchill discussed their wartime partnership and postwar plans. From this meeting, the Allies also assured Iran of postwar independence and financial aid.

America and the Shah

After defeating Nazi Germany in 1945, the British found their nation economically and militarily depleted, opening the way for the United States to assume much of Great Britain's importance on the world stage. Immediately after the war, the United States used its influence to pressure the Soviets out of northwestern Iran. With Hitler no longer a common enemy, the American/Soviet/British "Grand Alliance" quickly deteriorated, as the Soviet Union squared off against the United States and Great Britain.

The United States in Iran

The rivalry that developed between the United States and Soviet Union caused each side to jockey for position in smaller countries. For Iran, alliance with the United States was a way of checking Soviet expansionism, while for the United States, Iran was a strategic base of operations in Moscow's backyard. In addition, partnership with Tehran would open the way for American companies to develop the full potential of Iran's vast oil fields.

For centuries, most Iranians viewed the Anglo-Iranian Oil Company (AIOC)—born out of a 1901 deal between the Qajars and a British businessman—as a remnant of British imperialism. In 1951, the Majlis nationalized Iran's oil industry, removing what they saw as the last vestiges of foreign control. In response to the newly established National Iranian Oil Company (NIOC), London severed diplomatic ties with Tehran. Within a year, Iran's oil industry was at a standstill, as nationals lacked the technical skills needed to operate wells and refineries. By the mid-1950s, petroleum production was turned over to several European and American companies, with the understanding that half of their revenues would be given to Iran.

Cold War Connections

As Washington and Moscow battled for international influence, the United States secured its position in Iran by covertly assisting the shah (who up to this point had been subservient to the prime minister). Through an apparent partnership between British and U.S. intelligence agencies, an angry mob was paid to topple Iran's anti-Pahlavi Prime Minister Muhammad Musaddiq. With Musaddiq's removal in 1953, the U.S.–backed Shah Muhammad Reza Pahlavi established absolute control, but for decades to come, Iranians questioned his foreign connections.

FACT

Between 1953 and 1967, Iran received about $600 million in economic and military aid from the United States.

Through the latter half of the 1950s, the Middle East became a political battleground for American and Soviet ideologies. After the Egyptians aligned themselves with the communists, Washington passed a 1957 resolution known as the Eisenhower Doctrine. Under this resolution, the United States promised to aid any Middle Eastern regime that might be threatened by communism. For Iran, this offer was extremely attractive, as its economy and military would be improved by American support, and its borders would be protected from the Soviets. Through the late 1950s and early 1960s, Tehran and Washington continued to develop strong ties, as demonstrated by the 1959 American-Iranian Defense Agreement and the U.S. aid received by the shah.

Seeds of Revolt

With oil revenues flowing, and the United States sending substantial support, Iran's economy was on the rebound. Though this upturn generated new wealth, most Iranians saw the rich getting richer and the poor getting poorer. Recognizing the growing resentment among Iran's impoverished masses, U.S. President John F. Kennedy feared the pro-American shah would be overthrown.

Hoping to stabilize the Pahlavi regime, Washington encouraged the shah to deal with his nation's social problems. The resulting 1963 White Revolution forced Iranian owners of large estates to sell portions of their land to the government. These properties were then divided into small farms and distributed to the less fortunate. In addition, the shah introduced Western-inspired reforms that affected Iran's education system and promoted women's rights.

Though about 4 million families were given property, Iran's mullahs (religious leaders) denounced the shah's actions. Because many of the dissolved estates were religious endowments and most of the shah's policy changes challenged long-standing traditions, conservative clerics criticized the modern monarch. The White Revolution managed to deal with a portion of Iran's problems, but with many viewing the shah as an anti-Islamic, Western-sponsored dictator, Muhammad Reza Pahlavi's troubles were far from over.

In 1964, the shah deported a sixty-two-year-old ayatollah (highest rank for a Shi'ite cleric) by the name of Sayyid Ruhollah al-Musavi al-Khomeini. Though Khomeini was deported because of anti-Pahlavi rhetoric, in exile he was able to inspire an Iranian revolution.

By the late 1960s, Iran's oil revenues were in excess of $20 billion a year. With new wealth at his fingertips, the shah began a rapid and costly program of modernization aimed at catching Iran up to the West. Though his measures resulted in economic growth, improved living conditions, and new technologies, they also had serious repercussions. Culture shock, large-scale urbanization, and inflation were just a few of the things that led

Iranians to resent the Pahlavi ruler. In addition, the authoritarian manner with which the shah implemented his changes infuriated many.

Aware of his subjects' growing dissatisfaction, the shah used secret police (known as Savak) to find and punish opposition leaders. Through the early and mid-1970s, Savak agents managed to catch some dissidents, but the shah's dictatorial and "anti-Islamic" actions led many to look for a savior. By the late 1970s, many had discovered the teachings of a man they believed to be a liberator. For students of the Ayatollah Ruhollah Khomeini, salvation would be found in a pure Islamic state, led by Shi'ite jurists and guided by God.

Khomeini's Student Revolution

Since his deportation in 1964, the Ayatollah Khomeini sought refuge in neighboring Iraq. While living in the Shi'ite holy city of an-Najaf (burial site of the revered caliph Àli), Khomeini developed a doctrine known as the Rule of the Jurist. At the heart of this ideology was the belief that secular governments should be replaced by theocracies, in which God's laws would be administered by divinely appointed *mujtahids* (experts in Islamic theology and law). As an ayatollah (translated "miraculous sign of God"), Khomeini had attained the most honorable title within the *mujtahids,* one that motivated millions to accept his every word.

Growth of a Movement

In 1978, Saddam Hussein ejected Ruhollah Khomeini from Iraq, leading the Shi'ite holy man to seek refuge in France. In Iran, growing opposition to the shah brought the kingdom to the verge of civil war. Taking advantage of widespread dissatisfaction with the Pahlavi royals and their Western allies, Khomeini used a network of about 12,000 loyal students to propagate his revolutionary ideas. By recording the Ayatollah's sermons onto master audiotapes in France, smuggling them into Iran, then duplicating them, Khomeini's followers organized a strong national movement. Though not all Iranians embraced Khomeini's conservative religious views, many saw him as one who could liberate Iran from the Pahlavis.

By January 1979, opposition to the shah had risen to frenzied levels. With riots and demonstrations popping up across the nation, millions rallied behind the battle cry, "Death to the shah," forcing the Pahlavi monarch to flee for his life. Two weeks later, the Ayatollah Khomeini triumphantly returned to a nation embroiled in revolutionary fervor. Khomeini's students quickly made their presence known by executing members of the shah's notorious Savak secret police and hundreds of others who resisted the Islamic Revolution. With the shah out of the picture and most of Iran's Shi'ite mullahs and laymen behind him, Khomeini's theoretical Rule of the Jurist was becoming a reality.

A "Holy" State and Stately Hostages

On April 1, 1979, a constitution based on Islamic principles was adopted, and Iran was named a theocratic Islamic republic. After forming the Council of Guardians (a group responsible for preserving the republic's Islamic nature), Khomeini gave himself the lifetime position of *faqih,* or expert jurist. As supreme spiritual leader of the modern Middle East's first Islamic republic, the Ayatollah strategically shaped his new state according to strict religious regulations. The republic's new laws included mandatory dress codes, a prohibition of all alcoholic beverages, capital punishment for prostitution and adultery, as well as other mandates aimed at upholding morality. In addition, the conservative regime attempted to purify Iran's foreign policy by ending partnerships with Western and non-Muslim governments.

FACT

In 1980, the phrase *Allahu Akbar* ("God is Great") was added to Iran's flag to recognize the Islamic republic and its supreme leader, the Ayatollah Ruhollah Khomeini.

Though Iran's Islamic Revolution caused great concern in Washington, diplomatic and economic relations continued until November 1979. When the ousted Shah Muhammad Reza Pahlavi was allowed into the United States, some Iranians feared Washington was planning to reinstate him as Iran's leader. In what they viewed as a pre-emptive strike, a group of

Khomeini's students stormed the U.S. Embassy in Tehran. Taking seventy hostages, the group demanded the deposed shah be returned to Iran for trial. Despite continued negotiations, condemnation from the United Nations, threats of military intervention, a failed U.S. attempt to extract the hostages, and the ex-shah's death in July of 1980, Khomeini's militant students held their captives for more than a year.

In the midst of this international crisis, Khomeini endorsed the students' militant actions and accused America of being the "Great Satan." For most Westerners, this episode was instrumental in shaping a view of Iran as a fanatical terrorist state. Unaware of Washington's dealings with the deposed Pahlavi family and previous CIA-sponsored actions inside Iran, most Americans concluded that the Ayatollah was leading a nation of Muslim madmen bent on destroying freedom and democracy. To this day, many Westerners continue to see Iran through the prism of fear, anger, and confusion that was formed during this unfortunate affair.

Ayatollahs and Politics

About one month after the American hostages were taken in Tehran, the Soviets invaded Afghanistan. With Cold War rivalries complicating matters, the Islamic Republic of Iran found itself precariously situated between the superpowers. Was Moscow hoping to use Afghanistan as an eastern staging area for an all-out invasion of Iran? If so, would the Americans overlook the hostage crisis to aid Tehran against the Soviets? Believing Soviet leaders were planning to seize Iran's oil reserves, Washington issued the 1980 Carter Doctrine, warning that any outside attempt to control the Persian Gulf would be viewed as an assault on U.S. interests and would be met with military force. Whether or not the USSR was planning to occupy Iran, Soviet troops remained in Afghanistan for nearly a decade of costly conflict.

Though threats from Washington and Moscow were of great concern, Iran's attention was quickly diverted next door, to Baghdad. With Shi'ite Muslims accounting for more than half of the Iraqi population, Iran's Shi'ite-led Islamic revolution was an exciting and inspirational event. In addition, Khomeini's intentional efforts to spread the revolution into Iraq made Saddam Hussein's secular regime extremely nervous. With Iran's conservative religious government calling the Iraqi regime "infidels" and the Iraqi administration supporting Iran's Kurdish and Arab separatists, regional tensions quickly escalated.

Iran's official language, known as modern Persian or Farsi, is also widely spoken in Afghanistan (where it is called Dari) and Tajikistan (where it is simply referred to as Tajik).

Nasty Neighbors

By the summer of 1980, a type of political/religious population exchange was underway, as the Iraqi government deported thousands of Shi'ites (many of them Iranian nationals) to Iran, while Iranian counterrevolutionaries traveled to Iraq to fight against their nation's new Islamic regime. For several months, sporadic skirmishes broke out in border areas until Iraq launched a full invasion on September 21.

Though the conflict was initially a dispute between neighboring nations, it quickly grew into a regional and international conflict. In the eyes of many around the globe, this was a clash between secularism and religious revivalism. Though some attempted to paint the conflict as Arab versus Persian or Sunni versus Shi'ite, most looked beyond ethnic or denominational distinctions. Many Arabs and Sunnis supported the Ayatollah as a symbol of pure Islamic resurgence, while many others stood behind Saddam Hussein as the defender of secular nationalism.

Given the Islamic Republic of Iran's apparent volatility, most Western governments sided with Iraq's Ba'th Party as the more stable regime. With American hostages being held in Iran, Washington covertly supplied the Iraqis. By the summer of 1981, the Reagan administration had also complied with a number of Iran's requests (including a large sum of cash and weapons), and the hostages were released. Though this arms-for-hostages arrangement gave Iran a boost, increased American aid to Iraq created a bloody balance of power.

Trouble in Paradise

With Iran at war with Saddam and friends, the Islamic republic's administration was threatened from the inside. Though the Faqih or "Leader of the Islamic Revolution" enjoyed supreme authority over the state, in December 1979, a new constitution created the office of president to oversee certain administrative affairs. In January 1980, Abolhassan Bani-Sadr (a Western-educated liberal) was elected president, while conservative clerics won the majority in Iran's parliament.

FACT

The British novelist Salman Rushdie released a book entitled *The Satanic Verses* in 1988. Because of the book's portrayal of Muhammad, the Qur'an, and Islam, the Ayatollah Ruhollah Khomeini issued a fatwa, or religious ruling, in 1989 calling for the author's death. Though Rushdie is neither of Iranian descent nor nationality, Khomeini's ruling continues to threaten this controversial writer wherever he goes.

Opposed to Bani-Sadr's "un-Islamic" policies, the clergy-run parliament appointed a like-minded prime minister. Within a year, Bani-Sadr was pushed from power and Prime Minister Rajai took over the presidency. Two months later, the new President Rajai was assassinated, and by October 1981 the Ayatollah Ali Khamenei had been elected as Iran's third president.

To curtail Iraq's massive petroleum exports, the Islamic republic expanded its efforts to include oil tankers and platforms in the Persian (Arab) Gulf. As a result, both the Iraqi and Iranian oil industries were brought to a grinding halt. With the flow of Middle Eastern oil threatened, international involvement increased throughout the 1980s. After eight years of hardship and the war with Iraq, Iran's economy was in ruins, hundreds of thousands were dead, and close to a million others were wounded. Eager to stop the madness, Iran's citizens convinced their leaders to make peace with the Iraqi "infidels."

Switching Supreme Leaders

On June 4, 1989, less than a year after ending the war with Iraq, Iran's eighty-seven-year-old supreme leader passed away. With Khomeini's death, President Ayatollah Ali Khamenei was appointed supreme leader of the revolution. The following month, Ali Akbar Hashemi Rafsanjani was elected as the republic's fourth president. Himself a moderate cleric keen to implement modernization, Rafsanjani was forced to balance personal views with those of his conservative colleagues. While walking a fine line between compromise and conviction, the new Iranian president expanded his powers, eliminated the office of prime minister, and improved relations with several Western governments.

Though relations with the United States improved slightly during the early years of Rafsanjani's presidency, by the mid-1990s allegations of an Iranian nuclear arms development program changed everything. In 1995, U.S. President Bill Clinton cut all ties with Iran, accusing the Islamic republic of developing weapons of mass destruction and supporting international terrorism. The following year, a U.S.–sponsored trade embargo made it illegal for any company (American or otherwise) operating in the United States to do business with Iran. Despite the embargo, Russia agreed to build a nuclear power plant in southwestern Iran.

Iran's attempts to acquire enriched uranium for its atomic energy program have raised international suspicions that the Islamic republic may be seeking to develop nuclear weapons as well. In 2003, the International Atomic Energy Agency (IAEA) challenged the Iranian leadership to make their nuclear aspirations clear or face serious repercussions.

Winds of Change

Though the people of Iran transformed their nation from a constitutional monarchy to an Islamic republic, the leadership of Iran transformed a "theocracy" into a clerical dictatorship. After the death of Ayatollah Ruhollah Khomeini in 1989, popular support for the new supreme leader,

Ayatollah Ali Khamenei, and his conservative mullahs quickly dwindled. By the early 1990s, even the former supreme leader's son, Ahmad Khomeini, opposed Iran's leadership. In response, Khamenei's regime had Ahmad Khomeini assassinated on March 18, 1995.

A New President

In 1997, Iran elected Muhammad Khatami as the republic's fifth president. Having campaigned on a platform of tolerance and social reform, this moderate Shi'ite cleric touched on the pulse of a population ready for change. Though Khatami was the son of an ayatollah and was himself a *hojatolisalm* (distinguished Shi'ite title, just below that of ayatollah), his theological and philosophical studies produced more moderate views than those of his predecessors.

As Iran's new head of government, Khatami appointed a moderate cabinet, loosened restrictions on certain books, newspapers, films, and so on, and allowed new political parties to be licensed. In addition, President Khatami sought to improve damaged relations with the United States and other Western nations. Though conservative mullahs continued to impose repressive laws on an increasingly unhappy population, Khatami's reforms gave many Iranians hope for the future.

FACT

Today about 90 percent of Iranians are Shi'ite Muslims and 9 percent are Sunni Muslims, while Christians, Jews, Zoroastrians, and members of the Baha'i movement together make up 1 percent of the population.

Through the late 1990s, Khamenei's totalitarian rule caused many Iranians to reject his authority and that of the Council of Guardians. Despite growing dissatisfaction on the Iranian streets, conservative clerics continued their oppressive acts into the twenty-first century, leading four prominent ayatollahs to deny Khamenei's position as supreme leader of the Islamic Revolution.

Ripe for Reform

In 2003, the late Ayatollah Khomeini's grandson—Husayn Khomeini—voiced his opposition to Khamenei and his mullahs, calling them "the world's worst dictatorship." As a symbol of his defiance, the prominent Shi'ite figure moved from Iran to Iraq, where he declared, "Iran needs democracy and separation of religion and state." In addition, Khomeini warned of an eminent popular movement in which Iran's clerical regime would be removed.

With members of the deposed Pahlavi family campaigning around the world for a democratic Iran, the conservative clerics might have reason to be concerned. As exiles in the National Council of Resistance of Iran (NCRI) make detailed plans to replace their nation's theocracy with a representative government, the "godly" governors are likely grumbling. The continued deployment of American troops to his east, in Afghanistan, and to his west, in Iraq, should leave the supreme leader slightly scared. Accusations from the Ayatollah Khomeini's grandson might create a bit of anxiety, but it is the frustration of roughly 70 million Iranian citizens that could bring an end to Khamenei's fanatical fraternity.

As the thirteenth century Persian poet Sa'di Shirazi put it,

All human beings are in truth akin;
All in creation share one origin.
When fate allots a member pangs and pains,
No ease for other members then remains.
If, unperturbed, another's grief canst scan,
Thou are not worthy of the name of man.

Whether or not Iran's conservative Islamic regime is replaced through a popular uprising, the leadership of this nation must respect the people they are leading, including those with different ideologies and ethnicities.

Chapter 18

Turkey—Modern and Democratic

For nearly 500 years, Istanbul stood as the center of Ottoman power, until the twentieth century, when the empire went down in flames. From these ashes, Ankara rose as the capital of a new and vibrant Turkish republic. Only eighty years after its triumphant birth, the Republic of Turkey is a young developing nation with the potential to rise above its neighbors as the first successful Middle Eastern democracy.

Young Turk Takeover

After nearly 600 years of Ottoman rule, many of the empire's European subjects exchanged their imposed "Ottoman" identity for an ethnically based national consciousness. In 1912, these sentiments led to a war of independence in the Balkans, which produced the sovereign states of Bulgaria, Greece, Montenegro, and Serbia. In North Africa, French troops occupied the former Ottoman territories of Algeria and Tunisia, while Italian forces took what is now Libya as well as the Dodecanese Islands in the Aegean Sea.

With the new Balkan nations formed from his northwest territories, European-controlled North Africa eroding his southwestern lands, and the Italians occupying the Aegean region on his western shores, the Ottoman sultan was threatened by Arab nationalism throughout his southeastern territories. In addition, the sultan was challenged at his doorstep, as Turkish nationalism spread through the streets of Istanbul and the villages of Anatolia.

Known to outsiders as "Young Turks," the Committee of Union and Progress (CUP) was an underground movement of fierce Turkish nationalists. Opposed to the sultan's tyrannical rule, CUP members sought to expel the despotic Ottoman family and re-establish the 1877 Constitution, while reviving the ancient glory of the Turkish people.

Nationalism

Nationalist-inspired pan-Turkism, or "pan-Turanism" (derived from "Turan," name of the Central Asian Turkish motherland), celebrated Turkish culture and ethnicity, but the movement also looked to establish a Turkish homeland stretching from Eastern Europe to western China. With ethnically Turkic populations in Austrian-administered Hungary, Ottoman Anatolia, Russian-ruled Central Asia, Qajar-controlled Persia, and the newly established Republic of China, the massive pan-Turkish nation would have to be taken by force.

By 1913, the CUP members' control of the parliament had placed their own leaders above the sultan. Looking to strengthen the empire's military capabilities, CUP leaders worked closely with Great Britain and Germany.

Before Turkish nationalists could extend their powers into Turkic Central Asia and beyond, trouble in the Balkans set off an international conflict of global proportions.

Fatal Friendship

As World War I erupted in the summer of 1914, Istanbul's nationalist regime remained neutral. Through the first months of the war, Berlin wooed CUP leaders to its side, while London made several moves that disappointed the Turkish administration. By November, the Ottoman Empire had sided with Berlin and the Central Powers over the Allied Nations, which included Russia, a longtime Ottoman enemy, as well as Italy, France, and Great Britain, all occupiers of Ottoman territories.

Known for centuries as Asia Minor or Anatolia, the modern nation of Turkey (*Türkiye* in Turkish) was so named because of its large population of ethnic Turks.

Though Istanbul's alliance with the Kaiser led to a series of blistering defeats and, ultimately, the fall of the empire, Turkish forces scored one decisive victory in 1915 at the Dardanelles Strait. As the first stage of an elaborate plan to link Allied supply lines in the Mediterranean with Russia's Black Sea ports, British commanders sent lightly armed men from the Australia New Zealand Army Corps (ANZAC) to take the beaches of Gallipoli.

Foreseeing limited Ottoman resistance at the Dardanelles, British planners believed Turkish defenses would be concentrated at Istanbul's Bosporus waterway. To their surprise, ANZAC forces met heavy fire from Turkish artillery. After eight months of intense fighting and a quarter of a million Allied casualties, the invaders were forced to flee. As commander of this important victory, Mustafa Kemal became the champion of Turkish nationalism and (after the fall of the Ottoman Empire) the harbinger of postwar independence.

From the Ashes of Empire

In the fall of 1918, Germany accepted defeat, bringing an end to World War I. As one of the conquered Central Powers, the Ottoman Empire was forced to cede its predominately Arab provinces to the British and French, while accepting the presence of foreign troops in Istanbul and throughout Asia Minor. In 1920, with the empire's territory reduced to non-Arab Anatolia and a small piece of southeastern Europe, the sultan sent representatives to France to discuss a postwar resolution. Instead of offering Istanbul reasonable terms for a peaceful settlement, the Allies (minus Russia and the United States) presented their firm plans to dissolve the remaining imperial lands. Known as the Treaty of Sèvres, the treaty accepted by the Ottoman emissaries included the following points:

- Greece would gain the empire's remaining Eastern European lands, as well as most of Anatolia's Aegean coast.
- Italy was to be given southwestern Anatolia and its Mediterranean coast.
- France would connect south-central Anatolia to its existing Syrian Mandate area.
- Eastern Anatolia would be divided into independent Armenian and Kurdish states (monitored by the French).
- A swath of land connecting the important Bosporus and Dardanelles waterways (including the city of Istanbul) was to be under international control.
- A Turkish-controlled region would remain in a small portion of central Anatolia.

Picking Up the Pieces

Though the sultan embraced this treaty, Turkish nationalists refused to accept the division of their homeland. With the world's most powerful governments arrayed against them, patriotic Turkish men and women rallied behind their celebrated war hero, Mustafa Kemal, in a war of independence. After establishing a new parliament, known as the Turkish Grand National Assembly, Kemal and his followers set out to reclaim their territories and establish a Turkish state. By the summer of 1922, after winning several important victories in western Anatolia, Turkish forces stormed the city of Smyrna (now Izmir), pushing the Greek military into the sea.

After reclaiming the entire Aegean coast, Kemal's patriots looked north to the Dardanelles and Istanbul, where Allied troops were protecting the "international" waterway. Recognizing the rising tide of Turkish resistance, Allied forces fled their northern positions, followed soon by troops in the southern Italian zone and the French areas. Using his World War I hero status, Mustafa Kemal concentrated the popular power of Turkish pride to out-spirit, outwit, and outmaneuver the world's most powerful nations. Utilizing his new role as savior, Kemal encouraged the Turkish Grand National Assembly to end the more than six centuries of Ottoman rule. On November 1, 1922, the sultanate was abolished.

Republic Rising

With Turkish nationalists controlling most of Anatolia, a new peace conference was held in Lausanne, Switzerland, to replace the failed Sèvres arrangement. By the summer of 1923, after eight months of deliberation, the Treaty of Lausanne was signed, ensuring Turkish sovereignty in Anatolia and a portion of southeastern Europe. In addition, Turkish and Greek officials arranged a "population exchange," in which Greek-speaking Christians in Western Anatolia were uprooted from their homes and sent to Greece, while Turkish-speaking Muslims were pulled from Greece and transported to Anatolia.

FACT

In the early 1920s, Turkish and Greek leaders organized a "population exchange" in which more than a million ethnic Greeks were forced to leave Turkey, while close to 500,000 ethnic Turks were compelled to vacate their homes in Greece.

With the Ottoman regime removed, nationalism at frenzied levels, and Turkish sovereignty recognized by the world's most powerful nations, the empire's ashes were stirring. On October 29, 1923, new life arose as the

Grand National Assembly (GNA) declared the long-awaited Republic of Turkey, with Mustafa Kemal as its first president. Because Istanbul had been the center of Ottoman might for nearly five centuries, the GNA chose the city of Ankara, deep within Turkish Anatolia, as the infant republic's capital.

Atatürk's Radical Reforms

As president, forty-two-year-old Mustafa Kemal assumed the arduous task of rebuilding an impoverished nation, depleted by years of war, decades of poor administration, and (in his estimation) centuries of social stagnation. At his core, Kemal believed Western civilization was superior to the Ottoman state's Islamic civilization. In his view, the Ottomans had forsaken their rich Turkish heritage for backward Arab customs and ideologies. By reviving ancient Central Asian culture and embracing European constructs, the new republic would join the great nations of the world as a proud and prosperous Turkish state.

Though Kemal was the son of Turkish-speaking parents, he was born and raised outside of Anatolia, in the Ottoman-controlled city of Salonika (contemporary Thessaloniki, Greece). As a young officer in the Ottoman army, Mustafa learned to despise the empire's inefficient bureaucracy and archaic traditions. At the same time, the young Turk developed a fascination with modern Western nations and their successful secular regimes. While studying the works of Enlightenment-era philosophers and political theorists (such as Jean-Jacques Rousseau and Thomas Hobbes), Kemal solidified his belief in the separation of religion and state, as well as many other physiological, sociological, and political principles.

Influenced by the controversial Turkish nationalist and sociologist Ziya Gökalp, Kemal decided to avoid the slow and less abrasive process of making small-scale modern adjustments. Instead, the patriotic citizens of Turkey were given a type of "civilization transplant," affecting nearly every area of their lives. Of Kemal's many revolutionary reforms, the disentanglement of religious and public life was his first and most passionate order of business.

The Assembly's Disassembly

Similar to Islamic Iran's devotion to its divinely guided supreme leader, the Ottomans secured their subjects' complete devotion by combining the royal position of sultan and the divinely endowed office of caliph. Though the GNA abolished the Ottoman sultanate in 1922, the caliph was allowed to remain as a religious figurehead. Despite the caliphate's pan-Islamic significance, Turkey's secular regime viewed it as a symbol of outmoded Ottoman theocracy. On March 3, 1924, the GNA abolished the caliphate along with several other religious/political offices.

The abolition of the pan-Islamic office of caliph was a massive cultural shakeup in Turkey. From the 1928 birth of Egypt's antisecularist Muslim Brotherhood to Osama bin Laden's current contempt for Turkish "apostasy," the aftershocks of this cultural temblor continue to rock the Middle East and the world.

With the most important Ottoman political and religious institutions removed, Kemal and the GNA continued their secularization campaign by abolishing state-sponsored Islamic schools and courts, dissolving the Ministry of Waqfs (religious endowments), banning religious brotherhoods, and closing sacred shrines. Though Ottoman reformers had introduced some European-style laws, the GNA entirely replaced the nation's "God-given" laws with secular European codes. In this widespread regulatory overhaul, polygamy was outlawed, Muslims were given the right to change their religion, and women were given equal rights in certain areas.

In 1925 the state moved further into its citizens' private lives by outlawing the fez (a flowerpot-like head covering worn by Muslim men throughout the Ottoman Empire) and forcing men to wear Western-style brimmed hats. For conservative Muslims, brimmed hats were unacceptable, as they would hamper proper prostration during prayers. In addition, Kemal encouraged Turkish women to leave their veils at home. For traditionalists, this request was as risqué as asking Western women to bare their breasts.

New Speak—Renewed Identity

Though the Turkish language has been spoken for thousands of years, it was without a written form until migrating Turks met Arabic-speaking Muslims. As a result, Turkish was rendered on paper for the first time with Arabic characters. Viewing the Arabic script as a cumbersome foreign influence, Kemal adopted the Latin alphabet used by most Western nations. Seeing the Arabic language as archaic and alien, the Turkish president ordered the Qur'an to be translated into Turkish, while the call to prayer (recited throughout the world in Arabic) was to be done only in the Turkish language.

As part of Kemal's ardent nationalist agenda, the Turkish language was to be "purified" of non-Turkish words borrowed from Arabic and Persian. Cities with non-Turkish names were given Turkish names. Thus, the Greek city of Smyrna was called Izmir, Armenian Antep became Gaziantep, and so on. History books were rewritten to present Turkic tribes as the source of world civilizations and to establish an ancient Turkish presence in Anatolia. Though his nationalist predecessors envisioned a massive pan-Turkic nation, Kemal focused on a much smaller Anatolian Turkish homeland.

FACT

Though experts say the first Turkic tribes migrated from Central Asia to Anatolia as early as A.D. 1000, many Turks believe ancient Anatolia's Hittite peoples (2000 to 1200 B.C.) were Turkish.

With an increasingly unified national identity, Turkey continued to synchronize itself with European ideologies and institutions. Among Kemal's many changes was the calendar. The lunar Islamic calendar (based on Muhammad's escape from Mecca to Medina) was replaced by the internationally recognized solar Gregorian calendar (centered on the birth of Jesus Christ). In a further attempt to align Turkey with Western markets, Kemal established the Saturday and Sunday "*vikend,*" making the Friday prayer day a workday. As if these changes didn't make the point abundantly clear, the clause recognizing Islam as Turkey's state religion was deleted from the country's constitution in 1928.

New Names

From his personal affection for Western clothing and entertainment to his love for Turkish *raki* (a distilled liquor with strong anise flavor) and *meze* (Middle Eastern–style dips and appetizers), Mustafa Kemal was a man of modern ambitions and ethnic pride. As a testament of this unique fusion of philosophies, in 1934 a law was passed requiring all citizens to adopt Turkish surnames. Though last names were a Western phenomenon, this directive was also meant to unify the nation with a single Turkish identity.

In accordance with the surname law, Kemal took on the name *Atatürk*, meaning "Father of the Turks." Though the term "Father" is a fitting title for someone who secures a national homeland, no word or phrase can express the undying respect, admiration, and love most Turks feel for this man. Though Atatürk departed this world on November 11, 1938, his grand vision and attitudes are alive to this day.

Kemalist Clergy

After Atatürk's untimely death, his right-hand man Ismet Inönü and other like-minded leaders continued preaching the message of modernism, secularism, and nationalism. As the protectors of Kemal's adolescent secular nation, Turkey's leaders were left with many difficult decisions. Though Atatürk's sweeping changes paved the way for a future Western-style democracy, many social and economic issues stood in the way.

Despite popular support for Kemal's secular system, the threat of Islamic extremism worried the green administration. Atatürk's efforts to create a strong national identity encouraged most citizens to place tribal and ethnic allegiances on the back burner, but subversive movements continued to menace Turkish national unity (especially in the east). Believing the young state was not yet ready for full democracy, Kemal's successors implemented strict controls over their citizens.

On July 25, 1951, Turkey adopted Statute 5816, which states, "Anyone who publicly insults or curses the memory of Atatürk shall be imprisoned with a heavy sentence of between one and three years." While this may seem harsh, more severe punishments are doled out for defacing or destroying statues, busts, or representations of the late Mustafa Kemal Atatürk.

Out of the Darkness into the Fire

For nearly a decade, xenophobic and ethnocentric leaders closed Turkey off to many outside influences, curbing Kemal's cosmopolitan vision. After World War II a ray of light was allowed in as Turkey became a charter member of the United Nations. The following year, in 1947, Turkey accepted economic and military aid from the United States, which hoped to gain Ankara's allegiance against the communists. While administrators tried not to take sides in the Soviet-American Cold War competition, things changed as Turkish troops entered the Korean War. By 1951, after a year of bloody conflict against communists, Turkey made its position abundantly clear by joining the anticommunist North Atlantic Treaty Organization (NATO).

In 1950, Turkey's first open elections saw the opposition Democratic Party defeat President İnönü and the ruling People's Republican Party. Over the next decade, Prime Minister Adnan Menderes and the Democrats relaxed many of Atatürk's secularist policies while at the same time creating new laws to ensure the absolute authority of the state. Focusing on health care, education, and infrastructure, the new government moved to modernize both the cities and villages of Anatolia. These massive development programs inched Turkey closer to Kemal's modernist dream, however Ankara's habitual overspending created devastating inflation and left many laborers unpaid.

By 1960, a deteriorating economy and dissatisfaction among Turkey's emerging young intellectuals and professionals had moved Prime Minister Menderes to seek the support of Turkey's more conservative rural populations. As a result, the Democratic Party moved further away from Atatürk's secularism toward a more pro-Islamic stance. Concerned by the government's blatant disregard for foundational Kemalist principles, the Turkish military stepped in to protect their savior's secular state.

Politicians, God, and Generals

On May 27, 1960, a second Turkish republic was born as General Cemal Gürsal and his National Unity Committee wrested power from the deviant Democrats. To punish those who had strayed from Kemal's pure path, the High Court of Justice was established. In the end, close to 600 Democratic leaders were found guilty, leading to the execution of Prime Minister Menderes and eleven others.

In an effort to avoid future wandering from the true Kemalist track, a new constitution was drafted, the GNA was split into a two-chamber parliament, and a protective Constitutional Court was created. Though former President Inönü was narrowly re-elected as Turkey's premier, just four years later the conservative Justice Party (basically a revamped Democratic Party) and its leader, Suleyman Demirel, were voted into power.

Over the next five years, Turkey's political situation spiraled out of control. Clashes between rightists (often Sunni Muslims) and leftists (largely from the heterodox Alevi tradition) left thousands dead, threatening the unity of Kemal's secular state. Recurring urban terror attacks, growing unrest among the impoverished, and violent Kurdish separatist groups challenged the government's authority and competency. In 1971, the military once again used its might to secure the floundering state, as martial law was imposed and Prime Minister Demirel was forced to resign.

After the fall of the Soviet Union, Turkish nationalists revived pan-Turkic passions by establishing ties with the newly independent Central Asian republics. As the ancestral Turkic homeland, Turkey gave financial and logistical support to countries such as Kazakhstan and Turkmenistan. In addition, Ankara hoped these nations would see Turkey as a secular, modern, and Muslim example.

The 1973 elections brought the People's Republican Party and its leader, Bülent Ecevit, into power. Within a year, Turkey was at war in Cyprus over Greek plans to annex the island's largely Turkish northern region. Though Turkish victories in Cyprus revived nationalist pride, political, religious, and ideological differences ignited a new period of civil unrest within the year. This ended in 1980 with yet another military coup and period of martial law. With General Kenan Evren in charge, civil order was restored, thousands (including GNA leaders) were arrested, a new constitution was created, and the parliament was reduced to a single chamber.

Following the 1983 elections, civilian rule was re-established as the new Motherland Party gained control of the Grand National Assembly. As centrists, the Motherland Party sought to end Turkey's internal feuds (conservative versus liberal, East versus West, and religious versus secular) by focusing on compromise and reconciliation. In the words of Motherland Party leader and former Prime Minister Turgut Özal, "Turkey has no further need of reforms or continual revolution . . . Freedom of thought and speech, freedom of religion together with secularism as its guarantee, and freedom of enterprise will lead us to become a great civilized and civilizing power once again."

Internal Struggle—East or West?

From the birth of the republic, Mustafa Kemal clearly stated his desire to see Turkey Westernized and modernized to the level of European nations. Though Atatürk died before realizing his dream, others proudly carried the baton. As a founding member of the United Nations and the only predominately Muslim nation in NATO, Turkey became an important bridge between the Muslim East and Christian West. By 1959, formal economic bridges were also extended westward as Turkey applied for full membership in the newly established European Economic Community (EEC). Without granting Turkey full membership, the 1963 Ankara Agreement and 1970 Protocol paved the way for Turkey's gradual integration into the EEC.

In 1993, European Economic Community (EEC) members formed the supranational European Union (EU). As the EEC's longest standing associate member, Turkey applied for full membership in the new coalition. Though the EU continued to strengthen ties with Turkey, a number of social and economic concerns kept the European powerhouse from giving Ankara a definitive answer. While many Turks believed membership in the EU would cure Turkey's economic crisis, some looked east to Islam for their salvation.

ALERT!

Many Americans are surprised to hear that Turkey has surpassed the United States in its empowerment of women. In 1993, Tansu Çiller was elected as Turkey's first female prime minister, while Washington has yet to see even a female vice president.

Example or Disgrace?

In the 1995 elections, East/West differences came to a head as the pro-Islamist Welfare Party ousted Tansu Çiller (Turkey's first female prime minister) from power. In response, two moderately conservative parties formed a coalition against the victorious Welfare Party, temporarily keeping the Islamists from controlling the government. Within a year this partnership fell apart, allowing Necettim Erbakan and his Welfare Party to set up the Turkish republic's first pro-Islamic government.

Statements from Prime Minister Erbakan like, "We will create an Islamic currency . . . an Islamic United Nations, an Islamic NATO, and an Islamic version of the EU," startled European leaders already hesitant about bringing Turkey into their ranks. Erbakan's promises to reclaim Jerusalem for Islam and save Turkey from the European "infidels" worried leaders around the world. With Atatürk likely turning over in his grave, Turkey's Kemalist generals once again intervened, forcing Erbakan to step down in 1997. In the following year, Kemalists banned Erbakan's Welfare Party (the largest group in Parliament), moving the elderly Bülent Ecevit back to the post he had filled in the 1970s.

The Kurdish Question

As Kemalists worked to salvage their damaged image in the West, the opportunity arose to capture republic enemy number one, Kurdish guerilla leader Abdullah Öcalan. Though Öcalan's arrest and punishment would likely ruffle the feathers of European human rights groups and politicians, Kemalists' hatred for this man was greater than any political or economic concerns.

Since the early 1980s, Öcalan and his Kurdistan Worker's Party (PKK) militia had waged a bloody war of independence in Turkey's eastern provinces. Viewed as terrorists by most Turks and as freedom fighters by many Europeans, the Kurdish question was an extremely touchy issue for both sides. In the face of imminent European condemnation, Turkish commandos (likely with the aid of American and Israeli operatives) extracted the Kurdish leader from his refuge at the Greek embassy in Nairobi, Kenya. A truly international affair, Öcalan's arrest touched off a global firestorm of finger-pointing and scolding, but in Turkey it was celebrated as if they had won the World Cup.

ALERT!

Head coverings mean different things for women in different countries. If an Iranian woman wears a veil, she may or may not be a pious Muslim. As a citizen of the Islamic Republic of Iran, she is following the norm for women in her country. If a Turkish woman wears a veil, she is more than likely making a statement of her conservative Islamic views. As a citizen of the secular Republic of Turkey, her modest dress is going against the modernist grain.

After Turkey's celebrations subsided, and the "terrorist" mastermind was issued a death sentence, European pressure (and Öcalan's willingness to do anything to save his neck) moved Ankara to reduce his punishment to life in prison. With their leader's life secured, PKK rebels ended more than fifteen years of armed struggle as they laid down their weapons and agreed to work peacefully within the Turkish political system. Ironically, the year that began with harsh European criticisms of Ankara's actions ended with a conditional invitation for Turkey to eventually become a full member of the European Union.

Sacred and Secular Synthesized?

The dawn of the twenty-first century produced more of the same as the pro-Islamic Virtue Party was banned from the GNA but the Islamic-based Saadet Party was born. Hoping to improve their chances for EU membership, Turkish officials abolished the death penalty, removed laws recognizing men as "head of the household," gave women full legal equality, and lifted restrictions on Kurdish broadcasting and education.

After winning the 2002 elections, the pro-Islamic Justice and Development Party replaced the aged Bülent Ecevit and his secularist People's Republican Party. Though viewed with suspicion by many in the West, Justice and Development Party leaders unveiled a synthesis of East/West orientations, promising to promote Islamic values while adhering to the secular principles of Turkey's constitution. As prime minister, Recep Erdogan set out to bridge the gap between modern secular urbanites and the more traditional and conservative rural populations. Though many continue to question the sincerity of the Justice and Development Party's secularist claims, it seems for now that they have reached a healthy balance between Turkey's cultural and ideological extremes.

One Nation Looking Forward

As one of the Middle East's most strategic nations, Turkey sits on the edge of two continents and two civilizations. Turkey's pro-Western and secular foundations are unique for the region, but the nationwide esteem for Mustafa Kemal Atatürk is the republic's most distinctive quality. Just as religious texts are interpreted in many ways, Kemal's vision for Turkey has been construed in many ways over the past seven decades.

Many Questions

With the people of Turkey intimately attached to Atatürk's memory, the nation's future will be based in some fashion on Kemalist ideologies, but what will that look like? If Kemal envisioned a secular state, is there any role for Islam in that state? If Atatürk wanted his nation to be modern, what exactly is modernity for this Middle Eastern nation? If the "Father of the Turks" desired democracy, should the Turkish people be allowed to choose an Islamic republic? These are just a few of the questions that arise as leaders attempt to marry Atatürk's noble plans with Turkey's contemporary complexities.

Since Persian and Greek armies clashed on the Aegean coast nearly 2,500 years ago, Anatolia has remained a vital link between Europe and Asia. Though Ankara is allied with the United States, Washington's regional plans are often at odds with Turkish public opinion. Once again in the middle, Turkish leaders are placed in the precarious position of maintaining their valuable relationship with the United States, while avoiding unpopular decisions that could create instability and give extremists a platform for critique.

**E
ALERT!**

Though European culture has greatly influenced Turkey, today the tides are changing. In 2003, Turkish pop star Sertab Erener surpassed artists from twenty-five other nations to win the coveted Eurovision title. Known as "Turkey's Shakira," Sertab is one of several Turkish superstars, like male vocalist Tarkan or the edgy punk rock group Athena, who have gained huge success in Europe and around the globe.

Improving relations with Greece (Turkey's traditional enemy to the west) and renewed ties to Iran (the despised radical regime to the east) provide a glimpse of the powerful role Turkey could play in the region. Though Ankara has loosened restrictions on its ethnic and religious minority groups, many Europeans feel the republic has a long way to go before it can be a stable partner. With widespread unemployment and hyperinflation leaving the Turkish economy well below European standards, many wonder if this nation will ever meet the criteria set by EU officials.

Poised for Success

In the face of Turkey's perplexing problems, one word encapsulates this proud people—potential! No matter how bad things have been, Turkey has the tools to become one of the world's most powerful nations.

Turkey's highly educated, free thinking, and cosmopolitan thirty-something crowd is eagerly waiting to make its mark as the authoritarian ways of an aged political establishment are proving inadequate. With more than half of Turkey's citizens under the age of twenty-five, a massive population of intelligent, techno-savvy, and stylish youth is preparing for change.

FACT

In 1970, fourteen Turkish lira (TL) were equal to one U.S. dollar. Today, as a result of hyperinflation, one dollar will now get you about 1.5 million TL.

If twentieth-century totalitarian tactics are forsaken, and a new generation is empowered with "freedom of thought, speech, religion, and enterprise," then these words of Motherland Party's Turgut Özal will be more than rhetoric. Though ethnic and religious distinctions may have threatened the Turkish identity eighty years ago, today these differences can be celebrated within one powerful and self-confident nation. When the multiethnic and multireligious people of Turkey are allowed to live freely without fear, then Atatürk's dream will finally become a reality, and Turkey will lead the region into a new era of peace and prosperity.

Chapter 19

E Tackling the Tough Issues

Now that you've been introduced to the Middle East's heritage, peoples, cultures, history, and politics, it is necessary to examine a few of the larger concepts that define the region and perplex the West. From the shame/honor-based worldview, which can move a father to kill his beloved daughter in the name of family honor, to the monumental issues moving Western and Islamic civilizations to the brink of catastrophe, this chapter will provide valuable insights into this unsettling new millennium.

Understanding Shame/Honor Societies

If you were raised in Europe or North America, you were more than likely taught to value truth and despise deception. As a Westerner, you probably base your decisions on your concept of right and wrong. You do, say, and act as you feel, as long as it doesn't break the law or hurt anyone. If you properly follow the rules, you are innocent; if you knowingly go against these directives, you are guilty.

Though most of the world's cultures recognize a difference between right and wrong, other factors may be of greater importance in their daily lives. For instance, in many African and South American tribal societies, fear of the spirits/gods causes individuals to base their actions on what will anger or appease these powerful beings. If sacrificing an innocent child will convince the gods not to destroy a village, then the infant is killed. By Western standards, the tribal leaders are guilty of murder, but in a fear-based culture they are revered for their heroism.

Some cultures are focused on maintaining honor and avoiding shame. In others, fear of more powerful supernatural forces guides the society, while still others see punishing the guilty and protecting the innocent as their number-one aim. Though most cultures are based on one of these three perspectives, aspects of all three play some role in every civilization.

In the Middle East, India, and most of Asia (including China, Korea, and Japan), yet another worldview places honor above all things. While these societies may fear the wrath of a higher power and punish lawbreakers, they are most concerned with maintaining honor and avoiding shame. Consequently, telling a lie could be viewed as neither right nor wrong but as an honorable action, if it was meant to protect one's group. However, if the deception was selfishly motivated, then it would be considered a shameful act.

Coffee and Confederation

In the Middle East, personal friendships and tribal alliances are fully dependent upon issues of honor and shame. While mutual respect can forge honor-based unions that remain strong for generations, these associations can self-destruct because of a single dishonorable action. The symbolic use of coffee in traditional Bedouin diplomacy provides a clear illustration of this time-honored relational system.

As a sign of his honor and to uphold the reputation of his tribe, a Bedouin man will offer a cup of rich coffee to any passerby. This first cup, known as *salaam* (meaning "peace"), communicates the host's hospitable and nonaggressive intentions. After a period of conversation, the guest may be offered a second cup of coffee, called *sadaqa* (meaning "friendship"). Through this cup, the host recognizes the guest's honorable qualities and conveys his desire to pursue a friendship. If the guest continues to show himself respectable and sincere, then the alliance is sealed with a third cup of coffee. Known as *issayf* (translated "the sword"), this final drink shows the host's willingness to fight alongside his new friend. Unless this person dishonors the host or his tribe, the host is obligated to protect and stand by his friend, even to death.

From the tent of an Arab nomad to the villa of a Turkish nightclub owner, your mannerisms, choice of words, and countless other actions will communicate your level of respect for those around you and the degree to which you should be respected. From insisting that a guest take the best seat in your house to the chair you choose when visiting another person's home, a litany of gestures will convey your desire to honor or dishonor others.

Group Dynamics

In this society, the opinions and norms of one's group often overshadow an individual's personal desires. Whether family, tribe, ethnic group, religious community, or nation, one member's shameful act or victimization dishonors every member. As a result, the group is responsible for restoring its honor. By covering or compensating for the shameful act, honor can be restored, but if this is not an option, the group is obliged to take revenge. Though this arrangement usually ensures stability within a group, tribal/sectarian feuds are often produced by each side's duty to deal with damaged honor.

E ALERT!

There's no "me" in "we"! In shame/honor-based societies, the entire group will feel the repercussions of one member's offense. For instance, if your sister is accused of being promiscuous, and you are engaged to be married, your future in-laws would likely call off the wedding to avoid union with your family's shame.

Because each side feels the need to restore its honor, third-party intervention is often the only way intergroup conflicts can be resolved. In the case of Iraq, Saddam Hussein's tyrannical regime used ruthless measures to maintain order. By suppressing conflicting ethnic, religious, and tribal groups, dictators use fear to dissuade opposing parties from fighting one another. However, if an oppressive ruler is removed or unable to exercise his power, age-old conflicts quickly re-emerge.

While Middle Eastern dictators have employed terror to ensure temporary stability, other leaders have used traditional mediation techniques to reach lasting resolutions. From the wisdom of King Solomon, seen in his response to two women arguing over one baby, to Muhammad's skillful mediation between warring tribes in Arabia, impartial and intelligent leaders have resolved complex conflicts for thousands of years.

In the traditional Palestinian peacemaking process, known as *sulha,* a mediator is chosen not only to determine guilt or innocence but also to uphold familial honor. If the accused is found innocent, the accusers are forced to pay a fee to the accused and their family as a way of restoring damaged honor. If the accused is found guilty, the perpetrator is punished, while his or her family is compelled to pay a fee to the victim and their family. In the end, tribal feuding is averted, as the perpetrator's family is shamed and the victim's family has its honor restored, leaving the shamed group to determine how it will restore honor within itself.

FACT

Though Jordan is in many ways a modern country, with trendy nightclubs, a regional center for human rights, and a king whose first language is English, government officials look the other way as hundreds are killed in the name of family/tribal honor each year. In contrast, many Jordanians, who look to the United States as an example of modernity and human rights, are appalled by the legality of abortion in America and the millions of fetuses aborted each year.

Is Islam a Violent Religion?

If you were in the United States after September 11, 2001, you more than likely heard your share of people asking and answering the question, "Is Islam a violent religion?" Though you likely heard some people explaining the events of September 11 as a natural outgrowth of Islam's inherently militant nature, it is just as likely that you remember others presenting Islam as a religion of peace. So which is it? Can Islam be violent and peaceful at the same time?

This is a difficult question that could be asked of any of the world's major religions. Can any religious tradition be branded "violent" or "peaceful"? A quick review of history reveals periods of violence and peace in nearly every religious tradition. You might be thinking, "What about the battles Muhammad fought—didn't he teach his followers to fight for Islam?" This may be true, but in the Hebrew Scriptures, the Book of Joshua (revered by Jews and Christians alike) is full of death and destruction, with men, women, and children dying at the hands of God's holy warriors. Does this make Judaism an inherently violent religion? Were the Crusades a natural outgrowth of violence condoned by passages in the Bible? What about World War I? With a combined total of 37 million casualties, this European war claimed many more lives than any of Muhammad's desert skirmishes.

Throughout history, billions have died at the hands of Jews and Christians, but few would label Judaism or Christianity as violent religions. Some would argue that God instructed Joshua and his men to kill pagans for a specific purpose and time and that today, Judaism is focused on morality, faith, and peace. Others would say that Jesus Christ introduced nonviolence and personal sacrifice as an alternative to ancient Judaism's "an eye for an eye and a tooth for a tooth" mentality. Nevertheless, individuals from each tradition continue to participate in their nations' armed forces with what they believe to be scriptural and divine backing.

A Matter of Interpretation

In the twenty-first century, most Muslims look to violence found in the Qur'an as something that was necessary for a time. Now that Islam is no longer in danger of extinction, more peaceful methods should be the norm. Though Muhammad fought to resist the enemies of Islam in the seventh century, today the vast majority of Muslims believe their struggle is one of personal purity and devotion.

The Qur'an does call for violence in some circumstances, but it also instructs devotees to be merciful and to seek peaceful resolutions to conflict. Just as a Christian or Jewish person may be compelled to protect his/her nation or family, many Muslims are ready to do the same. This in no way makes Islam, Christianity, or Judaism violent religions. However, because Islamic and Hebrew scriptures reference bloodshed at various points, these traditions may not be wholly considered "peaceful" religions either.

Rather than examining a certain religion's scriptures or history, one may choose to explore the actions of its current adherents. Though the Hebrew and Islamic scriptures apparently condone violence, and though Jews, Christians, and Muslims have taken part in many violent battles, the vast majority of today's Jewish, Christian, and Muslim worshipers are concerned with morality, spirituality, prosperity, and peace. Nevertheless, minorities from each of these traditions believe they have a divine obligation to fight those who oppose or contradict their religious beliefs.

Consider Your Sources

No matter what you see in the news or hear from "experts," not all Muslims are terrorists. Through the media, Westerners have been shown the Muslim hijacker, the Muslim car bomber, and the wild-eyed Muslim revolutionary with Kalashnikov and burning American flag in hand. These are the exception and not the rule. Muslim terrorists do exist, but they only make up about 3 percent of the global Muslim population. Unfortunately, extremists receive most of the media's coverage. Even American terrorists from Christian backgrounds who shoot abortion doctors, bomb government buildings, and massacre their classmates get a good deal of airtime. Does this mean all Americans from Christian backgrounds are terrorists? No. These incidents are seen through the perspective of your everyday experiences dealing with peace-loving Americans.

FACT

According to the U.S. State Department, eleven American civilians are killed each year on average as a result of terrorist attacks outside the United States. By comparison, an average of 20,000 murders occur annually in the United States, and close to 2,000,000 violent crimes are committed each year in this country.

Explosions and acts of terror in the Middle East are newsworthy, but spice-shop owners offering tea and coffee to tourists or poor farmers giving foreigners a meal and a place to sleep don't get the ratings. Without experiencing this hospitality firsthand, it is impossible to fully grasp the peaceful nature of this region. Most Muslims will give you the benefit of the doubt no matter what your nationality or religion. The United States has more violent crime than any Muslim country. Does that mean you should be afraid to step out of your front door? Of course not! Nor should you be fearful of visiting the Middle East. You probably shouldn't run through Gaza City waving an Israeli flag, but you wouldn't drive through an African-American community flying a Confederate flag, either.

Islamic Revivalism and Militancy

Though most Muslims want to live righteous and peaceful lives, some are violently opposed to the West and its influences on the Muslim world.

These revivalists advocate a return to more traditional Islamic values, with many attempting to resurrect seventh-century Arabian civilization. These revivalists believe life was the way God intended it to be during Mohammed's time. Thus they seek to rebuild a type of medieval society in which women are suppressed, men are forced to grow beards, and foreign influences are forbidden.

In addition, individuals with this mindset want their secular governments to give way to theocratic systems in which Islamic law would govern all areas of life. Revivalists are most prevalent in Saudi Arabia, Sudan, Iran, Pakistan, and Algeria, but they can be found in just about any Muslim nation (and many non-Muslim lands). Though most revivalists are willing to accomplish their goals through peaceful methods, they may also take up arms in their religious quest.

A Planet Divided

For extremists, the world is divided into the "House of Islam" (Muslim-controlled areas) and the "House of War" (non-Muslim–controlled lands). In their minds, Muslims must use any means necessary to expand the House of Islam around the globe. If peaceful methods succeed in furthering the cause of Islam, then so be it, but if the spread of Islam is hampered or the Islamic way of life is threatened, "true Muslims" are obliged to fight nonbelievers and apostate Muslims.

QUESTION?

Are many Muslims also part of Al-Qaeda?
Though the media may make it sound otherwise, out of the world's estimated 1,300,000,000 Muslims, only about 5,000 are members of Al-Qaeda.

For Osama bin Laden and his Al-Qaeda cronies, militancy is an honorable answer to the shame brought on their lands by Western cultural, economic, and political dominance. Though most Muslims consider the killing of innocent civilians to be evil and un-Islamic, militant revivalists believe non-Muslims and "backsliding" Muslims are part of an evil conspiracy to rule the world. In their view, a cosmic war is playing out on earth between the forces of good and evil. In this great struggle there are no civilians; everyone is either a partner or an enemy of God. What fair-minded Muslims and non-Muslims view as cowardly acts of terror combatants consider the only honorable response to Western oppression and corruption.

Between Frustration and Aggression

Apart from obvious cultural and religious differences, historical and political barriers have been erected between Middle Eastern and Western peoples. Though most Muslims are not militant revivalists, many are frustrated by what they see as a history of Western domination and exploitation. For millions, the line between frustration and aggression is becoming thinner, though most continue to pursue justice through peaceful methods.

The Crusades began more than 900 years ago, but the memory of this European Christian offensive remains fresh in the minds of many Muslims, Jews, and Middle Eastern Christians. As a symbol of Western aggression, the Crusades are often referenced by present-day clerics who believe American and European governments are against Islam. As the flames of frustration are fanned, many express their anger, but few are ready to kill civilians.

The history of European colonialism is yet another sore point for many. From right-wing fanatics to leftist nationalists in the Middle East, the embarrassment caused by this period has left deep ruts of resentment throughout the region. Blaming colonialists for widespread poverty and political weakness, many Muslims believe the region could thrive if Western "puppet-masters" would cut their strings.

Combined with constrictive controls put in place during the British and French mandates, broken promises and double-dealing during postwar peace conferences have created a shroud of shame across the Middle East that remains to this day. Though Western-inspired nationalist movements eventually produced independent states, most of these countries have been or are currently controlled by repressive regimes (often supported by Western governments).

In the American and European guilt/innocence way of thinking, "collateral damage" (the death of civilians) is excused because the killing is unintentional. In the Middle East's honor/shame mentality, however, it is irrelevant whether or not a person intends to take a life. If someone is killed intentionally or accidentally, their family is not only grieved but also dishonored. The perpetrator is held responsible for their loss, and this death must be avenged.

Clashing Civilizations or Civilized Collaboration?

Since the September 11 attacks, you have more than likely heard people talking about the possible "clash of civilizations." In this scenario, Islamic and Western civilizations would find their differences insurmountable, and because of diametrically opposed agendas, the world would erupt into a global conflict of apocalyptic proportions. Though many doomsday theorists and some religious extremists believe these differences are destined to summon Armageddon, current small-scale tensions don't necessarily spell out World War III.

Though individuals on the edges of the Western and Islamic mainstreams are likely to continue their inflammatory statements and fanatical forecasts, these two great civilizations were formed on the same planet and have the potential to coexist peacefully on that same rock. Sure there are fundamental differences between our cultural constructs, but there are also similarities that can serve as bridges of understanding. The Middle East may never adopt a Western-style democracy, and the United States may never have a Muslim majority, but each can respect the citizens of the other as human beings.

While many Americans are concerned with developing morality, character, and family values, these are already strong points in the Middle East and much of the Muslim world. At the same time, many Middle Easterners admire Westerners for their successful businesses and flourishing economies. If individuals from each camp could focus on their common concerns, each society would benefit, and certain barriers could be dissolved.

These distinct worldviews can work together to avoid a cultural catastrophe, but if they are to enjoy peace and prosperity tough decisions must be made. For the West, this means addressing Middle Eastern frustrations, some of which trace their roots back to the Crusades and colonialism. By recognizing and removing economic, political, and social roadblocks that currently feed popular Middle Eastern disdain, Western governments could help pave the way for a peaceful future. For the Middle East (and the larger Muslim world), peace and prosperity could be realized if the moderate majority decided to reclaim its destiny from the militant minority. Though there are many other factors to consider in this complex issue, one thing is certain. If a clash of civilizations is to be averted, civilized nations must collaborate to see that peace (without terror) and justice (without oppression) are available for all.

Chapter 20

Where's the Peace?

Y ou may be wondering why powerful bodies such as the United States or United Nations can't encourage lasting peace. You may even feel the people of this region are simply choosing war over peace. In reality, the current conflicts are perpetuated by a matrix of complicated factors. In this final chapter, you will be challenged to consider these roadblocks to peace while using your understanding of the region to develop informed opinions and possible resolutions.

Border Disputes

As the twenty-first century moves forward, border disputes continue to breed bloody conflicts in the Middle East. Though the entire region is not ablaze with war, several conflicts are currently raging, a number of others are temporarily in a lull, and many more have the potential to erupt if certain issues are not resolved. Of all the hot spots, the future of Israel/Palestine will guide the future of the entire region.

Though there are many interconnected factors contributing to the Arab-Israeli conflict, the issue of land is one of the most important. For the Arab world, the State of Israel is believed to be wrongfully occupying territories that have been inhabited by Arab Palestinians for more than 1,000 years. In addition, Arab and non-Arab Muslims around the globe believe Jerusalem's Dome of the Rock and al-Aqsa Mosque (located on what is often called the Temple Mount) should be under complete Muslim control, as it is the third holiest site in Islam. At the same time, many Israelis believe the West Bank and Gaza Strip are of strategic importance to Israel's national security. Also, there are many Jews who believe God gave these lands (including the Temple Mount) to the Jewish people and that they are the rightful inhabitants.

ESSENTIAL

The traditional two-state solution calls for a "viable Palestinian state" to be created alongside the existing State of Israel. However, logistical realities hamper this plan, as either the State of Palestine (consisting of the West Bank and Gaza Strip) would be separated by Israeli territory, or the Jewish state would be divided by a Palestinian access road connecting the West Bank and Gaza.

In addition to the ongoing struggle between Arabs and Israelis, the region has been plagued by violent territorial disputes in Western Sahara, Morocco, Algeria, Egypt, Sudan, Yemen, Lebanon, Syria, Turkey, Iraq, Iran, Afghanistan, Pakistan, and more. Within the past fifty years, virtually every nation in the Middle East has been involved in some sort of conflict related to the possession of land. Though several nations have resolved their differences, tensions remain high, and the potential for large-scale war remains ever-present.

So why can't everyone simply agree on a set of internationally recognized borders and move forward in peace and prosperity? As an educated student of the Middle East, you can explore this question by critically evaluating each situation according to its historical, ethno-linguistic, and religious realities. As border disputes continue to breed bloody conflicts, it may be productive for these nations to rethink some of the more problematic political boundaries, which were drawn by Western governments at the close of World War I. Though no one outside of the region should attempt to decide the future borders of these nations, the citizens of the world can use their experiences and ideas to provoke dialogue and inspire creative new pathways for peace.

Ethnic Divisions and Religious Differences

As you now know, the Middle East is not a monolithic Arab Muslim entity. Rather, this region is an ethnic and religious mosaic with vastly different peoples and cultures. Though this diversity has made the Middle East an enchanting and flavorful area, it has also produced a region rife with conflict. When considering the prospects of peace in this corner of the globe, ethnic and religious differences are among the most important issues to understand.

Today most Americans celebrate their nation's ethnic and religious diversity, but less than 150 years ago, Native Americans were slaughtered and forcibly displaced from their ancestral homelands. African-Americans were bought and sold as property, and Irish Catholic immigrants were despised by America's "native" Protestant citizens. Because of ethnic and religious differences, the young nation was nearly torn apart, as civil war and political corruption challenged the unity of the United States. Given time, the United States eventually found ways to work through its problems, emerging as a melting pot of all the world's peoples and cultures.

Similarly, the young nation-states of the Middle East are facing the growing pains of adolescent nationhood. Just as the United States forged through awkward and trying times, the governments of the Middle East are dealing with their own difficult circumstances. Though the international community will play some role in the development of these nations, given time, lasting peace and stability will likely emerge from within.

FACT

In Martin Scorsese's film *Gangs of New York*, the audience is reminded of an often-forgotten period in the mid-1800s when violence and chaos ruled the streets of America's largest city. As corrupt politicians employed crooked cops and powerful gang leaders, bloody street battles raged between those born on American soil and those arriving from Ireland. With the nation descending into civil war, ethnic and religious differences threatened the unity of the United States. Similar circumstances are at work in the Middle East today.

Post-Saddam Iraq

With the destruction of Baghdad's Ba'thist regime, ethnic and religious diversity is now at the center of postwar planning efforts. Unlike Afghanistan, Iraq has many educated people who desire to realize their vision for a post-Saddam Iraq. While many of these individuals and their groups will find common ground and purpose, some ideological divisions could be irreconcilable.

Many experts believe Saddam Hussein's totalitarian rule allowed Iraq to survive as a unified nation despite deep ethnic and religious divides. In fact, some say this type of administration is the only way most Middle Eastern leaders can retain control of their lands. In the case of Saddam's regime, he and the majority of the Revolutionary Command Council were both Arab and Sunni. Ethnically, about 75 percent of Iraqis are Arabs and, as far as religious affiliation, as few as 32 percent are Sunni Muslims. Because of these demographics, there is a constant threat to any regime that would seek to lead these diverse peoples within the current borders of Iraq.

As for the Kurdish regions of Iraq, the question of independence from Arab rule has driven many to resist Baghdad's authority. After years of bloodshed, many Kurds in Turkey have opted for a peaceful existence within the Republic of Turkey in exchange for increased cultural freedoms. However, their brothers and sisters across the border in Iraq have taken a different approach.

Iraqi Kurds have reacted to both Saddam's brutality and American protection by forming a semiautonomous region. Washington's support for Kurdish liberation from Iraq, coupled with the U.S./Kurdish partnership in Operation Iraqi Freedom, have given many a clear view of statehood. Tasting this level of independence has brought most Iraqi Kurds to a point (unlike Kurds in Turkey) where it seems unthinkable to return to any type of long-term non-Kurdish rule.

FACT

Though Washington deems Kurdish separatists in Iraq to be freedom fighters, Kurdish fighters in Turkey are considered terrorists.

With an Iraqi population that is 65 percent Shi'ite, 32 percent Sunni, and 3 percent Christian, religious differences are a major factor in this nation. Since Iraq's birth, Sunnis have ruled over a Shi'ite majority, but with the establishment of the interim Governing Council in July 2003, Shi'ite politicians now hold a majority in the cabinet. Nevertheless, many have denounced these moderate Shi'ite leaders as puppets of the West. In their place, many would like to see more conservative mullahs (religious leaders).

Though many of Iraq's conservative Shi'ites want to see mullahs in power, Western leaders and non-Shi'ite Iraqis fear this scenario would result in an oppressive theocracy. Though a Shi'ite-led Islamic state may be attractive to many of Iraq's 16 million Shi'ites, nearly 9 million Sunnis and other non-Arabs and non-Muslims are not willing to live in a religious Shi'ite state.

ALERT!

Most Shi'ites are not fanatics. Though Americans and Europeans often associate Shi'ites with Iran's Islamic Revolution of 1979 and the ensuing hostage crisis, many modern Shi'ites are moderate and even liberal in their interpretation of Islam.

Currently, Iraqis from varied ethnic and religious backgrounds are unified in their desire to see Western forces withdraw from their country as soon as possible. But what will happen when this common cause is realized and each faction begins to pursue its own goals? If significant differences are not resolved, civil war could be an unavoidable reality for the people of this diverse land. Civil war in Iraq could then lead to the creation of two or even three nation-states representing the country's major religious and cultural factions. On the other hand, Iraqis could find creative ways to avert war and ensure that all major ethnic and religious groups are represented and empowered within a unified Iraq. Either way, the future of Iraq is intimately connected to its various cultural and religious groups.

ESSENTIAL

After World War I, British officials combined the ethnically and religiously distinct Ottoman provinces of Mosul (predominately Kurdish), Baghdad (largely Sunni Arab), and Basra (mostly Shi'ite Arab) into one mandate area. Currently, this volatile nation known as Iraq continues to divide along these same ethnic and religious lines.

Israel/Palestine: Whose Holy Land?

Though much of the Arab-Israeli conflict is focused on issues of territory, security, nationalism, and basic human rights, there is an ethnic/religious dimension to this quarrel. Jews and Arabs are believed to be cousins through Abraham's sons Isaac and Ishmael (Isma'il), but after thousands of years, little cultural or ethnic similarities remain.

While most Arabs have lived in the Middle East for millennia, most Jews migrated to Europe and other parts of the world following the Diaspora of the first century. While some Jews remained in the region, the Jewish people, culture, and religion evolved (for the most part) outside the Middle East. As a result, Arabs and Jews have developed very different ethnic identities. Among other things, these ethnic divisions contribute to the current conflict, as each group sees itself as superior.

In addition, religious differences contribute to the struggle in Israel/Palestine as certain individuals from each side are convinced that God has chosen them to control the Temple Mount (al-Haram al-Sharif), Jerusalem (al-Quds), and the surrounding areas. While religious beliefs lead some Israeli Jews to discriminate against Muslim and Christian Palestinians, many Israelis consider their occupation of the West Bank and Gaza Strip as an issue of national security rather than divine promise. Though many Palestinian Muslims have rallied around a religious battle flag for the liberation of Jerusalem, many are more concerned with ending the Israeli government's humiliating grip on their daily lives.

Ideological Differences and Political Agendas

Although ethnic and religious differences are at the core of current conflicts in the Middle East, political ideologies and agendas contribute to their complexity. Political leaders in the Middle East are often categorized as being doves or hawks. The term "dove" is often used to describe those who are willing to make painful territorial compromises to achieve lasting peace. The term "hawk" is often reserved for those who hold to their rigid principles regardless of the human cost. Although these terms are generalizations of the ideological struggle that exists within Middle Eastern governments, they help to categorize the major perspectives on the issue. Many feel that if the doves had their way, any peace that was achieved would be temporary. The population at large may feel they compromised too much and, as a result, may grow disgruntled and bitter. Peace would then be disrupted as they blamed their former enemies or even their leaders for forcing them to sacrifice their principles. In contrast, many feel that if the hawks were to control their destiny, the current bloodshed would increase, and the region would become even further divided along religious and cultural boundaries.

As you can see, resolving the current conflicts in the Middle East will require reconciliation between rival religious and cultural groups as well as the political leaders who claim to represent them. If the hawks and the doves cannot compromise and find a common ground, they cannot hope to bring their peoples to compromise with their neighbors.

ALERT!

Though the Bush administration has set forth what's known as the Road Map to Peace for the Israeli-Palestinian conflict, not everyone sees it as a positive path. Osama bin Laden's right-hand man, Ayman al-Zawahiri, referred to the peace plan as America's "road map to hell." Many Jewish settlers living in the West Bank and Gaza Strip also oppose Washington's peace efforts, as it may require the forfeiture of their homes and property.

Historical Memory

To further complicate the prospects of peace in this part of the world, memories of past clashes and wrongdoing create longstanding feuds, deep-seated hatred, and great distrust. From the animosity between Armenians and Turks produced by the Armenian Genocide to the cycle of vindictive hatred that has driven Israelis and Palestinians to kill one another for more than fifty years, the past is not easily forgotten. Though the Ottoman Empire was dismantled more than eighty years ago, many Arabs continue to resent the Turks as arrogant apostates, while a large number of Turks see Arabs as ignorant desert dwellers.

Not only do memories shape relations between Middle Eastern peoples, they also color the way most Middle Easterners view foreign governments. Stories of the Crusades leave Muslims, Jews, and Eastern Christians with a powerful image of Western Christian brutality. Recollections of European colonialism led many Middle Easterners to blame the West for their own impoverishment. Fresh memories of post–World War I British and French mandates guide the hearts and minds of many who see current American and European actions as part of a larger plan to dominate the region.

Because of former invasions, periods of occupation, broken promises, and decades of exploitation, most individuals in the Middle East do not trust the motives of Western governments. As a result, Middle Eastern leaders must walk a fine line between powerful Western nations (which can provide much needed resources and political muscle) and their citizens, who will view pro-Western leaders as traitors.

Given these complications, you can see why U.S. and even U.N. involvement can be a tricky issue for politicians and an uncomfortable prospect for the average Middle Easterner. With so many issues intertwined in this web of war, peace will require time and patience. These conflicts will not likely be resolved overnight by a single military operation or a cleverly orchestrated plan. Though the vast majority of Middle Easterners desperately long for peace and prosperity, a great chasm lays between desire and reality. There is no easy answer for peace in this region, but that does not mean it is impossible.

Your Place in This World

You can be part of the process! More than likely, you will not be at the negotiating table with world leaders, but with what you now know, you can still play an important role. With your informed understanding of the Middle East, you can begin to build bridges over the deep canyons of misunderstanding that have set our cultures at odds.

You may decide to help your coworkers and neighbors understand the barrage of troubling images they see in the news. You might choose to be a voice of balance amid those who present extreme points of view. You can use your vote to support leaders who are committed to finding solutions to these problems. You can even travel to the Middle East to develop your perspectives through hands-on experience. Unlike many Americans and Europeans, you now have insights that will help you converse in coffee shops and municipal parks from Marrakech to Kabul.

Tips for Tasteful Travelers

Though you can now relate more effectively with individuals in this region, as a cultural outsider there are certain issues you will need to remember if you choose to be a guest in the Middle East. To have the most effective cross-cultural experience, fact-finding mission, or tourist trip, remember the following words—modesty and respect! Cultural norms vary greatly between countries, but whether you are in the conservative Kingdom of Saudi Arabia or the more liberal land of Turkey, err on the side of respect and modesty. By placing these concepts at the forefront of your mind you will not only keep from offending your hosts, you will help to correct some of the misconceptions that Middle Easterners may have about you or your country. In addition, you will be graced with hospitality unlike any other. Enjoy!

Though Middle Eastern cultural norms may seem restrictive, being sensitive to them will be to your benefit. In addition, you will help to break down unsavory stereotypes perpetuated by Hollywood and unknowingly reinforced by many tourists.

Pulling It all Together

Positive change for this region will require input from the world's concerned and informed citizens. Ultimately, however, the fate of the Middle East rests with those who call these lands home. The information you have drawn from this resource can help you to be a part of something much bigger than yourself. By expanding your knowledge, seeking new experiences, and challenging preconceived notions, you will find the tools to be a peacemaker.

May the information you have acquired in these pages be more than facts for your head but inspiration for action as well. Whatever you decide to do after reading this book—seek Salaam, support Shalom, and pursue peace! Ⓔ

Timeline: Prehistory to the Present

Prehistory—Ancient Monotheists: Adam, Enoch (Idris), Job (Ayyoub), Noah (Nuh), etc.

7000 to 3500 B.C.—Sumerians develop world's first civilization in southern Mesopotamia (contemporary Iraq)

5500 to 3500 B.C.—Egyptians develop civilization along Nile River (northeast Africa), establishing northern and southern kingdoms

3500 B.C.—Sumerians invent wheel

3200 B.C.—Sumerians create world's first written language

3100 B.C.—Egyptian kingdoms united by Pharaoh Menes

2800 B.C.—Papyrus writing sheets invented by Egyptians

2500 B.C.—Phoenicians settle along northeastern Mediterranean coast

2500 B.C.—Sumerian *Epic of Gilgamesh* written

2200 B.C.—Hittites establish civilization in Anatolia (present-day Turkey)

2100 B.C.—Abraham (Ibrahim) born in Mesopotamian city of Ur

2050 B.C.—Isaac (Is-haq) born in Canaan (present-day Israel/Palestine)

2000 B.C.—Jacob (Yakub) born in Canaan

2000 B.C.—Babylonian civilization established in central Mesopotamia

1900 B.C.—Joseph (Yusuf) born in Canaan

1850 B.C.—Israelites enslaved in Egypt

1800 B.C.—Birth of Assyrian Empire in northern Mesopotamia

1750 B.C.—Assyrian Empire conquered by Babylonians

1700 B.C.—King Hammurabi develops detailed law code for Babylonian Empire

1530 B.C.—Babylonian Kingdom destroyed

1520 B.C.—Moses (Musa) born in Egypt

1440 B.C.—Israelites's Exodus from Egypt/Conquest of Canaan

1440 to 1400 B.C.—Moses receives Ten Commandments and pens Torah

1350 B.C.—Pharaoh Amenhotep IV rejects polytheism

1200 B.C.—Hittite Kingdom destroyed

1200 to 800 B.C.—Assyrian Empire slowly re-established

1000 B.C.—Persian prophet Zoroaster preaches monotheism

1000 B.C.—Kingdom of Saba' (Sheba) established in southwestern Arabia

1000 to 950 B.C.—Kingdom of Israel established, Jerusalem built, and Temple of Solomon erected

930 B.C.—Kingdom of Israel splits: Israel (north) and Judah (south)

722 B.C.—Israel destroyed by Assyrians

700 B.C.—Assyrian capital moved to Nineveh (present-day Mosul, Iraq)

612 B.C.—Assyrian Empire conquered by Medes

605 B.C.—King Nebuchadnezzar establishes Neo-Babylonian (Chaldean) Empire

600 B.C.—Medes establish empire in northern Mesopotamia and Aryana (Iran)

586 B.C.—Judah conquered by Neo-Babylonians (Chaldeans) and population exiled to Babylon

550 B.C.—Median Empire conquered by Persians/ Persian Empire established

539 B.C.—Babylon conquered by Persians

538 B.C.—Citizens of Judah (Jews) return from exile in Babylon

500 B.C.—Nomadic Arab "Nabataeans" settle in present-day southern Jordan

490 to 479 B.C.—Greco-Persian Wars

331 B.C.—Alexander the Great conquers Persian Empire; Greek Empire born

264 B.C.—Punic Wars begin between Carthage and Rome

146 B.C.—Rome captures Carthage

133 B.C.—Roman Empire controls North Africa

100 B.C.—Nabataeans establish the city of Petra

27 B.C.—Roman Empire's Pax Romana begins

3 B.C.—Jesus son of Mary (Esa ibn Marium) born in Bethlehem

A.D. 30—Jesus' crucifixion

A.D. 40 to 95—Christian Scriptures written

A.D. 50 to 70—Persecution of Christians in Judea/Spread of Christianity

A.D. 70—Destruction of Jerusalem Temple and expulsion of most Jews of Judea

A.D. 135—Rome removes all remaining Jews from Province of Judea

A.D. 224—Sassanians revive glory of Persian Empire

A.D. 284—Roman Empire divided into East and West

A.D. 303—Great persecution of Christians by Emperor Diocletian

A.D. 312—Roman Emperor Constantine converts to Christianity

A.D. 325 to 451—Series of Church Councils determine Christian Orthodoxy

A.D. 330—Constantinople becomes capital of "Christian" Roman Empire (Byzantine Empire)

A.D. 447—Attila the Hun takes Balkans and Asia Minor (minus Constantinople) from Byzantines

A.D. 476—Rome destroyed by Germanic warriors

A.D. 527—Justinian expands and strengthens Byzantine Empire

A.D. 570—Muhammad ibn Abdullah born in Mecca, Arabia

A.D. 610—Muhammad receives first revelation of Qur'an

A.D. 622—Muhammad and his followers escape to Yathrib (later renamed Medina)

A.D. 632—Muhammad's death; Revelation of Qur'an ends

A.D. 632—Abu Bakr becomes leader; Medina is capital of Islam

A.D. 634—Abu Bakr dies; Ùmar leads Muslim community

A.D. 640—Muslim armies conquer Persia, Egypt, and eastern Mediterranean

A.D. 644—Ùmar assassinated; Ùthman in command

A.D. **656**—Ùthman killed; Àli becomes supreme leader

A.D. **661**—Àli assassinated—last of the "Rightly Guided Caliphs"

A.D. **662**—Umayyad Dynasty established; Muslim capital moved from Medina to Damascus

A.D. **680**—Husayn killed in city of Karbala

A.D. **685**—"Dome of the Rock" built in Jerusalem

A.D. **733**—Umayyads expand Islamic domains stretching from Spain to India

A.D. **750**—Abbasid Dynasty takes control from Umayyads; capital of Islam moved to Baghdad

A.D. **900**—Small Umayyad kingdom established in Spain

A.D. **969**—From Cairo, Fatimids establish rival dynasty to Abbasids

1040—Seljuk Turks move into Mesopotamia and Syria

1054—Separation of the Eastern "Orthodox" and Western "Catholic" churches

1055—Fatimids occupy Abbasid Baghdad

1071—Seljuks defeat Byzantines in eastern Anatolia, capture Emperor

1097—Start of Western "Christian" Crusades in Middle East

1169—Salah al-Din (Saladin) expels Crusaders from Egypt

1187—European colonialists expelled from Jerusalem by Saladin

1250—Mamluks take Fatimid Egypt, establish dynasty

1258—Mongols destroy Baghdad and Abbasid Dynasty

1291—Last Crusader colonialists expelled from the Middle East

1299—Osman's Turkic tribe expands power from northwestern Anatolia

1370—Ottomans (Osmanli) establish dynasty, move into Eastern Europe

1402—Timur "the Lame" (Tamerlane) defeats Ottomans, captures Sultan

1448—Ottomans regroup and take Kosovo in Balkans

1453—Ottoman Sultan Mehmed conquers Constantinople; end of Byzantine Empire

1492—Spanish Inquisition displaces many Jews and Muslims

1500s—European kingdoms develop economic ties with Muslim world

1501—Safavid Dynasty set up in Persia and Central Asia

1517—Mamluk Dynasty toppled; Ottomans gain most of Arab world

1526—Mughal Dynasty begins in present-day India, Pakistan, and eastern Afghanistan

1529—Sultan Süleyman besieges Vienna; Ottoman "Golden Age" begins

1555—Peace-treaty signed between (Sunni) Ottomans and (Shi'ite) Safavids

1600s—European colonies established in Americas, Africa, and Southeast Asia

1623—Safavid Shah Abbas takes Ottoman city of Baghdad

1631—Taj Mahal built by Mughal emperor

1683—Ottomans besiege Vienna again

1700s—European navies control the world's seas

1735—Weakened Ottomans lose territory to Russia

1757—Islamic Mughal Empire conquered; India controlled by Great Britain

1790s—Ottoman Empire known as "Sick Man of Europe"

1795—Safavid Dynasty overthrown by Turkic Qajar tribe in Persia

1800s—European powers move into Muslim North Africa, Persia, and Central Asia

1839—Ottomans Westernize and reorganize

1880—Zionism (Jewish nationalism) born out of European nationalistic fervor

1882—British occupy Egypt

1882—First migration of European Jews to Palestine

1896—Publication of Theodor Herzl's *Der Judenstaat* ("The Jewish State")

1901—British granted oil rights in Persia

1906—Constitutional Revolution in Persia

1908—Young Turk Revolution

1913—Ottomans lose most of European territories to nationalist movements

1914—World War I sparked by assassination in former Ottoman Balkan lands

1914—Ottomans join Germany and the Central Powers

1915—Hussein-McMahon correspondence

1915—Ottoman victory at Gallipoli; Mustafa Kemal becomes Turkish hero

1916—Sykes-Picot Agreement

1917—Balfour Declaration

1918—Arabia, Syria, and Mesopotamia fall from Ottoman to British control

1918—Ottomans withdraw from war/Central Powers surrender, ending World War I

1919—Paris Peace Conference determines European influence over Middle Eastern lands

1919—British and French mandate areas replace Ottoman *vilayet* system

1919—Egyptian nationalist Wafd Party established

1920—Faysal named king of Syria by Arab nationalists; French expel him

1920—Treaty of Sèvres; Turkish War of Independence

1921—Jewish Haganah formed

1921—Faysal named king of Iraq; Abdullah made king of Transjordan

1922—British protectorate terminated; Egypt first independent Arab state

1923—Turkish republic declared with Mustafa Kemal as president

1924—Turkey abolishes pan-Islamic caliphate

1925—Reza Khan topples Qajars; becomes shah of Persia

1926—Saudi family takes Hijaz region from Hashemites

1928—Islam no longer recognized as state religion in Turkey's constitution

1928—Muslim Brotherhood formed in Egypt

1929—Massacre of Jews in Jerusalem

1932—Iraq becomes independent state

1932—Saudi family announces united kingdom of Saùdi Arabia

1934—Mustafa Kemal takes name Atatürk

1935—Persia formally called "Iran"

1935—Oil discovered in Arabian Peninsula

1936—Iraqi military coup makes Hashemite king figurehead

1938—Kemal Atatürk's death

1939—"White Paper" ends British support for Zionism; Palestinian state promised

1939—Beginning of World War II

1941—Iran sides with Germany; British and Russians invade Iran

1941—Iraq sides with Germany; British troops invade Iraq

1942—Pro-Allied administration formed in Iraq

1943—New shah sides with Allies

1945—Birth of Arab League; end of World War II; birth of United Nations

1946—French mandate ends; Syria and Lebanon granted independence

1946—Zionist terrorists bomb Jerusalem's King David Hotel

1948—Massacre of 245 Palestinians in the village of Dayr Yasin

1948—Jewish State of Israel declared; Arab-Israeli war begins

1949—Jordan and Egypt sign cease-fire agreement with Israel

1950—Turkish troops part of U.N. force in Korean War

1951—Turkey joins NATO

1951—Iran's oil industry nationalized

1952—Egyptian Free Officers' Revolution

1953—Apparent CIA-supported removal of Iranian prime minister

1953—Arab Republic of Egypt declared

1954—Gamal Abdel Nasser named president of Egypt

1955—Baghdad Pact signed

1956—Nasser nationalizes Suez Canal

1956—British, French, and Israeli forces attack Egypt

1957—Eisenhower Doctrine put into action

1958—Egypt and Syria form United Arab Republic (UAR)

1958—Jordan and Iraq form Arab Union

1958—Iraqi Free Officers' Revolution; monarchy overthrown; republic declared

1959—American-Iranian Defense Agreement

1960—Birth of the second Turkish republic

1960—Organization of Petroleum Exporting Countries (OPEC) formed

1961—Syria pulls out of UAR

1961—Kuwait granted independence from Great Britain

1962—Egypt and Saudi Arabia clash over civil war in Yemen

1963—Short-lived Ba'th Party coup in Iraq; pan-Arabists take over

1963—Egypt helps to form Organization for African Unity (OAU)

1963—White Revolution in Iran

1964—Ayatollah Khomeini kicked out of Iran; settles in Iraq

1964—Arab nations agree to support Palestinians through PLO

1965—Yasser Arafat's Al-Fatah movement gains popular support

1967—Israel strikes Egypt; Six-Day War; Palestinian areas occupied by Israel

1967—U.N. Resolution 242 drafted

1968—Complete Ba'th Party takeover in Iraq; RCC formed; power to Tikriti clan

1969—Arafat becomes leader of PLO

1970—Nasser's death; Anwar al-Sadat new Egyptian president

1970—Aswan High Dam completed

1971—Bahrain, Qatar, United Arab Emirates, and Oman receive independence

1972—Palestinian militants kill Israeli athletes at Munich Olympic Games

1973—Egypt and Syria attack Israel on October 6 (Yom Kippur)

1973—Soviet-American sponsored cease-fire and U.N. Resolution 338

1974—Turkey at war with Greece over island of Cyprus

1975—Iraq and Iran agree on disputed territories

1975—Start of civil war in Lebanon

1977—Egyptian President Sadat speaks to Israeli parliament

1978—Ayatollah Khomeini deported from Iraq

1978—Camp David Peace Accords

1979—Israeli-Egyptian Peace Treaty; Egypt kicked out of Arab League

1979—Islamic Revolution in Iran, American hostages taken

1979—Afghan-Soviet War begins

1979—Saddam Hussein named president of Iraq

1980—Start of Iran-Iraq War (first Gulf War)

1980—Turkish generals take over government; martial law instituted

1981—Israel destroys Iraqi nuclear reactor outside Baghdad

1981—Sadat assassinated; Hosni Mubarak new Egyptian president

1981—Syria's Golan Heights annexed by Israel

1982—Israel invades Lebanon; 800 Palestinians massacred at Sabra and Shatila refugee camps

1983—Bombing of U.S. Marine barracks in Beirut

1984—Civil war starts between Kurdish PKK guerillas and Turkish military

1985—First Saudi Arabian citizen in space

1985—Israeli forces pull out of Lebanon

1987—Palestinian intifada begins

1988—Iran-Iraq War ends; Iraqi Kurds gassed by Saddam Hussein's regime

1988—Egyptian author Naguib Mahfouz awarded Nobel Prize in Literature

1989—Egypt readmitted to Arab League

1989—USSR pulls troops out of Afghanistan, ending long and bloody war

1989—Ayatollah Khomeini's death

1990—Iraq invades Kuwait/ Nation declared Iraq's nineteenth province

1991—U.S.–led Operation Desert Storm (second Gulf War); Kuwait liberated; sanctions and "no-fly zones" imposed on Iraq

1993—Turkey elects first female prime minister

1993—Oslo Peace Accords; Palestinian intifada ends

1994—Israel and Jordan Peace Treaty; Oslo II (Taba Accords)

1994—Saddam Hussein orders attacks on Shi'ites in southern Iraq

1995—United States cuts all ties with Iran

1995—Jewish extremist assassinates Israeli Prime Minister Yitzak Rabin

1996—Series of Palestinian bombings; clashes between Palestinians and IDF

1996—Osama bin Laden threatens U.S. soldiers in Arabia; bombing of U.S. facility

1997—Members of Gamaat al-Islamiyya massacre 58 tourists in Luxor, Egypt

1998—U.S.–led Operation Desert Fox in Iraq

1998—Osama bin Laden threatens all Americans around the world

1998—U.S. embassies in Kenya and Tanzania bombed; Al-Qaeda targets struck in Sudan and Afghanistan

1998—U.S.–sponsored Wye River Peace Deal

1999—Gamaat al-Islamiyya signs cease-fire with Egyptian government

1999—Kurdish Leader Abdullah Öcalan captured; Turkey given conditional invitation for EU membership

2000—Camp David II; fate of Jerusalem sticking point

2000—Ariel Sharon sparks second Palestinian uprising (the al-Aqsa Intifada)

2001—Ariel Sharon elected Israeli prime minister

2001—September 11 attacks in United States

2001—United States strikes Al-Qaeda with Operation Enduring Freedom in Afghanistan; Taliban removed from power

2003—U.S. President Bush unveils plan for Middle East free-trade zone

2003—U.S.–led Operation Iraqi Freedom removes Saddam Hussein and Ba'th Party from power

2003—Representative Governing Council formed in Iraq; ongoing suicide bombings and popular unrest; capture of Saddam Hussein

2004—Iraqi Governing Council members agree on temporary constitution

2004—Hamas founder Shaykh Ahmad Yasin assassinated by Israeli Defense Forces

Appendix B

Further Reading and Resources

Books

Atatürk: The Biography of the Founder of Modern Turkey, by Andrew Mango (The Overlook Press, NY: 1999)

Between Memory and Desire: The Middle East in a Troubled Age, by R. Stephen Humphreys (University of California Press, CA: 2001)

Coptic Egypt, by Jill Kamil (The American University Cairo Press, Cairo, Egypt: 1996)

Crescent & Star: Turkey Between Two Worlds, by Stephen Kinzer (Farrar, Straus and Giroux, NY: 2001)

The Crusades Through Arab Eyes, by Amin Maalouf (Schocken Books, NY: 1985)

From Beirut to Jerusalem, by Thomas L. Friedman (Anchor Books, NY: 1990)

A History of the Arab Peoples, by Albert Hourani (MJF Books, NY: 1991)

The Middle East: Fourteen Islamic Centuries, by Glenn E. Perry (Prentice Hall, NJ: 1983)

A Modern History of the Kurds, by David McDowall (I.B. Tauris, NY: 1997)

Sulha: Palestinian Traditional Peacemaking Process, by Elias J. Jabbour (House of Hope Publications, Shefar'Am, Israel: 1996)

We Belong to the Land: The Story of a Palestinian Israeli Who Lives for Peace and Reconciliation, by Elias Chacour (Harper Collins, NY: 1992)

Magazines and Journals

International Journal of Middle East Studies, edited by Juan R. I. Cole (Cambridge University Press, NY: 2003)

Islam and Christian-Muslim Relations, edited by John L. Esposito and David Thomas (Carfax Publishing, PA: 2003)

Journal of Palestine Studies, edited by Hisham Sharabi (University of California Press, CA: 2003)

Middle East International Review, Produced by Winning Communications (Dubai, United Arab Emirates: 2003)

Washington Report on Middle East Affairs, edited by Richard H. Curtiss (American Education Trust, Washington, D.C.: 2003)

Videos

Acts. Visual Entertainment, 1997 (*www.visualbible.com*)

Beyond the Mirage: The Faces of the Occupation. Americans for a Just Peace in the Middle East, 2002 (*www.ajpme.org*)

The Bombing, by Simone Bitton. First Run/Icarus Films, 1999 (*www.frif.com*)

Byzantium: The Lost Empire, by John Romer. Discovery Communications & Family Home Entertainment, 2000 (*www.familyhomeent.com*)

A Dangerous Man: Lawrence After Arabia. Anchor Bay Entertainment, 1998.

Islam: Empire of Faith. PBS Home Video, 2001 (*www.pbs.org*)

Israel's Shattered Dreams, by Victor Schonfeld. MPI Home Video, 1990.

Matthew. Visual Entertainment, 1997 (*www.visualbible.com*)

The Seven Wonders of the Ancient World. Questar Video, 2002 (*www.questar1.com*)

Tales from Arab Detroit, by Joan Mandell. ACCESS & Olive Branch Productions, 1995.

Travels in Europe: Turkey. Small World Productions, 1995.

Web Sites

Middle East Cross-Cultural Association
www.meccaresource.com

Middle East News—BBC World Service
http://news.bbc.co.uk

Middle East Newspapers and News Sites in English
www.world-newspapers.com/east.html

Middle East Religious Studies
Christianity (Orthodox)—*www.rbsocc.org*
Christianity (Protestant)—*www.gospeloutreach.net*
Christianity (Roman Catholic)—*www.vatican.va*
Islam (Sunni)—*www.viewislam.com*
Islam (Shi'ite)—*www.shia.org*
Modern Judaism—*www.jewfaq.org*

Middle East Research and Information Project
www.merip.org

Washington Report on Middle East Affairs
www.wrmea.com

Organizations and Associations

Americans for a Just Peace in the Middle East
P.O. Box 1086, Santa Barbara, CA 93102
www.ajpme.org

Campus Watch: Monitoring Middle East Studies on Campus
1500 Walnut St., Suite 1050, Philadelphia, PA 19102
www.campus-watch.org

The Fares Center for Eastern Mediterranean Studies at Tufts University
Cabot Intellectual Center, 160 Packard Ave., Medford, MA 02155
http://farescenter.tufts.edu

Middle East Cross-Cultural Association
P.O. Box 271707, Fort Collins, CO 80527
www.meccaresource.com

Middle East Studies Association of North America
1219 N Santa Rita Ave., The University of Arizona, Tucson, AZ 85721
www.mesa.arizona.edu

Index

Abbasid dynasty, 101–4
Àbd al-Malik, 99–100
Àbdullah, King of Iraq, 130, 135, 140, 212
Abraham (Abram), 24–25
Abu Bakr, 90–91
Afghanistan, 204, 205–7, 244
Ahura Mazda, 34
Alawites (Nusayri), 155–56
Alevi-Bektashis, 156
Alexander II, 37–38
Al-Fatah, 164, 165
Algebra, 102
Àli (son of Sharif Husayn), 130, 139
Àli ibn Abi Talib, 93
Alphabet, 21, 39
Al-Qaeda, 206, 276
Amorites, 23
Anatolia, 129–30, 134, 135, 136–37, 253. *See also* Ottoman Empire; Turkey; Turks (Turkic peoples)
Apostles, 61–63
Apostolic letters, 62–64
Arab Israelis, 171
Arab League, 181, 184–85
Arab Socialist Renaissance Party. *See* Ba'th Party
Arab Union of Jordan/Iraq, 217
Arabs, 8. *See also specific Arab countries*
Arafat, Yasser, 165, 169, 173
Aramaic (Syriac), 33, 150
Ark of the Covenant, 46, 47, 50
Armenians, 147–48
Aryan tribes, 33
Aryanism (of Hitler), 160
Asad, Bashar, 156
Asad, Hafez, 174
Assyrians, 28–31, 149–50, 214, 223
Astronomy, 15–16, 18, 38
Aswan High Dam, 184, 186–87, 192
Atatürk, Mustafa Kemal, 136–37, 139, 186, 238, 253, 254–59, 260
Attila, 75–76
Augustine of Hippo, 152
Ayatollah Ali Khamenei, 247, 248, 249
Ayatollah Khomeini
    death of, 247

expulsion from Iraq, 223, 242
Iran-Iraq War and, 224–26, 244–46
revolution of, 241, 242–44
rise of, 223, 224

Babylonians
    Chaldeans and, 31–33
    early civilization, 23–24
Baghdad, 212
Baghdad Pact, 216
Balfour Declaration, 132, 138
Barak, Ehud, 175
Basra, 212
Ba'th Party, 217–19, 222–23, 231
Bedouin, 83–84
Begin, Menachem, 161, 168–69, 188
Ben-Gurion, David, 161
Berbers, 152–53
Bin Laden, Osama, 190, 202–7, 276
Bush, George W., 231, 232
Byzantine Empire, 67–80
    Christian monastics and, 71–72
    Constantine conversion and, 68–69
    Constantinople and, 70–71, 111, 118
    Council of Chalcedon and, 74–75
    Council of Constantinople and, 72–73
    Council of Ephesus and, 73–74
    Council of Nicaea and, 69–70
    decline/fall of, 79–80, 117–18
    Emperor Justinian and, 77–79
    politics, religion and, 72–75
    religious freedom in, 69–71
    Sassanians and, 76–77
    Turkic challenges, 75–76
Byzantium, 70

Caliphs, 90–93
Camp David talks, 169, 188
Canaan, Hebrews and, 25–26, 47–50
Carter, Jimmy, 169, 187–88
Carter Doctrine, 244
Chaldeans, 31–33
Christianity, 53–66
    apostolic letters, 62–64
    Assyrians and, 150

Council of Nicaea, 69–70
Crusades and, 108–11, 114, 277
early persecution, 60–61
first-century Judaism and, 54–56
martyrs of, 60, 65–66
in Middle East today, 78
monastic movements, 71–72
moshiach, messiah, Christ and, 56–57
Paul and, 61–63
Romans and, 64–66
See also Byzantine Empire; Jesus
Çiller, Tansu, 263
Circassians, 148–49
Civilization, 13–26
    Babylonians and, 23–24
    components of, 14
    current world views, 278–79
    Egyptians and. *See* Egypt
    Hebrews and, 24–26
    Hittites and, 21–23
    Phoenicians and, 20–21
    Sumerians and, 14–17
Clinton, Bill, 173, 174, 231
Coffee, 98, 121, 183, 271
Compassionate imperialism, 36–37
Constantine the Great. *See* Byzantine Empire
Constantinople, 70–71, 111, 118
Copts, 151
Council of Chalcedon, 74–75
Council of Constantinople, 72–73
Council of Ephesus, 73–74
Council of Nicaea, 69–70
Crusades, 108–11, 114, 277
Culture/history overview, 9–10
Cuneiform, 16
Cyrus, 35

Darius, 35–36
Desert, 6–7
Diaspora, 26, 51, 64–65
Din, 95–96
Druze (Mowahhidoon), 156–57

Egypt, 179–93
    as African nation, 185

Egypt—continued
   Anwar Sadat and, 169, 186–88
   Arab name of, 180
   Cairo conversion, 115
   early civilization, 17–20
   Free Officers and, 182–83
   Gamal Abdel Nasser and, 182, 183–86, 192
   Hosni Mubarak and, 188, 190–93
   imperialism remnants of, 180–82
   independence of, 135, 139
   Islamic extremists and, 189–91
   Israeli friendship of, 192
   King Farouk and, 181–82, 183
   monumental constructs of, 192–93
   nationalism of, 135, 182–83
   1980s/90s unrest, 189–90
   1973 war and, 167–68, 187
   1967 war and, 165–67, 187, 201–2
   pan-Arabism and, 181, 183–86
   population of, 144, 179
   progressiveness of, 18–20
   pyramids of, 18, 39
   Suez Canal and, 164, 180, 184, 192
   supporting U.S.-led Iraqi operations, 191
   Upper/Lower, 17
   Yemeni war and, 185, 186, 187, 201
Egyptian Islamic Jihad group, 189–90
Empires, 27–40
   Assyrians, 28–31
   Chaldeans (Neo-Babylonians), 31–33
   compassionate imperialism, 36–37
   components of, 28
   Greeks, 37–39
   Medes, 33–35
   Persians, 8, 35–37
   See also Byzantine Empire; Ottoman
      Empire; Romans
Epic of Gilgamesh, 16
Erbakan, Necettim, 263
Essenes, 54, 65
Ethnic groups, 8–9
Europe
   colonialism of, 124–25, 277
   Crusades and, 108–11, 114–16, 277
   post-World War I influence by, 133–35
   World War II alliances, 215
European Economic Community (EEC), 262–63
European Union (EU), 263

Faisal, King of Saudi Arabia, 201–2
Far East, 2
Farouk, King of Egypt, 181–82, 183
Faysal, King of Iraq, 130, 135–36, 139, 212, 213,
   214

Faysal II, King of Iraq, 215, 216
Ferdinand, Archduke Francis, 129
Fida'yin (fedayeen), 163, 164
Filastin, 160
Free Officers, 182–83, 217
Fuad, King of Egypt, 180, 181

Gamaat al-Islamiyya, 189–90
Gaza Strip, 282
   failed occupation, 164
   occupation of, 166, 171
   occupation resistance, 167, 168, 171–72
   peace challenges, 287, 288
   refugee camps, 163
   Sharon acknowledging occupation, 176
   withdrawal plans, 172, 173
Genghis Khan, 110
Geographic boundaries, 6–7
Geography, 6–7
Ghazi, King of Iraq, 214–15
Golan Heights, 166, 167, 168, 171, 174
Grand National Assembly (GNA), 256, 257, 262
Greeks, 37–39
Gulf War (Iran-Iraq), 224–26, 244–46
Gulf War (Operation Desert Storm), 228–29
Gulf War (Operation Iraqi Freedom), 231–32
Gunpowder, 114–15

Hadith, 94–96
Hajj, 208
Hamas, 172, 173
Hannibal, 39
Harems, 4
Hashemites, 130–31, 139–40, 196, 212, 216–17
Hashish, 107
Hasmoneans, 54
Hebrews, 24–26
   in Egypt, 25
   origin of, 24–25
   as wanderers, 25, 44–45, 47
   See also Israel; Judaism
Hellenistic culture, 38–39
Hijaz, 196
Hittites, 21–23
Hizbullah, 170
Honor/shame societies, 270–73
Husayn, 99
Husayn, Sharif, 130–31, 132
Hussein, Saddam
   early years, 222
   ethnic cleansing by, 223, 226, 228–30
   executing top leaders, 223–24
   fall of, 231–32
   Iraq after, 232–34, 284–86

occupying Kuwait, 227–28
   rise of, 218–19, 222–24
   U.S. supporting, 225, 226
   See also Iraq

Ibn Sàud, King of Saudi Arabia, 196, 200
Iman, 95
Inönü, Ismet, 259, 260, 261
Intifada, 171–72
Intifada (second), 175–76
Iran, 235–49
   alliances of, 238–39
   Aryan connection, 237
   Ayatollah Ali Khamenei and, 247, 248, 249
   Ayatollah Khomeini and. *See* Ayatollah
      Khomeini
   Cold War and, 240, 244–45
   demographics of, 237, 248
   dynasties, divisions of, 236–39
   hostages, 243–44
   Iraq war, 224–26, 244–46
   Islamic Revolution (1979), 138
   Medes and, 33–35
   modernization of, 238–39
   Muhammad Khatami and, 248
   official language of, 245
   reform potential of, 249
   revolution within, 241–44
   Reza Shah Pahlavi and, 137–38, 237–39
   Safavids and, 122–23, 238
   as theocracy, 243
   U.S. relations, 239–41, 244–45, 247
   World Wars and, 238–39
   See also Persia/Persians
Iran-Contra Affair, 226, 245
Iraq, 211–19, 221–34
   Arab population, 224
   Assyrians and, 28–31, 149–50
   Ba'th party, 217–19, 222–23
   demographics of, 224, 284–86
   early twentieth century territories, 212–13
   flag of, 217
   formation of, 196
   future of, 234
   Governing Council of, 233
   independence of, 139, 213–14
   instability, revolutions, 216–17
   Iran war, 224–26, 244–46
   Marsh Arabs in, 229–30
   Operation Desert Fox, 231
   Operation Desert Shield, 227–28
   Operation Desert Storm, 228–29
   Operation Iraqi Freedom, 231–32
   post-Saddam, 232–34, 284–86

RCC, 183, 218, 222–23
as republic, 217
Russian alliance of, 224, 226
sanctions, hard times, 230
term origin, 212
U.S. perspective of, 227
WMDs, 231, 232
World War II alliances, 215
See also Hussein, Saddam
Iron, 21
Ishmael, 83
Islam, 81–96
    ancient Arabia and, 82–84
    basic beliefs, 95–96
    caliphs, 90–93
    desert nomads and, 83–84
    diverse lands/people and, 92
    frustration/aggression and, 277–78
    Hadith, 94–96
    Ka'ba, 84, 100
    Mecca and, 84–85, 207–8
    Nabataens and, 83–84
    offshoots of, 154–57
    overview, 81
    pervasiveness of, 9
    Qur' an, 92, 93–96
    revivalism/militancy of, 275–77
    rise of, 96
    Saba' and, 82
    violence and, 273–75
    Wahhabism and, 196–99, 207–8, 210
    See also Muhammad (ibn Àbdullah);
        Muslims; *specific sect names*
Islamic empires, 97–111
    Abbasid dynasty, 101–4
    Crusades and, 108–11, 114, 277
    Mamluks and, 105–6, 115–16
    Shi'ites, 106
    Turks, 106–7
    Umayyad dynasty, 98–101, 104–5
Islamic Revolution (1979), 138
Israel
    Arab resistance to, 161–62
    destroying Iraqi nuclear reactor, 225
    early expansion/division, 50–51
    Egyptian friendship, 192
    formation of, 140–41, 161
    Jacob as, 43
    Jerusalem, 51
    origin of, 43, 50
    tribes of, 19, 25–26, 29, 43
    World War II aftermath and, 160–61
    Zionism and, 128, 131
    See also Israel/Palestine; Judaism

Israeli Defense Forces (IDF), 168, 169
Israel/Palestine, 159–77
    freedom fighters/terrorists, 163, 167
    intifada, 171–72
    intifada (second), 175–76
    Israeli settlements, 168–69
    1956 war, 164, 184, 201
    1948 war, 161–62
    1993 breakthrough, 172–73
    1973 war, 167–68, 187, 202
    1967 war/cease-fire, 165–67
    Oslo Accords, 172–73, 174
    peace challenges, 286–87
    peace prospect, 176–77
    PLO and, 164–65, 167, 169–70, 173
    refugee camps, 162–63, 170
    religion and, 174
    World War II aftermath and, 160–61
    Wye River Memorandum, 174–75
    See also Gaza Strip; West Bank
"istan" suffix, 12

Jacob, 19, 25, 42–43
Jerusalem, 51. *See also* Israel; Israel/Palestine
Jesus
    ascending to heaven, 60
    as chosen one, 57–58
    death of, 59
    as moshiach, messiah, Christ, 56–57, 68
    prophesies surrounding, 56–57, 58–60
    rising from dead, 59–60
Jihad, 91
Jordan
    independence of, 140
    1967 war/cease-fire and, 165–67, 201–2
    Transjordan and, 134, 135, 136, 140, 196
Joseph, 42–43
Josephus, Flavius, 56
Joshua, 49–50
Judaism
    Diaspora, 26, 51, 64–65
    early evolution, 24–26
    Essenes and, 54, 65
    ethnicity of, 154
    in first-century, 54–56
    "Jew" word origin, 26, 43
    Joseph and, 42–43
    Joshua and, 49–50
    Levitical law and, 47–49
    Maccabeans and, 54
    Moses and, 44–49
    moshiach and, 56–57
    official symbol of, 50
    Pharisees and, 55–56, 64

Romans and, 64–66
Sabbath of, 49
Sadducees and, 55, 64–65
sons of Jacob and, 42–43
Tanakh of, 51–52
today, 153–54
Torah writings, 47–49
types of, 153–54
Zealots and, 56, 65
See also Hebrews; Israel; Israel/Palestine
Justinian, Emperor, 77–79

Ka'ba, 84, 100
Kemal, Mustafa. *See* Atatürk, Mustafa Kemal
Kerkorian, Kirk, 147
Khatami, Muhammad, 248
Kurdish Democratic Party (KDP), 216
Kurds, 145–47
    in Iraq, 215, 216, 217–18, 223, 226, 228–29,
        284–85
    Turkey and, 264

Lawrence, T. E. (Lawrence of Arabia), 130–31
Lebanon
    as battleground, 169–70
    independence of, 140
    Phalange revenge in, 169–70
    PLO in, 169
    U.S. marine barracks attack, 170
Leviticus, Book of, 48–49
Linguistic groups, 8–9

Maccabeans, 54
Magi religion, 34
Mahdi, 104
Mahfouz, Naguib, 5
Mamluks, 105–6, 115–16, 119–20
Manna, 46
Martyrs, 60, 65–66
Masjids, 98
Mecca, 84–85, 207–8
Medes, 33–35
Medina, 88–89
Mehmed, Sultan, 118–19
Mesopotamia
    Assyrians and, 28–31
    Chaldeans and, 31–33
    early twentieth-century territories, 212–13
Mevlana, 110
Middle East
    conservative/liberal definitions of, 11–12
    culture/history overview, 9–10
    defined (for this book), 12
    ethnic terms for, 8

MIddle East—*continued*
  ethnic/linguistic groups, 8–9
  geographic boundaries, 6–7
  media influencing view of, 2–3
  misconceptions of, 3–6
  Orient areas and, 2
  peace challenges. *See* Peace challenges
  religion and, 9
  social identity, 10–11
  term origin, 2–3
Modern Middle East, 143–57
  Alawites (Nusayri) and, 155–56
  Alevi-Bektashis and, 156
  Armenians and, 147–48
  Assyrians and, 149–50
  Berbers and, 152–53
  Circassians and, 148–49
  Copts and, 151
  diversity of, 143, 145
  Islamic offshoots and, 154–57
  Jews and, 153–54
  Kurds and, 145–47, 215, 217–18
  Mowahhidoon (Druze) and, 156–57
  urbanization, technology of, 144–45
Moguls, 122
Moses, 44–49
  early years, 44
  inspiration of, 44–45
  Levitical law and, 47–49
  mission of, 45–46
  Ten Commandments and, 45
Moshiach, 56–57
Mosul, 212, 214
Mowahhidoon (Druze), 156–57
Muàwiyya, 98
Mubarak, Hosni, 188, 190–93
Mughal (Mongol) Empire, 122–23
Muhammad (ibn Àbdullah), 81,
  85–90
  Abu Bakr and, 90–91
  death of, 90
  in Medina, 88–89
  as prophet, 86–87
  Quraish tribe and, 87–88
  revelation of, 85–86
  successors to, 90–93
  teachings of, 88–89
  varied roles of, 89
Muslim Brotherhood, 180–81, 182, 184
Muslims
  marrying Christians, 98
  presence of, statistics, 9
  Shi'ites. *See* Shi'ites
  Sufis, 100–101, 109, 155

  Sunnis. *See* Sunnis
  Wahhabis, 196–99

Nabataens, 83–84
Nasser, Gamal Abdel, 182, 183–86, 192
Nationalism, 135–38, 139–41
Near East, 2
Nebuchadnezzar, 31–32
Neo-Babylonians, 31–33
Netanyahu, Benjamin, 174–75
Nile, commerce on, 18–19
1956 war, 164, 184, 201
1948 war, 161–62
1973 war, 167–68, 187, 202
1967 war, 165–67, 187, 201–2

Oil
  Iran and, 237, 239–40, 241, 246
  Iraq and, 218, 224, 227
  Persian Gulf region, 140
  Saudi Arabia and, 199–202
1,001 Arabian Nights, 3–4
Operation Desert Fox, 231
Operation Desert Shield, 227–28
Operation Desert Storm, 228–29
Operation Iraqi Freedom, 231–32
Organization of Petroleum Exporting Countries
  (OPEC), 202
Orient, 2
Orientalism, 3–6
  harems and, 4
  mythology, marketing and, 5–6
  1,001 Arabian Nights and, 3–4
  Shriners and, 4–5
Oslo Accords, 172–73, 174
Oslo II, 173
Osmanli, 116, 126
Ottoman Empire
  conquering Mamluks, 119–20
  decline/fall of, 124–26
  ethnic evolution, 118–19
  ottoman footstools and, 126
  rise/expansion of, 116–21
  Safavids and, 122–23, 238
  Sultan Süleyman, 120–21

Pahlavi, Reza Shah, 137–38, 237–39
Pahlavi, Shah Muhammad Reza, 240, 241–42
Palestine
  dividing, for Israel, 140–41, 160–61
  ethnicity of, 160
  as Jewish refuge, 138–39, 160–61
  peace challenges, 282

  See also Gaza Strip; Israel/Palestine; West
    Bank
Palestine Liberation Organization (PLO),
  164–65, 167, 169–70, 173
Palestinian Liberation Army (PLA), 165
Pan-Arabism, 181, 183–86
Paul (Saul), 61–63
Pax Romana, 40
Peace challenges, 281–90
  border disputes, 282–83
  ethnic/religious divisions, 283–87
  historical memory, 288–89
  ideologies/political agendas, 287–88
  Israel/Palestine, 286–87
  post-Saddam Iraq, 284–86
  your contribution to, 289–90
Persia/Persians, 8, 34, 35–37, 236–37. *See also*
  Iran
Pharisees, 55–56, 64
Philistines, 160
Phoenicians, 20–21
Political boundaries, 6–7
Pyramids, 15, 18, 39

Qur' an, 92, 93–96
Quraish tribe, 87–88

Rabin, Yitzak, 173–74
Rafsanjani, Ali Akbar Hashemi, 247
Refugee camps, 162–63, 170
Religion, peace and, 283–87
Revolutionary Command Council (RCC), 183,
  218, 222–23
Reza Shah. *See* Pahlavi, Reza Shah
Romans, 39–40, 64–66
Rushdie, Salman, 246

Saba' (Sheba), 82
Sabaens, 82
Sadat, Anwar, 169, 186–88
Sadducees, 55, 64–65
Safavids, 122–23, 238
Sahara, 6–7
Said, Edward W., 3
Sassanians, 76–77
Sàud, King of Saudi Arabia, 200–201
Saudi Arabia, 195–210
  conservative garb of, 198
  defense systems of, 208–9
  early history of, 196
  Egypt and, 201
  evolution of, 208–10
  formation of, 140
  fractured fraternities of, 201–2

Mecca and, 84–85, 207–8
1973 war and, 202
oil and, 199–202
Operation Desert Shield and, 227–28
Osama bin Laden and, 190, 202–7, 276
religious police of, 209
September 11 and, 206–7
Wahhabism and, 196–99, 207–8, 210
Yemeni war and, 201
Sàudi family, 131, 139–40, 196
School, birthplace of, 16
September 11, 206–7
Shame/honor societies, 270–73
Shamir, Yitzaq, 161
Sharon, Ariel, 169, 170, 175–76
Shi'ites
Alawites as, 155
Cairo ridding, 115
early years, 99, 103–4, 106, 107, 109–10
empire of, 106
Hajj and, 208
in Iraq, 212, 223, 224, 228–30, 285
as Islamic offshoot, 155
origin of, 90
state of. See Iran
Shriners, 4–5
Simeon of Antioch, 72
Sinai Peninsula, 164, 166, 167, 168, 186
Six-Day War (1967), 165–67
Social identity, 10–11
Solomon, 26, 50
Spain, 104–5
"stan" suffix, 12
Stern Gang, 139, 161, 163
Suez Canal, 164, 180, 184, 192
Sufis, 100–101, 109, 155
Süleyman, Sultan, 120–21
Sumerians, 14–17
astronomy, gods and, 15–16
evolution of, 14–15
influence of, 28
inventiveness of, 16–17
Sunnis, 90, 107, 155
in Cairo, 115
Hajj and, 208
in Iraq, 212, 214, 215, 216, 224, 285
Wahhabi (conservative), 196–99, 207–8, 210
Sykes-Picot plan, 132
Syria
Assyrians and, 150
independence of, 140
1973 war, 167–68
1967 war/cease-fire, 165–67, 201–2

not recognizing Israel, 166
as UAR member, 184–85

Taj Mahal, 122
Tanakh (Old Testament), 51–52
Ten Commandments, 45
Terrorism
Al-Qaeda and, 206, 276
early Jewish, 139, 161
Egyptian-based, 189–90
fighting against, 191, 206–7
freedom fighting vs., 163
Islam and, 273–75
1967 war spawning, 167
Osama bin Laden and, 190, 202–7, 276
September 11 and, 206–7
technology fighting, 144
Wahhabism and, 197
World Trade Center attacks, 190
Timeline, 291–99
Timur the Lame, 117
Torah writings, 47–49
Toshka Project, 193
Transjordan, 134, 135, 136, 140, 196. See also Jordan
Travel tips, 289–90
Treaty of Sèvres, 136
Tribes of Israel, 19, 25–26, 29, 43
Turkey, 251–67
abolishing caliphs, 257
Atatürk and, 136–37, 139, 186, 238, 253, 254–59, 260
early years, 252
East/West struggle, 262–65
Grand National Assembly of, 256, 257, 262
independence of, 139, 254–56
joining NATO, 260
Kurds and, 264, 284–85
nationalism of, 252–53
secularization of, 256–59, 262–63
today forward, 265–67
turbulent 1960s-1980s, 261–62
World War I and, 253–54
See also Ottoman Empire; Turks (Turkic peoples)
Turkish cigarettes, 5
Turks (Turkic peoples)
attacks by, 75–76, 106–7
Attila, Christians and, 75–76
defined, 8
Ottomans. See Ottoman Empire
Safavids and, 122–23, 238
See also Turkey

Umayyad dynasty, 98–101, 104–5
United Arab Republic (UAR), 185, 216–17
Ùthman ibn Àffan, 92–93

Wahhab, Muhammad ibn Abd al-, 196–97
Wahhabism, 196–99, 207–8, 210
Weapons of mass destruction (WMDs), 231, 232
West Bank
failed occupation, 166
occupation of, 166, 171
occupation resistance, 168, 171–72
peace challenges, 282, 287, 288
refugee camps, 163
Sharon acknowledging occupation, 176
withdrawal plans, 172, 173, 174
Wheel, invention of, 16
Wilson, Woodrow, 132–33
World War I
alliances, 129–30, 131–32
betrayed agreements after, 133–35
casualties, 129
European-influenced territories after, 133–35
events leading to, 129
land agreements after, 131–32
Paris Peace Conference, 133
T. E. Lawrence and, 130–31
Zionism and, 128, 131
World War II
Arab League and, 181–82
Israel/Palestine and, 160–61
Wye River Memorandum, 174–75

Yasin, Shaykh Ahmad, 172
Yemeni war, 185, 186, 187, 201

Zealots, 56, 65
Zionism, 128, 131
Zoroaster (Zarathustra), 34
Zoroastrianism, 34, 36

THE EVERYTHING SERIES!

BUSINESS

Everything® **Business Planning Book**
Everything® **Coaching and Mentoring Book**
Everything® **Fundraising Book**
Everything® **Home-Based Business Book**
Everything® **Leadership Book**
Everything® **Managing People Book**
Everything® **Network Marketing Book**
Everything® **Online Business Book**
Everything® **Project Management Book**
Everything® **Selling Book**
Everything® **Start Your Own Business Book**
Everything® **Time Management Book**

COMPUTERS

Everything® **Build Your Own Home Page Book**
Everything® **Computer Book**
Everything® **Internet Book**
Everything® **Microsoft® Word 2000 Book**

COOKBOOKS

Everything® **Barbecue Cookbook**
Everything® **Bartender's Book, $9.95**
Everything® **Chinese Cookbook**
Everything® **Chocolate Cookbook**
Everything® **Cookbook**
Everything® **Dessert Cookbook**
Everything® **Diabetes Cookbook**
Everything® **Indian Cookbook**
Everything® **Low-Carb Cookbook**
Everything® **Low-Fat High-Flavor Cookbook**

Everything® **Low-Salt Cookbook**
Everything® **Mediterranean Cookbook**
Everything® **Mexican Cookbook**
Everything® **One-Pot Cookbook**
Everything® **Pasta Book**
Everything® **Quick Meals Cookbook**
Everything® **Slow Cooker Cookbook**
Everything® **Soup Cookbook**
Everything® **Thai Cookbook**
Everything® **Vegetarian Cookbook**
Everything® **Wine Book**

HEALTH

Everything® **Alzheimer's Book**
Everything® **Anti-Aging Book**
Everything® **Diabetes Book**
Everything® **Dieting Book**
Everything® **Herbal Remedies Book**
Everything® **Hypnosis Book**
Everything® **Massage Book**
Everything® **Menopause Book**
Everything® **Nutrition Book**
Everything® **Reflexology Book**
Everything® **Reiki Book**
Everything® **Stress Management Book**
Everything® **Vitamins, Minerals, and Nutritional Supplements Book**

HISTORY

Everything® **American Government Book**
Everything® **American History Book**
Everything® **Civil War Book**
Everything® **Irish History & Heritage Book**

Everything® **Mafia Book**
Everything® **Middle East Book**
Everything® **World War II Book**

HOBBIES & GAMES

Everything® **Bridge Book**
Everything® **Candlemaking Book**
Everything® **Casino Gambling Book**
Everything® **Chess Basics Book**
Everything® **Collectibles Book**
Everything® **Crossword and Puzzle Book**
Everything® **Digital Photography Book**
Everything® **Easy Crosswords Book**
Everything® **Family Tree Book**
Everything® **Games Book**
Everything® **Knitting Book**
Everything® **Magic Book**
Everything® **Motorcycle Book**
Everything® **Online Genealogy Book**
Everything® **Photography Book**
Everything® **Pool & Billiards Book**
Everything® **Quilting Book**
Everything® **Scrapbooking Book**
Everything® **Sewing Book**
Everything® **Soapmaking Book**

HOME IMPROVEMENT

Everything® **Feng Shui Book**
Everything® **Feng Shui Decluttering Book, $9.95 (15.95 CAN)**
Everything® **Fix-It Book**
Everything® **Gardening Book**
Everything® **Homebuilding Book**

All Everything® books are priced at $12.95 or $14.95, unless otherwise stated. Prices subject to change without notice.
Canadian prices range from $11.95–$31.95, and are subject to change without notice.

Everything® **Home Decorating Book**
Everything® **Landscaping Book**
Everything® **Lawn Care Book**
Everything® **Organize Your Home Book**

EVERYTHING®
KIDS' BOOKS

All titles are $6.95
Everything® **Kids' Baseball Book,
3rd Ed.** ($10.95 CAN)
Everything® **Kids' Bible Trivia Book**
($10.95 CAN)
Everything® **Kids' Bugs Book** ($10.95 CAN)
Everything® **Kids' Christmas Puzzle &
Activity Book** ($10.95 CAN)
Everything® **Kids' Cookbook** ($10.95 CAN)
Everything® **Kids' Halloween Puzzle &
Activity Book** ($10.95 CAN)
Everything® **Kids' Joke Book** ($10.95 CAN)
Everything® **Kids' Math Puzzles Book**
($10.95 CAN)
Everything® **Kids' Mazes Book**
($10.95 CAN)
Everything® **Kids' Money Book**
($11.95 CAN)
Everything® **Kids' Monsters Book**
($10.95 CAN)
Everything® **Kids' Nature Book**
($11.95 CAN)
Everything® **Kids' Puzzle Book**
($10.95 CAN)
Everything® **Kids' Riddles & Brain
Teasers Book** ($10.95 CAN)
Everything® **Kids' Science Experiments
Book** ($10.95 CAN)
Everything® **Kids' Soccer Book**
($10.95 CAN)
Everything® **Kids' Travel Activity Book**
($10.95 CAN)

KIDS' STORY BOOKS

Everything® **Bedtime Story Book**
Everything® **Bible Stories Book**
Everything® **Fairy Tales Book**
Everything® **Mother Goose Book**

LANGUAGE

Everything® **Inglés Book**
Everything® **Learning French Book**
Everything® **Learning German Book**
Everything® **Learning Italian Book**
Everything® **Learning Latin Book**
Everything® **Learning Spanish Book**
Everything® **Sign Language Book**
Everything® **Spanish Phrase Book,**
$9.95 ($15.95 CAN)

MUSIC

Everything® **Drums Book (with CD),**
$19.95 ($31.95 CAN)
Everything® **Guitar Book**
Everything® **Playing Piano and Key-
boards Book**
Everything® **Rock & Blues Guitar
Book (with CD),** $19.95
($31.95 CAN)
Everything® **Songwriting Book**

NEW AGE

Everything® **Astrology Book**
Everything® **Divining the Future Book**
Everything® **Dreams Book**
Everything® **Ghost Book**
Everything® **Love Signs Book,** $9.95
($15.95 CAN)
Everything® **Meditation Book**
Everything® **Numerology Book**
Everything® **Palmistry Book**
Everything® **Psychic Book**
Everything® **Spells & Charms Book**
Everything® **Tarot Book**
Everything® **Wicca and Witchcraft Book**

PARENTING

Everything® **Baby Names Book**
Everything® **Baby Shower Book**
Everything® **Baby's First Food Book**
Everything® **Baby's First Year Book**
Everything® **Breastfeeding Book**

Everything® **Father-to-Be Book**
Everything® **Get Ready for Baby Book**
Everything® **Getting Pregnant Book**
Everything® **Homeschooling Book**
Everything® **Parent's Guide to Chil-
dren with Autism**
Everything® **Parent's Guide to Positive
Discipline**
Everything® **Parent's Guide to Raising
a Successful Child**
Everything® **Parenting a Teenager Book**
Everything® **Potty Training Book,**
$9.95 ($15.95 CAN)
Everything® **Pregnancy Book, 2nd Ed.**
Everything® **Pregnancy Fitness Book**
Everything® **Pregnancy Organizer,**
$15.00 ($22.95 CAN)
Everything® **Toddler Book**
Everything® **Tween Book**

PERSONAL FINANCE

Everything® **Budgeting Book**
Everything® **Get Out of Debt Book**
Everything® **Get Rich Book**
Everything® **Homebuying Book, 2nd Ed.**
Everything® **Homeselling Book**
Everything® **Investing Book**
Everything® **Money Book**
Everything® **Mutual Funds Book**
Everything® **Online Investing Book**
Everything® **Personal Finance Book**
Everything® **Personal Finance in Your
20s & 30s Book**
Everything® **Wills & Estate Planning
Book**

PETS

Everything® **Cat Book**
Everything® **Dog Book**
Everything® **Dog Training and Tricks
Book**
Everything® **Golden Retriever Book**
Everything® **Horse Book**
Everything® **Labrador Retriever Book**
Everything® **Puppy Book**
Everything® **Tropical Fish Book**

All Everything® books are priced at $12.95 or $14.95, unless otherwise stated. Prices subject to change without notice.
Canadian prices range from $11.95–$31.95, and are subject to change without notice.

REFERENCE

Everything® **Astronomy Book**
Everything® **Car Care Book**
Everything® **Christmas Book, $15.00**
    ($21.95 CAN)
Everything® **Classical Mythology Book**
Everything® **Einstein Book**
Everything® **Etiquette Book**
Everything® **Great Thinkers Book**
Everything® **Philosophy Book**
Everything® **Psychology Book**
Everything® **Shakespeare Book**
Everything® **Tall Tales, Legends, &**
    Other Outrageous
    Lies Book
Everything® **Toasts Book**
Everything® **Trivia Book**
Everything® **Weather Book**

RELIGION

Everything® **Angels Book**
Everything® **Bible Book**
Everything® **Buddhism Book**
Everything® **Catholicism Book**
Everything® **Christianity Book**
Everything® **Jewish History &**
    Heritage Book
Everything® **Judaism Book**
Everything® **Prayer Book**
Everything® **Saints Book**
Everything® **Understanding Islam**
    Book
Everything® **World's Religions Book**
Everything® **Zen Book**

SCHOOL & CAREERS

Everything® **After College Book**
Everything® **Alternative Careers Book**
Everything® **College Survival Book**
Everything® **Cover Letter Book**
Everything® **Get-a-Job Book**
Everything® **Hot Careers Book**

Everything® **Job Interview Book**
Everything® **New Teacher Book**
Everything® **Online Job Search Book**
Everything® **Resume Book, 2nd Ed.**
Everything® **Study Book**

SELF-HELP/ RELATIONSHIPS

Everything® **Dating Book**
Everything® **Divorce Book**
Everything® **Great Marriage Book**
Everything® **Great Sex Book**
Everything® **Kama Sutra Book**
Everything® **Romance Book**
Everything® **Self-Esteem Book**
Everything® **Success Book**

SPORTS & FITNESS

Everything® **Body Shaping Book**
Everything® **Fishing Book**
Everything® **Fly-Fishing Book**
Everything® **Golf Book**
Everything® **Golf Instruction Book**
Everything® **Knots Book**
Everything® **Pilates Book**
Everything® **Running Book**
Everything® **Sailing Book, 2nd Ed.**
Everything® **T'ai Chi and QiGong Book**
Everything® **Total Fitness Book**
Everything® **Weight Training Book**
Everything® **Yoga Book**

TRAVEL

Everything® **Family Guide to Hawaii**
Everything® **Guide to Las Vegas**
Everything® **Guide to New England**
Everything® **Guide to New York City**
Everything® **Guide to Washington D.C.**
Everything® **Travel Guide to The Dis-**
    neyland Resort®, Cali-
    fornia Adventure®,

Universal Studios®, and
the Anaheim Area
Everything® **Travel Guide to the Walt**
    Disney World Resort®, Uni-
    versal Studios®, and
    Greater Orlando, 3rd Ed.

WEDDINGS

Everything® **Bachelorette Party Book,**
    $9.95 ($15.95 CAN)
Everything® **Bridesmaid Book, $9.95**
    ($15.95 CAN)
Everything® **Creative Wedding Ideas**
    Book
Everything® **Elopement Book, $9.95**
    ($15.95 CAN)
Everything® **Groom Book**
Everything® **Jewish Wedding Book**
Everything® **Wedding Book, 2nd Ed.**
Everything® **Wedding Checklist,**
    $7.95 ($11.95 CAN)
Everything® **Wedding Etiquette Book,**
    $7.95 ($11.95 CAN)
Everything® **Wedding Organizer,**
    $15.00 ($22.95 CAN)
Everything® **Wedding Shower Book,**
    $7.95 ($12.95 CAN)
Everything® **Wedding Vows Book,**
    $7.95 ($11.95 CAN)
Everything® **Weddings on a Budget**
    Book, $9.95 ($15.95 CAN)

WRITING

Everything® **Creative Writing Book**
Everything® **Get Published Book**
Everything® **Grammar and Style Book**
Everything® **Grant Writing Book**
Everything® **Guide to Writing Chil-**
    dren's Books
Everything® **Screenwriting Book**
Everything® **Writing Well Book**

Available wherever books are sold!
To order, call 800-872-5627, or visit us at everything.com

Everything® and everything.com® are registered trademarks of F+W Publications, Inc.